HOWARD KOTTLER

FACE TO FACE

HOWARD KOTTLER

FACE TO FACE

PATRICIA FAILING

UNIVERSITY OF WASHINGTON PRESS

Seattle & London

Library of Congress Cataloging-in-Publication Data
Failing, Patricia.
    Howard Kottler : face to face / by Patricia Failing.
        p. cm.
    Includes bibliographical references (p.   ) and index.
    ISBN 0-295-97356-0 (cloth); 0-295-97369-2 (paper)
    1. Kottler, Howard, 1930-1989—Criticism and
        interpretation.
    2. Ceramic sculpture—20th century—United
        States—Pacific Coast. I. Kottler, Howard,
        1930–1989. II. Title
NK4210.K62F35   1994
709' .2—dc20   93-50664

The paper used in this publication meets the minimum requirements of American National Standard for Information Sciences—Permanence of Paper for Printed Library Materials, ANSI Z39.48-1984.

Printed in Korea

Contents

List of Illustrations

PHOTOGRAPHERS

Eduardo Calderón, 1.11, 1.14, 1.16, 1.19, 1.20, 1.22, 1.24, 1.25, 1.28, 1.36, 1.37, 1.38, 2.9, 2.12, 2.25, 2.27, 2.39, 3.10, 3.11, 3.19, 3.20, 3.24, 3.28, 3.30, 3.35, 3.36, 3.37, 4.22, 4.23, 4.24, 4.25, 4.26, 4.30, 4.31, 4.32, 4.33, 4.42, 4.44, 4.52, 4.53, 4.54, 4.56, 4.57; William Eng, 2.37, 3.8, 3.29, 3.33; David Kerns, 4.43, 4.45; Paul Macapia, 3.12; Richard Nicol, 2.7, 3.14, 4.38; Roger Schreiber, 2.30, 2.36, 3.5, 3.6, 4.2, 4.3, 4.4, 4.5, 4.6, 4.7, 4.9, 4.10, 4.14, 4.48, 4.49, 4.50, 4.55; Judith Schwartz, 3.22, 3.23

All reproduced art works are by Howard Kottler, unless otherwise stated. Dimensions, where given, are in inches, height preceding width.

Foreword

It is not easy to convey the essential being that was Howard Kottler. Personality, style, character, intelligence, humor—all his many attributes were such an elusive, complex, and subtle set of vari ables that even though one might use wonderfully descriptive language or tell an evocative story, there would still always be something missing, something flat about suggesting who he was.

What would be missing, of course, would be experiencing the real thing—the nuances of his voice, his ever-changing body language, his provocative, sometimes demonic demeanor, his impish playfulness, his charm, his wit, the truth of his biting words, his sensitivity, his delight with the discovery of a piece of Noritake, his passion for work, his lasciviousness, his intelligent interpreta-tions of history, his trust, his loyalty to family. Sometimes it was overwhelming. For those seeking a narrow range of diversity and complexity in a relationship, such wide swings in behavior could be unnerving.

Many described him as difficult or aloof, and at times, no doubt, he was. But for me, such quirks were a small price to pay for being in the presence of a unique and unforgettable personality.

What was it about him? First of all, he created a singular visual impact. He was slight in both girth and height, and by wearing black tee shirts and jeans, he always appeared young and boyish. He enjoyed managing a marvelously cascading Fu Manchu moustache. Its lines and curves shaped his silhouette, and indeed, his own profile became a sort of trademark in his work as well as a verbal referent in the titles of numerous pieces.

There was a complex duplicity in Howard. He could be controlled and dignified when delivering one of his famous, thoroughly enjoyable, controversial, informative, and intellectual lectures; or he could skip down a street belting out a song, mimicking Ethel Merman.

In the five years since Howard's death, there has hardly been a day when I have not had some memory or recollection of my friend and mentor. In the thirty-year span of our friendship, I spoke with him often, wrote a Ph.D. dissertation on his satiric work, and saw him several times a year.

I first met him in 1960, when I took an introductory class in ceramics as an undergraduate at Ohio State University. He had just returned from a Fulbright year at the Arabia factory in Finland, and my initial impression was of a most unconventional, serious, and enormously talented graduate student. He was a very private person, but because he loved New York, and maybe because I was fresh from the Big City, we became immediate friends, discussing favorite restaurants, theater, opera, our love for travel, and, of course, art. I had no serious interest in clay at the time, but Howard was so charismatic that I found myself transfixed by his enthusiasm and vast knowledge. I will always be grateful to him for providing my introduction to clay.

He was exacting and meticulous about his work and, as I was later to discover, about every aspect of his existence, from his extremely ordered studio to his carefully crafted Art Deco home. Howard loved order, detail, craftsmanship, and, above all, ideas. He loved dinner parties, too, especially his own, because he could make his favorite chocolate cake and engage in his love for good conversation.

No one person knew the total Howard Kottler. The mysterious aspects of his private life were, perhaps, early learned survival tactics designed to supress knowledge of his sexual orientation in order to allow him to advance within the academic community. He led many compartmentalized existences, and I think he was exhausted by the extent to which he had to manipulate and hide during those early years of building his career.

Our field is still largely conservative. However hidden Howard's life may have been, Howard's work was always "on the line." He was an influential and powerful force in shaping and defining the direction and "look" of contemporary American ceramic sculpture, and we are all the richer for it.

Judith S. Schwartz, Ph.D.
New York University

Author's Note

This study of ceramist Howard Kottler's work and professional development is based primarily on my interviews with him in Seattle from April 1988 until January 1989, a few weeks before his death. Kottler initiated these sessions after he learned of his terminal illness, intending to provide me with background data for an overview of his professional career that links his work to other developments in American visual arts from the 1950s to the 1980s. The following chapters include many direct quotes from Kottler, but the text essentially presents my own observations of and reactions to our conversations. The subtitle of this book, *Face to Face*, is taken from one of Kottler's double self-portraits. It refers not only to the format of our conversations but also to the self-reflective voice Kottler assumed as he summarized his work and career.

I would like to express my gratitude to Arna Goffe, Judy Schwartz, and Dan Neish for their invaluable assistance in the preparation of this book. Special thanks also go to Patty Warashina and LaMar Harrington for their insightful reflections on Howard Kottler's life and work; to Susan Leslie for her help in facilitating photographs and documentation; to Naomi Pascal, editor-in-chief of the University of Washington Press; and to Gretchen Van Meter for her good humor and intelligent editing of my manuscript. This book is dedicated to Arna Goffe.

Patricia Failing
Seattle, Washington

HOWARD KOTTLER

FACE TO FACE

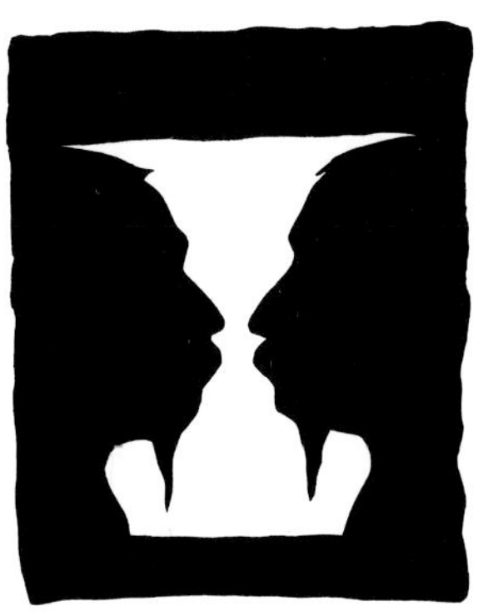

INTERDEPARTMENTAL

```
                                        16
                                         6
IS WEIRD WEIRD                          20
WEIRD
WEIRD IS HOW WEIRD                      14
  WEIRD, WEIRD.                         23
  WEIRD IS HOW WEIRD IS.                21
  WEIRD. WEIRD, WEIRD.                  16
  WEIRD IS WEIRD.                       11
WEIRRRRRD.                              20
  HOW WEIRD IS WEIRD                     7
                                       ----
                                        154
  WEIRD.                                17

  IS HOWARD WEIRD                       24
WEIRD IS HOW HOWARD IS.                 17
  WEIRD IS HOWARD                       16
HOWARD IS WEIRD                         21
HOW WEIRD IS HOWARD                      7
WEIRD.                                  19
HOWARD IS HOWEIRD                       20
HOWEIRD IS HOWEIRD                      10
                                       ----
                                        151
HOWEIRD.
```

Undated note in artist's files

Introduction

nvited to address a national ceramics conference in the mid-1970s, Howard Kottler strode to the lectern and, instead of speaking, sang the chorus of "Anything Goes." The song was ironically apropos, for Cole Porter's lyrics—"good's bad today, black's white today, day's night today"—encompassed the conflicting sentiments of both progressive and conservative ceramists. In concert with his iconoclastic visual production, such behavior established his professional persona as an irreverent provocateur who mercilessly goaded traditional ceramists. This cultivated notoriety, while it attracted curators and graduate students, served nonetheless to deflect attention from the range and sophistication of his artistic accomplishments. Many critics and ceramics historians, caught by the surface exuberance of his professional chutzpah, missed the point of Kottler's adventuresome and conceptually profound explorations of the 1980s, which took root in uncharted spaces of a newly expanded field.

Particularly during the last decade of his life, Kottler was driven by a decision to "put more of himself on the line." He formulated trenchant commentary throughout these years about the mutable boundaries of high art and kitsch, about surfaces that mask inner secrets, and about the vessel as a homoerotic medium. Elaborating his ideas in compositions that are frequently astonish-

ing, he created a body of late work that, in retrospect, has content and depth perhaps unparalleled in contemporary ceramics.

Given Kottler's untimely death from lung cancer in 1989, this book offers the first overview of his work as one of the West Coast ceramists who helped to redefine the entire field of contemporary ceramic art. Beginning his career with a traditional crafts orientation in the 1950s, Kottler established a rapport between his work and major new directions in mainstream painting and sculpture in the mid-1960s. By the 1980s he had become a conceptual artist who approached his materials as vehicles for art-historical commentary and physical eroticism, and as metaphors for probing the unbridgeable gap between the Self and the Other. Much of this late work was inspired by his observations about the fluid dynamics of control and submission in the evolution of human relationships—observations that call to mind the thinking of Michel Foucault.

In chronicling the development of Howard Kottler's art and his professional persona, it becomes evident that these two forms of production were not always in alignment. As a student, he was thoroughly trained in traditional ceramics techniques and glaze technology—his background included a Ph.D. in ceramics from Ohio State University, study with Maija Grotell at the

Cranbrook Academy, and a Fulbright grant for research in Finland. His 1964 Ph.D. dissertation indicates that, in the early 1960s, he divided academic ceramists into two camps: studio potters inspired by ceramics history, and artist-potters, like Peter Voulkos, who linked ceramics to the broader context of modern art. Kottler's sympathies were with the latter contingent, but his work was still deeply tied to the former.

After he initiated his teaching career at the University of Washington in the mid-1960s, his colleagues soon discovered that Kottler's conservative Ohio State production screened the incubation of an irreverent artistic personality. Captivated by Pop Art and San Francisco Bay Area Funk, he found the "freedom to let my craziness run amok" in the mid-1960s. Pop and Funk appealed to him as formal strategies, but he was even more impressed by the irony and double entendres that extended the literal content of the work. Like Robert Arneson, Kottler began to embrace professional practices frowned upon by traditional ceramists, conveying provocative messages to his peers through various forms of art-historical coding.

At the same time, he also claimed eroticism as a new frontier for his artmaking: in a series of organic vessels braced by punning titles, he opened up a new range of meanings that shift with the complexion of viewer desire. Compositions such as *Hole Grabber* (1967), a multimedia vase that combines a phallic tube, fur, rosebud decals, and casts of Barbie-doll arms, established Kottler's professional profile as an unpredictable iconoclast whose mode of address was innuendo rather than slapstick, the mode preferred by many of his 1960s colleagues.

During the 1970s Kottler's production broadened to include slip-cast assemblages, Art Deco–inspired pottery, and several series of decal plates, for which he is probably best known. The first plates were made in the late 1960s and dealt with subject matter rarely explored in contemporary ceramics—social and political commentary. As did the Berlin Dadaists, Kottler found the techniques of photocollage well suited to political expression: cutting up and recombining ready-made ceramic decals, he created absurd dislocations that paradoxically revealed facts of life in American culture.

In some plate compositions, such as the series based on decals of Grant Wood's *American Gothic,* the re-presentation of art-historical icons served as a vehicle for political commentary as well as a *de facto* statement about the commodification of high art.

During this decade Kottler also became intrigued by middle America's infatuation with simulated surfaces, such as wood-grain contact paper, a material he began to use in his own work. His forays into simulationism were partly inspired by an aversion to clay-as-clay partisanship within the field of ceramics, but he also began to think of these materials in metaphorical terms: the multiplication of fake surfaces in everyday life, he eventually decided, had an analogue in the disingenuousness of human relationships. Concealed desires, surface decorum, and the multiple facets of an individual personality became major themes for his sculpture of the 1980s, in which forms of irony related to his earlier production were combined with a nuanced expressionism that was rarely appreciated during his lifetime.

Kottler taught ceramics at the University of Washington for twenty-four years and became an effective and engaging teacher. Several of his successful graduate students, among them Irvin Tepper, Michael Lucero, and Mark Burns, influenced the development of his own work. In 1984 he hired Dan Neish as his technical assistant, and Neish executed many of Kottler's later compositions. This affinity for collaborative production signaled another repudiation of ceramics tradition: the *concept* is the locus of artistic expression, Kottler emphasized, not the artist's manual activity. With humor and sarcasm he waged constant warfare on mindlessness in contemporary ceramics, challenging his students and peers to "give crafts a good name" by inventing new forms that would reflect the realities of contemporary culture. In his own work of the 1980s Kottler reconsidered the vase as a homoerotic forum. Combining references to the ironic urbanism of Memphis design and the innocent decadence of Art Deco, he created a series of ball-and-shaft vessels that were not only exuberantly theatrical but were also coded for insiders in gay culture. This strategy of saying-but-not-saying began in his work

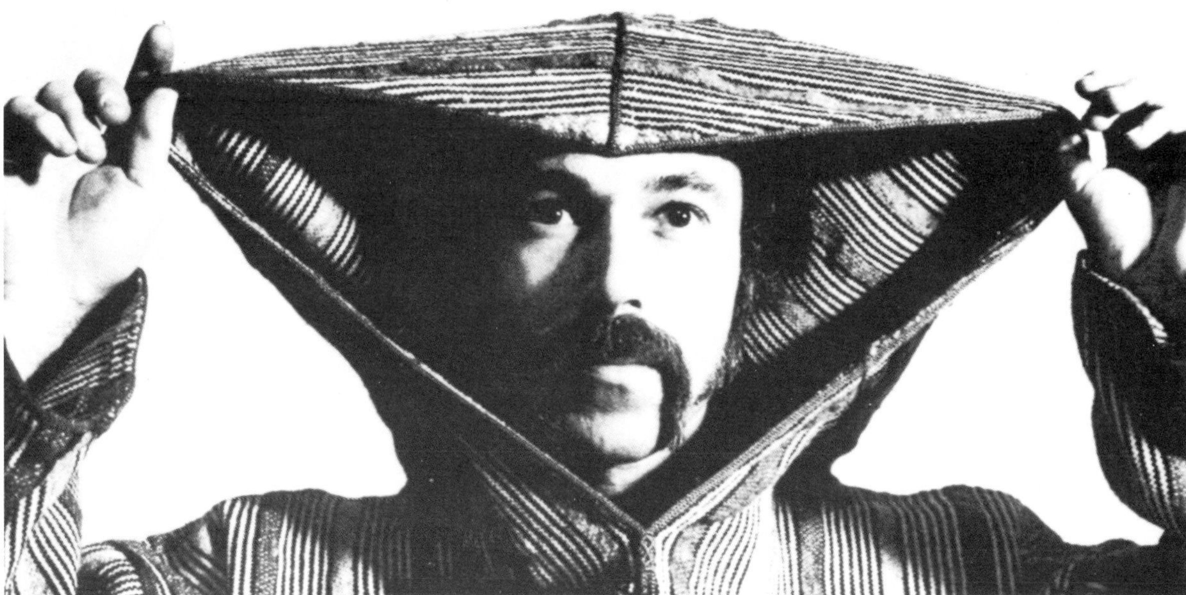

Howard Kottler

of the mid-1960s and assumed its most complex level of development in his large-scale ceramic sculpture of the 1980s.

Kottler's final body of sculpture illustrates several observations made by art historian Thomas Crow in his influential 1983 article about the avant garde and popular culture, "Modernism and Mass Culture in the Visual Arts." Reviewing the history of twentieth-century modernism in the West, Crow points out how subversive equations between high and low culture made by the artistic vanguard have kept the culture industry moving. Cubist collage and Pop Art conform most clearly to his model, but his argument can also be applied to developments in American ceramics in the 1960s and 1970s, when alexandrian craftsmanship based on oriental traditions was disrupted by an invasion of vernacular imagery, slapstick humor, and hobby-shop materials.

Kottler was an active participant in this invasion and he also, in effect, confirmed Crow's arguments about the mutable boundaries between high and low art in his late sculpture. In 1975 he began to collect Noritake porcelain, popular ceramic ware conceived by international designers in New York and manufactured in Japan. Much of the Noritake pottery produced between 1921 and 1941 was influenced by cubism and Art Deco, high art that descended into popular culture in the form of stylized animal figurines, powder boxes, candy dishes, and decorated plates. Kottler used these Japanese appropriations of cubism as a point of departure for his sculpture of the 1980s, thereby recycling Noritake cubism into the realm of high culture.

The enabling vehicles for this resurrection, however, were manufactured ashtrays and kitsch figurines. Could these vehicles be embraced by high culture too, along with their cubist formalism? Kottler posed this question in his late work, which draws parallels between situational definitions of high and low art and master-slave relationships among human beings. *Screwball* (1986), for example, is a four-and-one-half-foot blowup of a cubist Noritake dog figurine. This ceramic pet, covered with marble contact paper, has been chained by his master to a heavy ball-topped screw. The dog's body is made in sections that can be separated: concealed inside are his secrets, among them a dark human phallus. The dog gazes up at the master, who will inevitably bow to the demands of his pet, reversing the dynamics of dominance and submission. In *Bent* (1986), a double self-portrait sculpture with a cubist head, Kottler suggests that master and slave, high and low, can be bound together in a single personality; in other self-portraits, cubist faceting and two-sided profiles allude to multiple forms of self-identity.

In this late work, it could be argued, Kottler fully realized his own definition of the artist-potter by creating ceramics that engaged many of the issues explored by well-known artists associated with postmodernism. His work was barely appreciated on this level, however, and his expressionism almost escaped critical attention. In addition to his reputation as a prankster, his uneven production undoubtedly contributed to these oversights, but another factor played a role as well: as one of his friends explained, "Howard never crossed over or thought he should." A euphemism for fine artists who work in craft media or vice versa, the contemporary term "crossover artist" signals that the division between art and craft is still firmly ensconced, even if well-known artists can now move back and forth between the two categories.

Kottler's position on the arts/crafts dichotomy re-mained grounded in the idealistic presumptions of classic modernism: he simply assumed that good art would eventually be recognized as good art, even in a craft medium. As many crossover artists have discovered, however, if good art in a craft medium is to be understood and appreciated as good art, it must be shown in fine-arts institutions and discussed by fine-arts curators and critics. Kottler's work was rarely shown outside an institutional network primarily committed to values he did not share, and only minimally concerned with the ideas and issues that stimulated his late work. Professionally and personally, he remained an enigma even to most of his supporters, few of whom were aware either of the complexity of his involvement with gay culture or of the full scope of his artistic accomplishments. This enigma was ironically heightened by his decision to "put more of himself on the line" in his late work, for the self he put forward was a *poseur* with multiple identities, all of them genuine. In the interviews for this book Kottler adopted an academic voice, speaking for the record; his art, however, is polyphonous, and has even more to say.

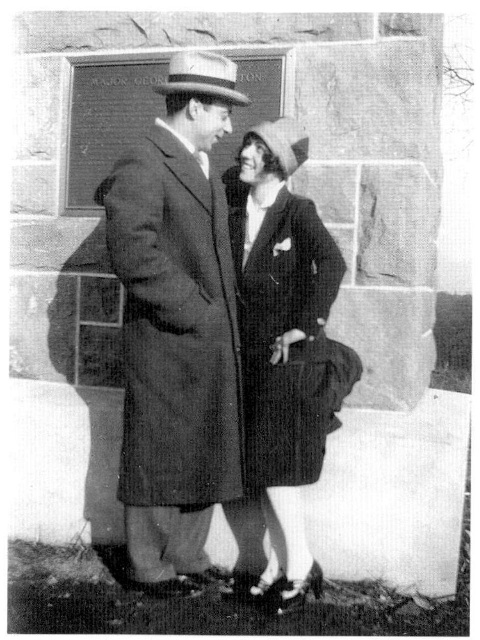

1.1 Paul Kottler and Nelly Novick just after their engagement in 1925

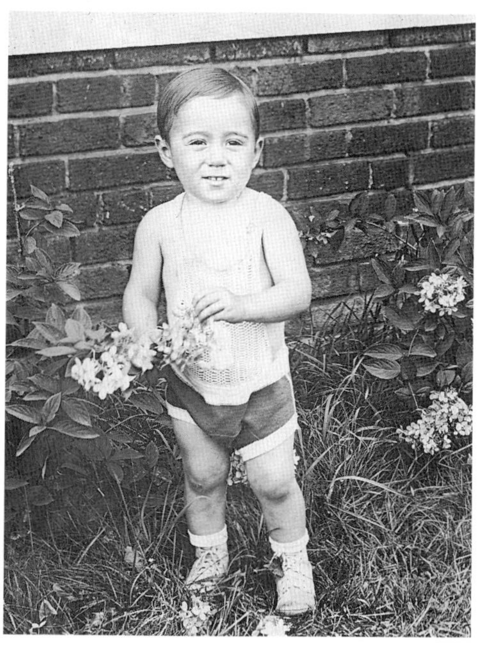

1.2 Howard Kottler, age 3

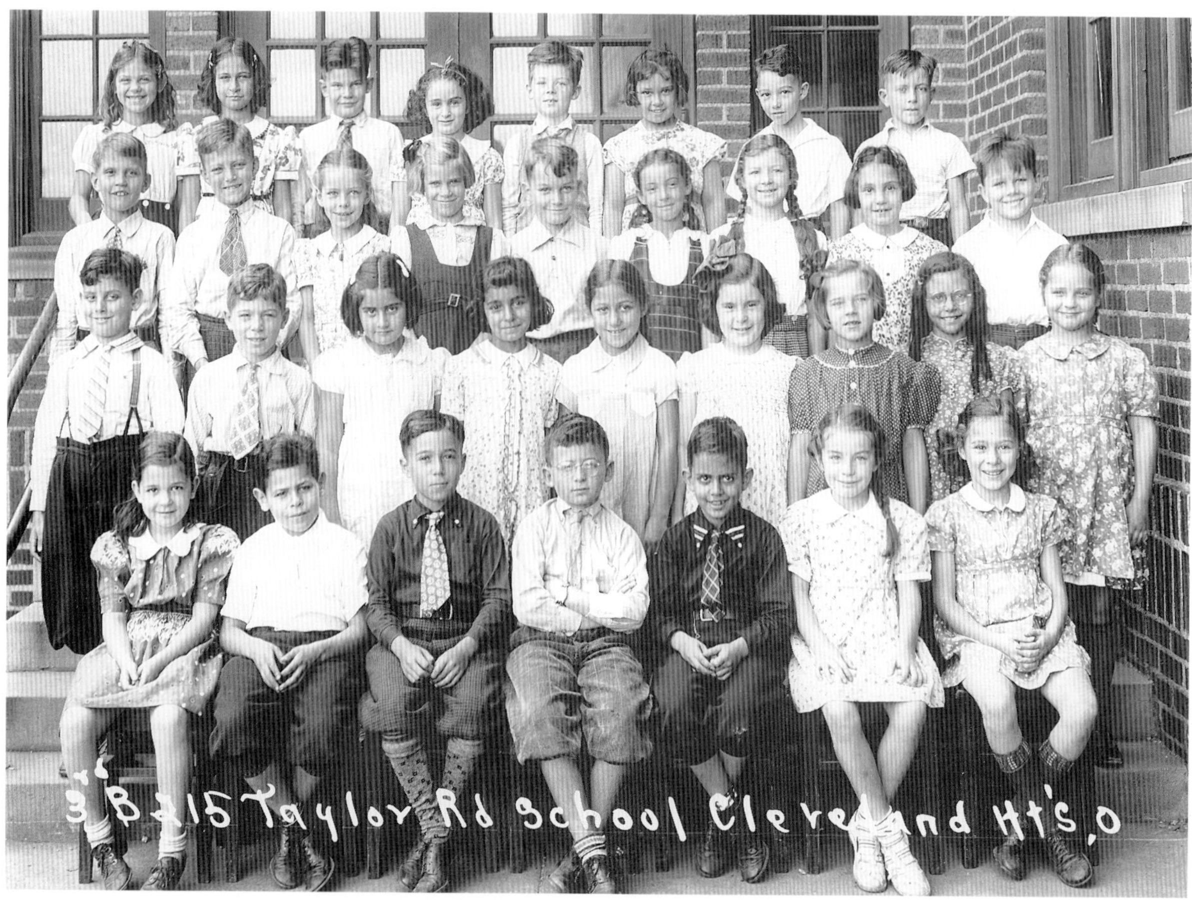

1.3 Howard Kottler (front row, third from the left) and his third-grade class, Taylor Road School, Cleveland, Ohio

ONE

Early Years in Ohio

In 1905, Howard Kottler's paternal grandfather, Wolffe Kottler, emigrated from Germany to Cleveland, Ohio, where he found work as a coppersmith in a shipbuilding yard. In 1910 he sent for his wife, Charlotte, and their two children, Paul and Clara, who settled with him in Cleveland. A few years later Kottler opened his own coppersmith's shop behind the family home at 5911 Lexington Avenue. When Wolffe Kottler died suddenly in 1929, his son Paul abandoned plans for a law career and took over the family business. Paul Kottler married Nellie Novick of Butler, Pennsylvania, in 1926; when he took over the shop, the couple was awaiting the birth of their first child, Howard William, who arrived on March 5, 1930 (figs. 1.1, 1.2).

As a young boy, Howard worked with his father in the coppersmith shop. "I was at my best with three-dimensional forms, whether it was pipe-bending or building with wood," he recalled. "Even in elementary school I knew I had a certain dexterity, and I was always good at making art. I enjoyed it a great deal, but I wasn't pushed in that direction. I was a typical kid from a Jewish family at a time when the general expectation was that sons would enter a profession. In my early childhood we lived in University Heights, which was an affluent area (fig. 1.3). I went to Saturday classes at the Cleveland Museum of Art which were great—very well organized. We would go up to the galleries and draw different kinds of objects, and we would make things as well.

"When I got older, I still did some drawing and watercolor on my own," Kottler continued. "I wasn't encouraged or discouraged by my family. I wasn't very inventive, but I was pretty good with color. For some reason I was attracted to oriental images. I remember going to the library and getting books with oriental pictures to copy. In high school I was enamored of Chinese lettering, even though I had no idea what most of the letters meant. I had this wonderful toy ball stuffed with strips of Chinese writing. Once I chose some of the letters I liked most and made them into a drawing, which I gave to my doctor. He hung it in his office until one day a Chinese patient saw it and started howling with laughter. Apparently I'd created some kind of nonsense that was really funny."[1]

In 1940, a business downturn forced Paul Kottler to sell the family's home in University Heights. Howard, his parents, and his sister Shirley, who was born in 1934, moved in with his grandmother and Aunt Clara in the house on Lexington Avenue (fig. 1.4). The house was a duplex, and the entire family crowded into the five-room downstairs unit. The move was traumatic for ten-year-old Howard; estranged from his grade-school friends, he became more self-conscious and introspective. He began

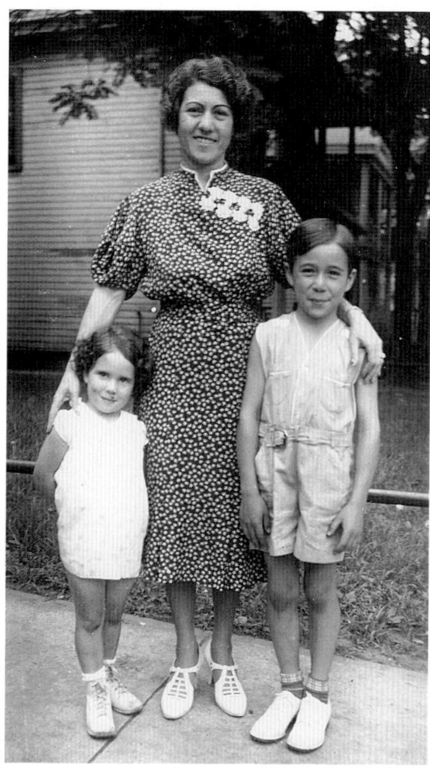

1.4 Kottler, his mother, and his sister Shirley in front of his grandmother's Lexington Avenue house, 1937

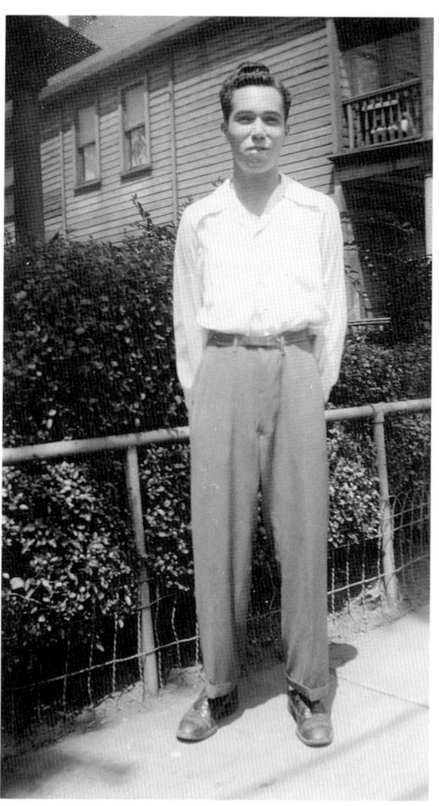

1.5 Howard Kottler, Cleveland, Ohio, 1946

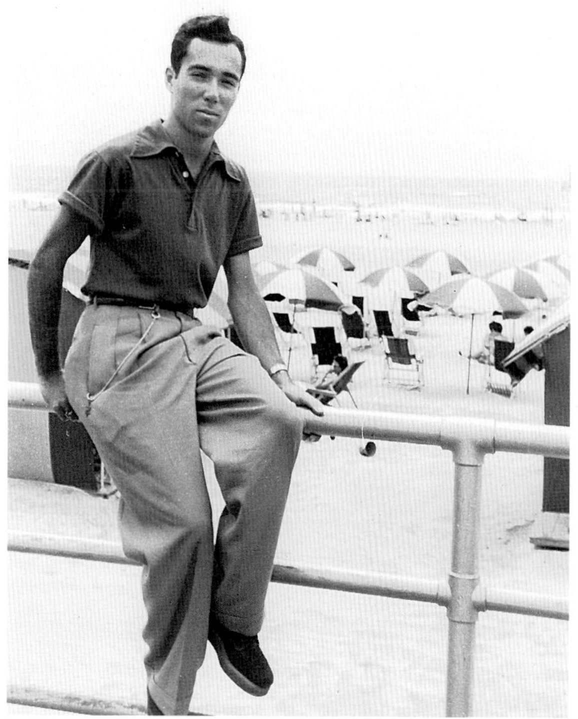

1.6 Howard Kottler, Atlantic City, New Jersey, 1948

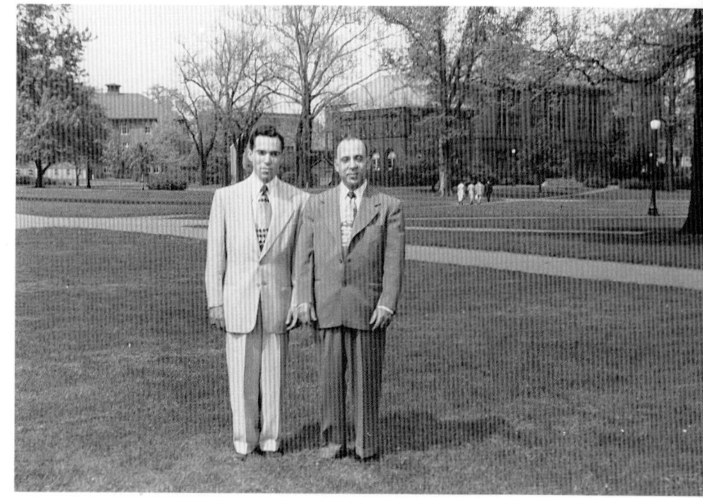

1.7 Howard Kottler and his father, Ohio State, 1950

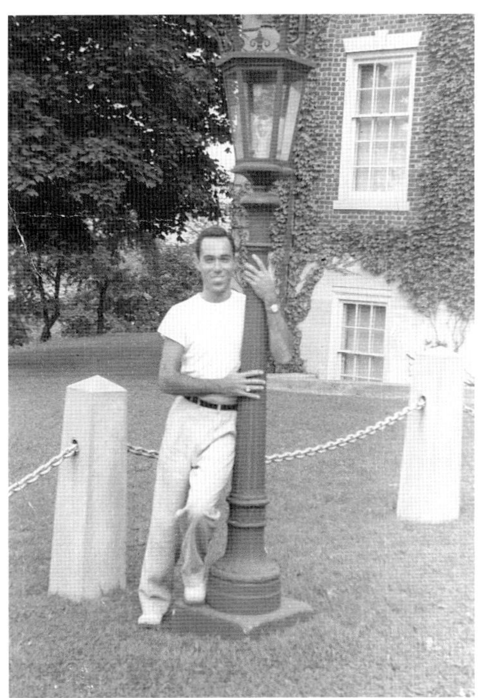

1.8 Howard Kottler, 1951

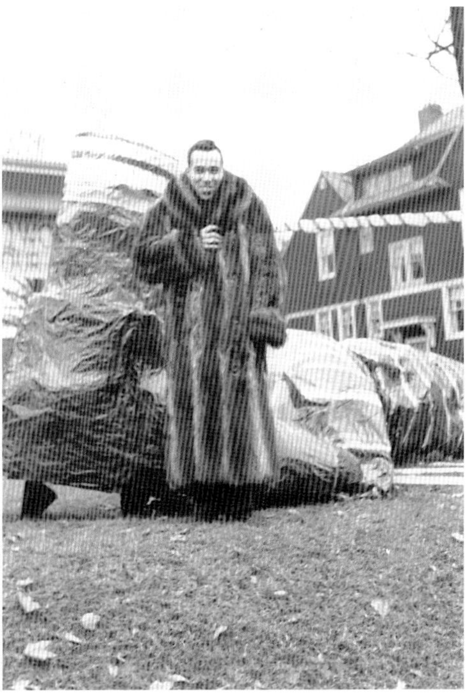

1.9 Howard Kottler at Tau Epsilon Phi fraternity house, Ohio State University Homecoming, 1951

to develop private amusements, such as collecting finger-nail cuttings in small boxes. "How weird [pun intended], you must be thinking," he wrote later. "Most boys at that age collect stamps or coins, but I was never your average collector. I went on to slightly larger boxes which I filled with pieces of icing from my Bar Mitzvah cake. Decorative icings entranced me, and for years I collected pieces of icings from special birthday, wedding, and anniversary cakes."[2]

The Kottlers all lived together on Lexington Avenue until the end of World War II. During the war the family business recovered, and in 1946 Kottler's father built a new home for his wife and children in Cleveland Heights. Howard attended Cleveland Heights High School and graduated in 1948 (figs. 1.5, 1.6). "Like my parents, when I graduated I just assumed I would enter a profession," Kottler observed. "But my parents were always lovely about it—they never dictated what I should do. I went to Ohio State University [OSU] in 1948 and got into the pre-med program (fig. 1.7). I graduated in 1952 with a B.A. in biological science.

"I look back on those years with a real feeling of dis-satisfaction. I wasn't good at science or math. I was very unhappy, but I continued to stay in the program. Ohio State was very gung ho on fraternities and sororities, and I joined a fraternity (figs. 1.8, 1.9). The fraternities were strictly divided into Jewish houses and Gentile houses. There were five or six Jewish fraternities and, socially, mine was near the bottom of the list. Most of the members were from New York and came to Ohio State to play—it was a big social school and easy in terms of studies. They planned to go into business or take over their fathers' businesses. Through my senior year in 1952 I basically conformed to the social life of the house. By then I knew I was gay, but I continued to act in a closeted situation. I was still dating, but I didn't enjoy it and was just putting on an act."[3]

In June 1952, Kottler needed one more elective course to complete his B.A. degree. "I decided—I don't know why—to take a ceramics course. Maybe it was because I often walked by the art building. It was summer term and I graduated in August. I hadn't done anything whatsoever in art as an undergraduate, even though I knew I was pretty good at making things. My first instructor was Eugene Friley, who was a very vibrant teacher, and I really enjoyed him."[4]

Kottler enrolled in Ohio State's optometry school in September 1952. "It was obvious that I didn't have the grades for medical school, so I chose optometry out of the blue. I had two fraternity brothers who were in optometry, and it seemed like a good profession. I could hardly have made a worse choice: optometry is based so much on math and physics, which were not my *métier* at all. I don't know why I didn't drop out right away, but I stayed on into the second year. But each quarter I took a ceramics course, even though you weren't supposed to do that in the professional program. I kept getting better and better and enjoying it more and more. The ceramics people wondered why I was still in optometry and felt I should make a decision about what to do. So I finally dropped out of optometry. This was during the Korean conflict, and because I was going backwards in my degree work, I was inducted. I flunked the physical because I'd had rheumatic fever as a child and had a leaky heart valve. The very next day I went back to Ohio State and enrolled in the B.F.A. program in ceramics."[5]

Together with Alfred University in New York, Ohio State had the most highly regarded university ceramics program in the United States in the early 1950s. The Ohio State program began in 1894, when the school initiated the country's first college-level classes in ceramics technology.[6] Faculty members during Kottler's years at OSU included, in addition to Eugene Friley, Edgar Littlefield, Margaret Fetzer, Paul Bogatay, and ceramics historian Carlton Atherton. The instructors were highly proficient in glaze technology, mold-making, and clay chemistry, and Kottler acquired a thorough grounding in traditional ceramic craftsmanship.[7] "I started to spend all my free time in the ceramics lab," Kottler said. "I loved every minute of it (fig. 1.10). I made up all the credits and was accepted into the M.F.A. program. I decided to do a thesis, and graduated with an M.A. degree in 1956."[8] A shift in Kottler's personal life also contributed to his elation. "After 1952 I really went out on my own socially. I

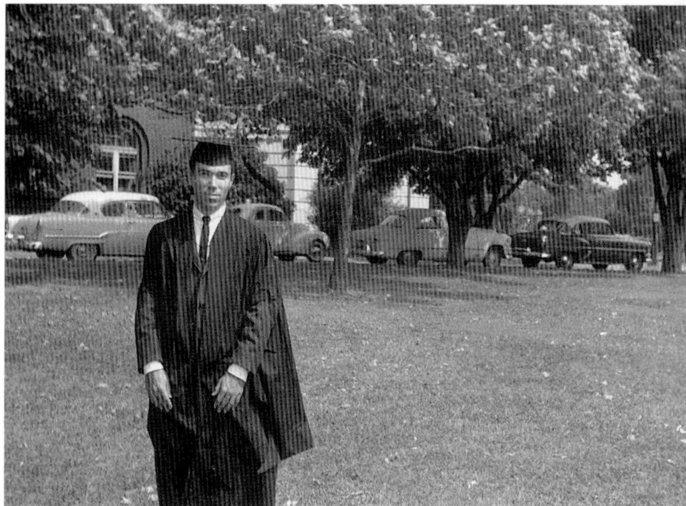

1.10 Howard Kottler, Ohio State Commencement, 1956

did go back to the fraternity occasionally, but at a certain point they realized I was gay and I could feel I wasn't welcome any longer. So I just dropped that part of my life completely and became totally involved in my art and the gay scene. Those were wonderful years for me."[9]

At first Kottler was a contented and unreflective student. "I just flowed with what was happening without much direction. In retrospect, something very positive was that in the beginning courses you were first taught hand-building. If you start with wheel-throwing, the wheel can become an end in itself rather than a tool. It's easy to get trapped—you are stuck with these symmetrical forms. With hand-building, you start thinking about the form first, and you begin to develop a form sensibility. Also, I think from the very beginning I had an affinity for hand-building in clay. Even though I came back to the wheel occasionally, the main thrust of my work was always hand-building."[10]

Kottler's first body of student work included a series of pinched and modeled semibiomorphic bowls (figs. 1.11, 1.12). "I think those forms came from two sources," Kottler observed. "First, I had a strong background in biology—I'd looked at a lot of protozoa. I also liked [Isamu] Noguchi's work, especially his amoeba-shaped tables. I took my first trip to New York in 1952 and I did a lot of drawing while I was there. I remember drawing some Noguchi-like things in a store window, because the

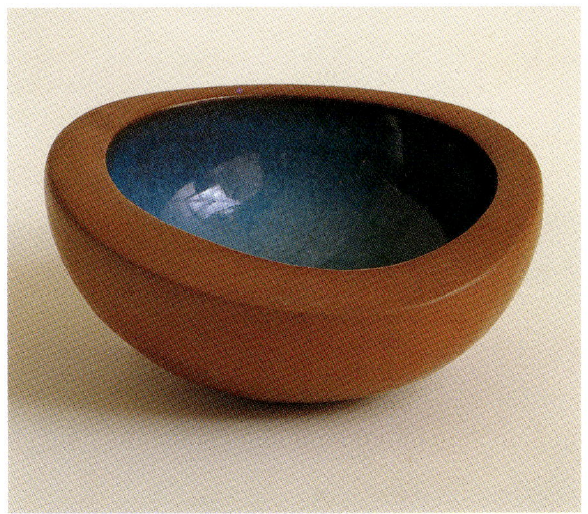

1.11 Bowl, Ohio State, 1953. Terracotta, 2 x 4½

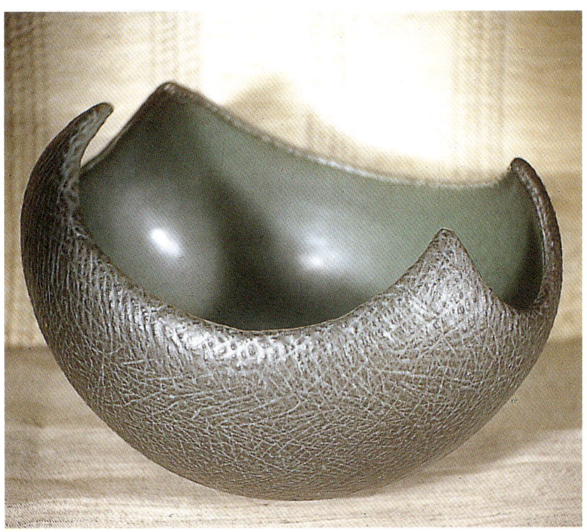

1.12 Bowl, Ohio State, 1954

owner came running out, very upset. He probably though I wanted to copy them for mass production."[11] The formal organization of these competent but unremarkable early vessels presages several trends in Kottler's later work. The outside and inside surfaces of the bowls are often treated separately; shiny glazes and decoration are applied to the interiors, while the exterior serves as a relatively neutral shell. This inclination to clearly divide his compositions into several different zones of reference and to treat exterior surfaces as shells for articulated inner spaces reappears in Kottler's work of the later 1960s

and asserts itself intermittently until the end of his career.

Kottler experimented widely as a student, however, and the only common denominator in the work is a taste for linear design and precise definition of edges and shapes. Influenced by Friley, he investigated mold-cast forms and, imitating Margaret Fetzer, he created a series of tiny globular vases with jewellike glazes (figs. 1.13, 1.14). "One of Fetzer's claims to fame was these incredibly small pieces she threw on the wheel using a toothpick," Kottler explained. "I used to tease her about them—I always said 'Well, Margaret, you can have your

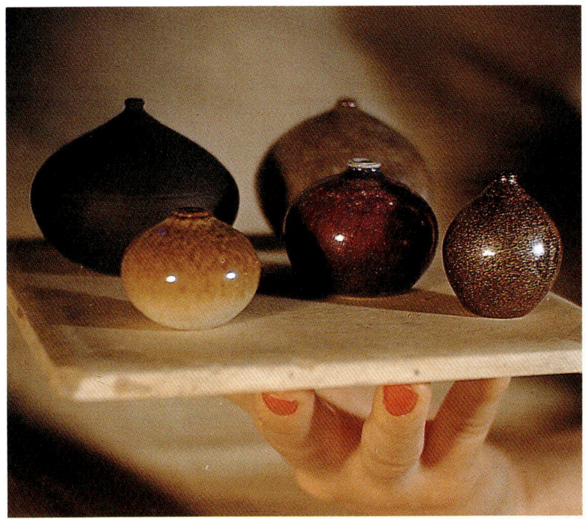

1.13 Vases, Ohio State, 1954. Stoneware, ca. 2 x 2

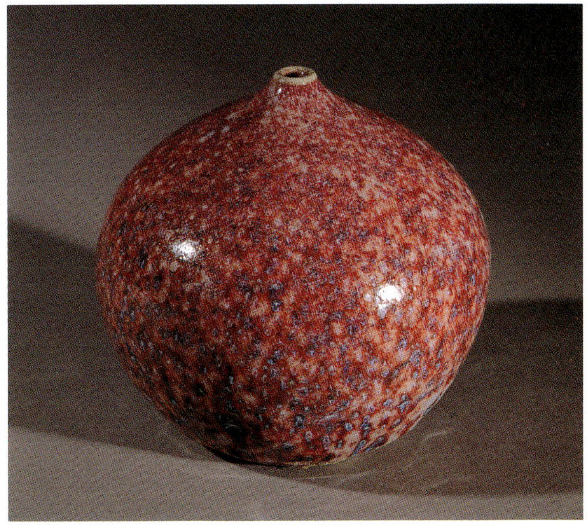

1.14 Vase, Ohio State, 1954

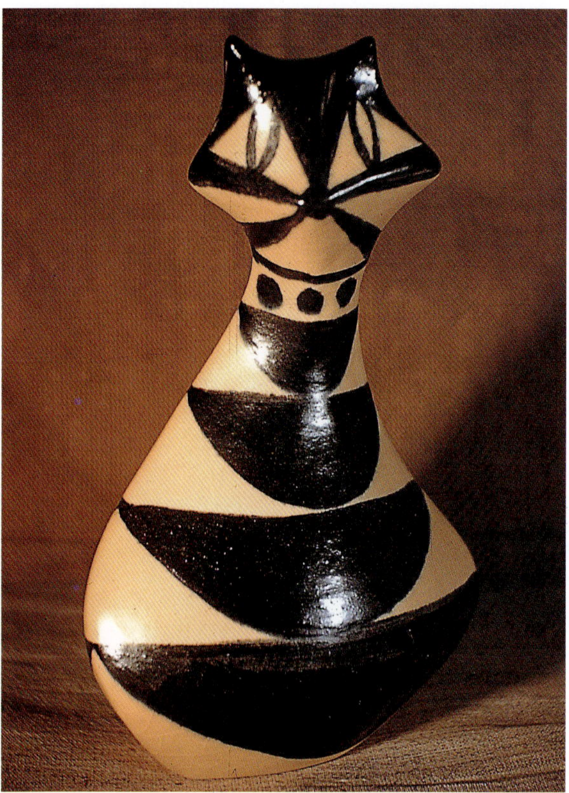

1.15 Cat, 1956. Stoneware, 6 h

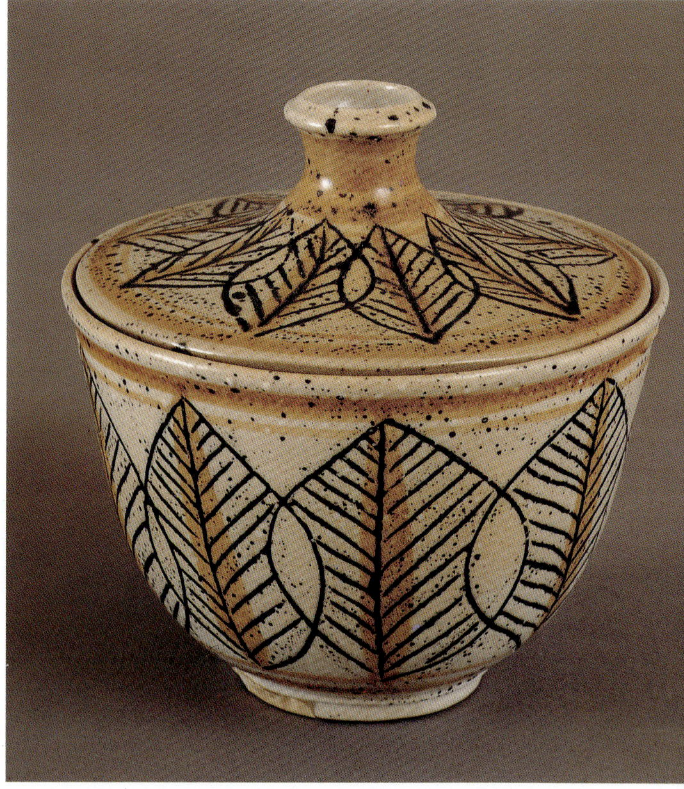

1.16 Lidded casserole, Ohio State, 1955. Stoneware, 7 x 6½

entire life's work in a cigar box.' The pieces were very lush and precious. I made some for myself, to poke fun at her a little because she was so serious about them."[12]

As a young ceramist, Kottler won an award for a cat figurine, which he laboriously mass-produced (fig. 1.15). The cat won second prize for ceramic sculpture at the 1956 Cleveland Museum annual May Show. The museum's director, William Milliken, was an enthusiast for ceramic sculpture with broad popular appeal. He praised the figurine as an "effective form, abstract in its implications [with] a fine glaze and a witty concept."[13] Kottler recalled that "once you were juried into the May Show you could sell the work right at the museum. I think I sold 200 cats. They were cast in stoneware, but they had a wax-resist glaze surface that took forever to do. In the firing no two pieces came out exactly the same, which I thought would be a plus. But some people wrote letters to complain, saying they didn't want their cat because it wasn't exactly the same as the piece in the show."[14]

In 1956 Kottler completed his master's thesis, *The Waisted Cylinder Form in the History of Ceramic Art*. The text surveys the historical evolution of the *albarello*, a pharmaceutical jar or spice pot, which appeared in the Western domain of the Islamic empire in the twelfth century. A "waisted cylinder" is a vessel with a concave cylindrical body: this shape was particularly well suited for a pharmaceutical jar, as Kottler pointed out, because the concavity of the body allowed each container to be easily grasped when rows of the albarelli were placed next to each other on a shelf.[15] For the production requirement of his thesis, Kottler created variants of traditional albarelli glazes which he applied to stoneware casserole dishes, lidded jars, bowls, and plates of his own design. He decorated these wheel-thrown forms with linear floral and leaf patterns or bird and animal figures based on early Persian designs (figs. 1.16, 1.17, 1.18).

"I don't remember exactly why I got into those drug pots," Kottler said, "but certainly I was influenced by my teacher, Carlton Atherton, . . . who had studied with

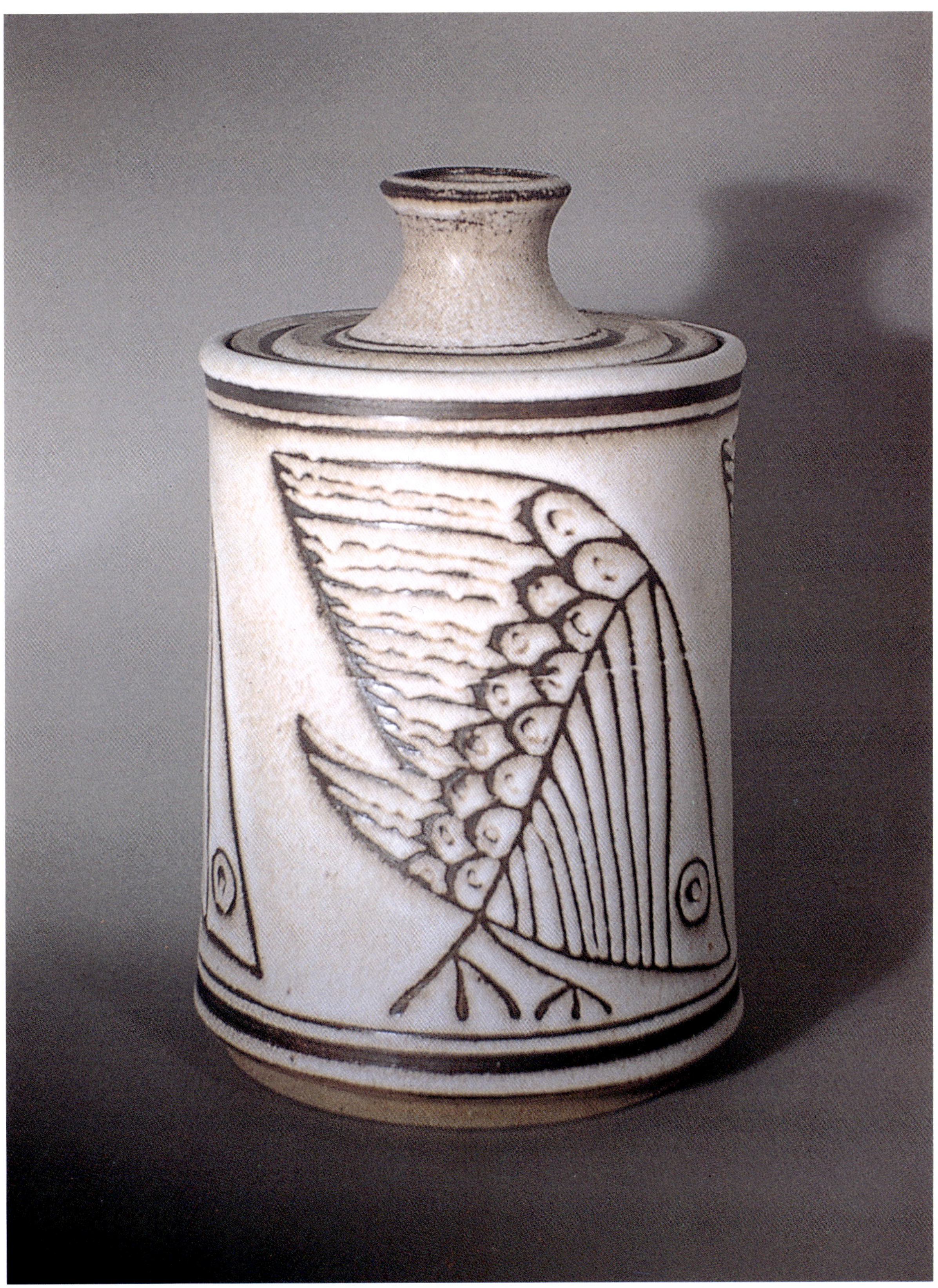

1.17 Cylindrical jar, Ohio State, 1956. Stoneware, 7 x 6½

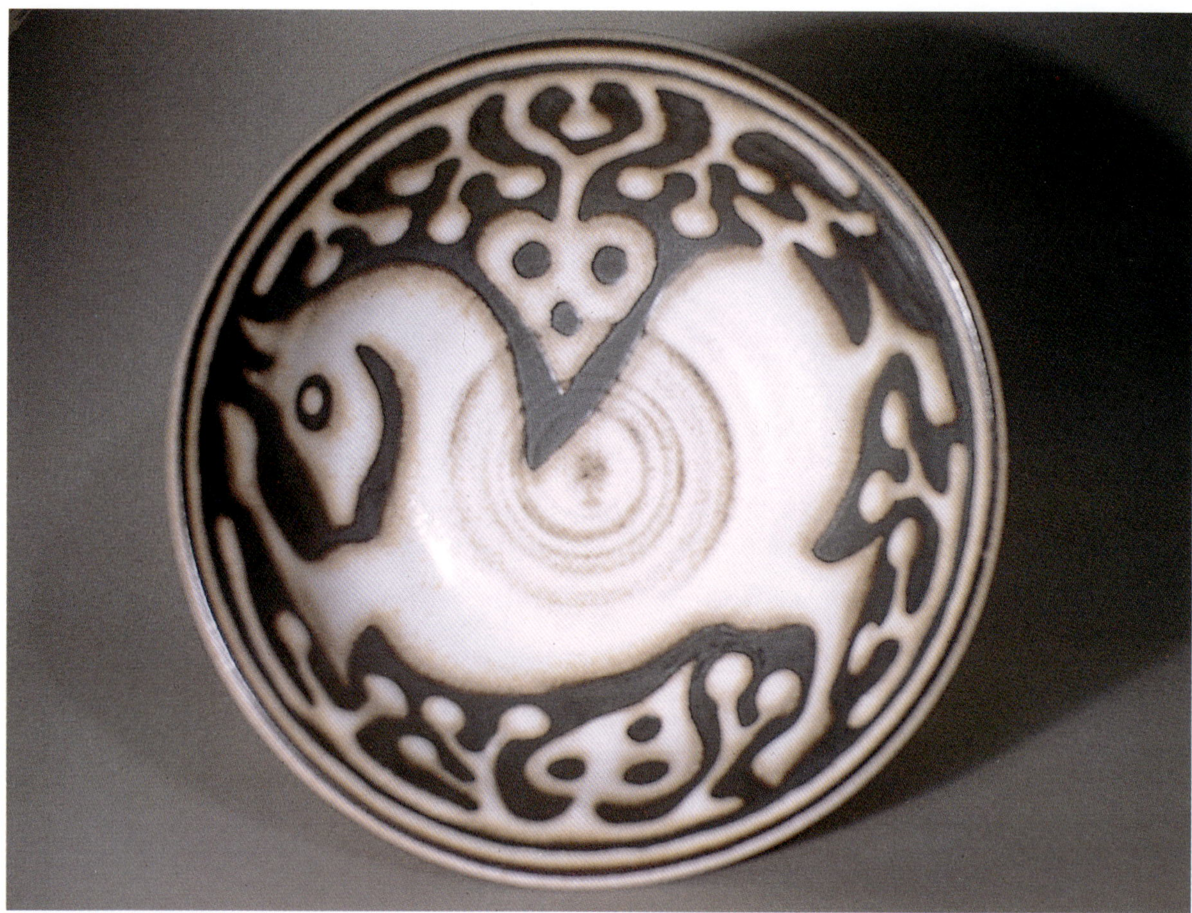

1.18 Plate, Ohio State, 1956. Stoneware, 2¼ x 6¼

Adelaide Robineau at Syracuse. He gave a very thorough course in the history of ceramics. As far as I know, Ohio State was the only major school at that point to offer, to ceramics majors, courses in the history of ceramics. He had a subtle way of putting things down he didn't like . . . pottery from the Ming dynasty on, for example. He generally didn't like anything with an elaborated surface—which seems strange, since he was very close to Robineau, whose work had highly elaborated surfaces. He wasn't interested in the twentieth century—he never mentioned Art Deco, for example. He mentioned Art Nouveau, but didn't really discuss that period. He had a fine but eclectic taste. I think it was centered, if anywhere, in an eighteenth-century French aesthetic, although he also had a great affinity for the work of Arthur Baggs. My taste was different from his, but I appreciated his teaching and historical perspective."[16]

Kottler, in his 1956 M.A. thesis, characterizes himself as a "studio potter engaged in the production of new ceramic forms." Reviewing the field in general, he observes that experimentation with form "is not a new concept in American ceramic ware, for it has its beginnings in the 1930s, when there was a return to the production of pottery which held closely to the basic shapes [sphere, cone, and cylinder]. This interest in form has steadily increased and has been augmented by a renewed regard for the ceramic art of other countries." The contemporary studio potter, he continues, must play a new societal role. "With the need for functional pottery being successfully filled by machines, the studio potter, once vitally concerned with the production of forms for utilitarian purposes, has been forced to reconsider his place in society. To continue the production of functional ware would not be practical in view of the machine, for mass-pro-

16

duced ceramics, when properly designed, can produce fine pottery at minimum cost to the consumer. As a result, the studio potter has searched for a release in another direction. . . .

"It is always difficult to pass judgment on art objects being currently produced," he adds. In time "it may be found that the ceramic forms of the studio potter of today were but passing fads—which in due course resulted in a return to functional shapes of the past." On the other hand, he wrote, "pottery might suggest a closer alliance between ceramics and ceramic sculpture, leaving functional pottery in the hands of the manufacturer and the creations of the studio potter in the realm of form with no reference to functional pottery. . . . Most observers find it exceedingly difficult to yield to the imaginative new forms, finding it easier to accept those from our remote past. In time, however, we must come to realize that such forms can be both strong and sincere expressions of the artist in his striving for a greater understanding of ceramic form which is intimately blended with the reality of today."[17]

In selecting the category of studio pottery as an umbrella for his own production, Kottler places himself within a tradition begun, according to ceramics historian Garth Clark, by the maverick Mississippi potter George E. Ohr (1857-1918), whose work was rediscovered in the 1970s. According to Clark, Ohr "was the first of the American studio potters and the first to achieve stylistic independence from Europe. He led the assault on the boundaries of applied and fine art, blurring the definition of what critic John Coplans so successfully terms 'the hierarchy of media.'"[18] In the early decades of the twentieth century, Clark identifies Charles Fergus Binns, founder of the New York School of Clayworking and Ceramics (later Alfred University), Mary Chase Perry, Henry Chapman Mercer, and Adelaide Robineau as leaders of the studio pottery movement. These independent spirits, he concludes, "developed strong personal aesthetics based on the interpretation and imitation of the monuments of ceramics history. This development was a mixed blessing. On the one hand, it resulted in an identity for ceramics based on its own roots and not on secondhand interpretation in clay of painting and sculpture. But this hermeticism meant that the revolutionary changes in concepts of surface and forms that were beginning to emerge in the modern art movement had no influence on the potter."[19]

Like most of his colleagues, Kottler had never heard of George Ohr in 1956. Along with studio potters like Binns and Robineau, he shared an aesthetic centered upon historical precedents in ceramics rather than major movements in modern art. Accurately evaluating his own Ohio State M.A. thesis show, Kottler later concluded that his vessels "were just too close to the historical precedents. There was some variation, but no real development of the waisted cylinder forms—some shifting of proportions, but that's about all. The surfaces were based on traditional Chinese glazes or Persian decoration, but I didn't really have a sensibility for that kind of drawing. . . . I was already in my mid-twenties and I didn't really know what I was doing. I worked hard every day and enjoyed it, but I wasn't coached to find my own direction. I came out of a science background, after all, and I didn't know much about art. By the time I arrived, most of the Ohio State faculty had crested—of the older people, only Paul Bogatay was actively working. It wasn't that the department wouldn't let you do what you wanted to do, but the program was basically oriented toward glaze technology and the oriental traditions promoted by Bernard Leach. Leach's *A Potter's Book*, I think, set back American ceramics for decades. We did a lot of experimenting with surfaces and tried to get a strong relationship between the glaze and the form, but the form was essentially treated as a surface. We had no contacts with the art movements developing in New York. I was drifting."[20]

After receiving his M.A. from Ohio State, Kottler received a scholarship to the Cranbrook Academy of Art, where he studied with Finnish ceramist Maija Grotell. "There's a funny story about the scholarship," Kottler said. "Grotell at some point in her career visited with Arthur Baggs, who came to teach at Ohio State in the late 1920s. She made some kind of *faux pas* in talking to Baggs about his work, and she wanted to make it up. Apparently I was the first person after that from Ohio State

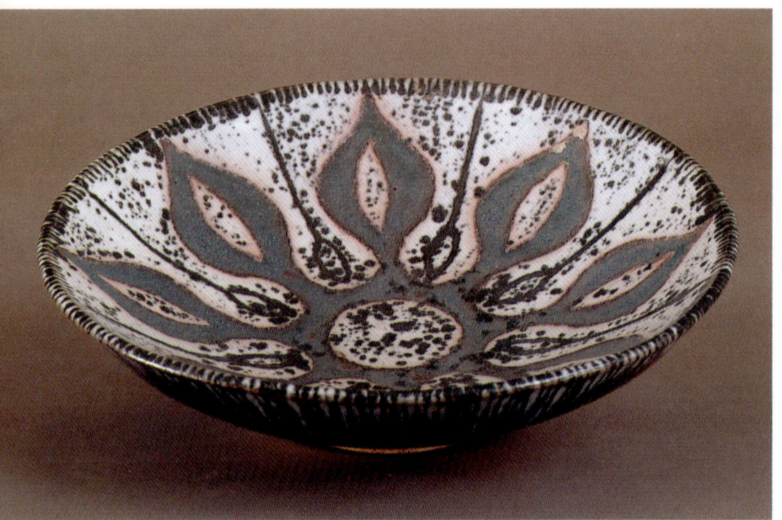

1.19 Inlaid plate, Cranbrook, surface technique in style of Grotell, 1957. Stoneware, 3¼ x 12

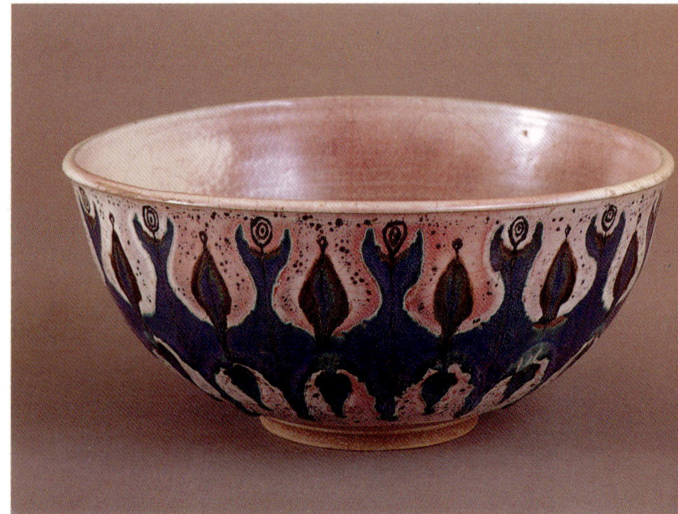

1.20 Inlaid bowl, Cranbrook, surface technique in style of Grotell, 1957. Stoneware, 6¾ x 14¼

who applied for a Cranbrook scholarship. Even though Baggs was dead by then, she still felt badly about it, and I got the scholarship."[21]

At Cranbrook, Kottler's work was strongly influenced by Grotell, but their personal relationship was tenuous. "We were not close at all and we didn't talk often," Kottler recalled. "It was easy for me to emulate her style, but I didn't really understand her work—it was a surface comprehension. This was certainly true for me later with Abstract Expressionism, too. I was like many students—enamored of a style and wanting to emulate it, but not being on the cutting edge because I didn't really understand the underlying concepts. Maija never said, 'Let's sit down and talk about what you are doing.' I had capabilities, but I still wasn't being directed in using them. I developed very, very slowly as a result." Furthermore, the strongest work at the Cranbrook Academy in the mid-1950s, in Kottler's view, was produced by painters, not ceramists. "Grotell wasn't working that much any more—she had health problems. In the painting department, though, was Fred Mitchell, who showed at the Howard Wise Gallery in New York. He was a good Abstract Expressionist painter who had a real commitment to innovation."[22]

Nevertheless, Kottler was highly impressed with Grotell's command of Art Deco motifs, her wax-resist surfaces and her inlaid glazes (figs. 1.19, 1.20). By 1957 his work was developing in two directions: traditional plate and bowl forms decorated *à la* Grotell, and elegant globular bottles modeled after the work of Honolulu ceramist Toshiko Takaezu (figs. 1.21, 1.22). Although the tubular spouts on the bottles were small and narrow, Kottler often accented these openings by highlighting the lip of the spout with shiny glazes that invaded the bottle interiors. "I discovered Takaezu's work and Voulkos's about the same time—in 1956-57," Kottler commented. "They were moving in opposite directions—big, direct, and spontaneous in the case of Voulkos, and toward refined simplicity and precision in the case of Takaezu. I didn't understand Voulkos then and instead I followed the lead of an artist I finally became opposed to. Takaezu's work now seems very mannered, but I was attracted by her sculpturesque approach."[23]

Kottler continued to produce similar asymmetrical, semibiomorphic vessel forms with multiple openings during his stay in Finland, which began after he received his M.F.A. degree from Cranbrook in 1957. Supported by a Fulbright grant, he spent seven months in Helsinki where he studied ceramics at the Central School of Arts and Crafts, and weaving and tapestry design at the Koke Studios (fig. 1.23). His contacts with artists at the Arabia Ceramics Factory, however, had the greatest impact on

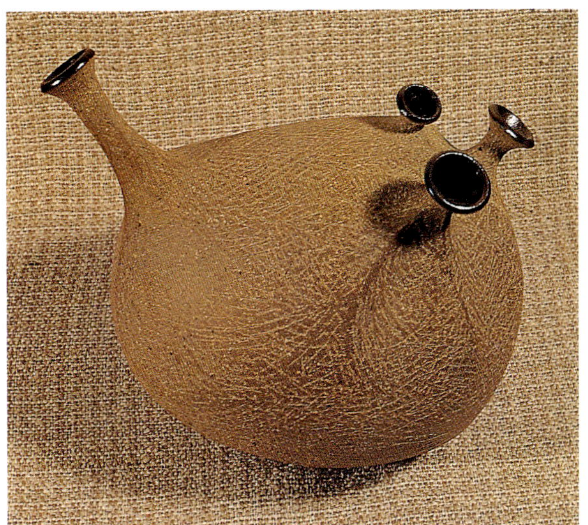

1.21 Multi-spout reed pot in style of Takaezu, 1957, 6½ x 7. Collection American Craft Museum, New York. Gift of Howard Kottler Testamentary Trust.

his future development. "I wanted to go to Finland because Grotell was Finnish and Finland was the top of the design world," Kottler said. "I'd seen articles about the Arabia factory in *Craft Horizons*, and it sounded very attractive. Arabia had fifteen artists who all had their own studios to produce whatever they wanted. The factory had a store in downtown Helsinki where only the work of these artists was shown and sold. The artists were paid a weekly salary that was never more than the top factory workers', and all their work became the property of the factory. They did a wide variety of things and brought Arabia great recognition—they were continually winning top awards in major European competitions. I had my own studio at the factory and, for me, it was an ideal place. I could stay closeted there or visit other studios, and I had access to all the factory expertise and equipment."[24]

The Arabia factory's collaborative production methods were a revelation for Kottler. "The artist-potters I knew all worked alone, basically—they didn't use assistants. At the Arabia factory, I could call from my studio for more clay and phone again for someone to pick up the work and take it to the kiln and return it when it was finished. That kind of efficiency was completely opposed to the Cranbrook experience, where you were supposed

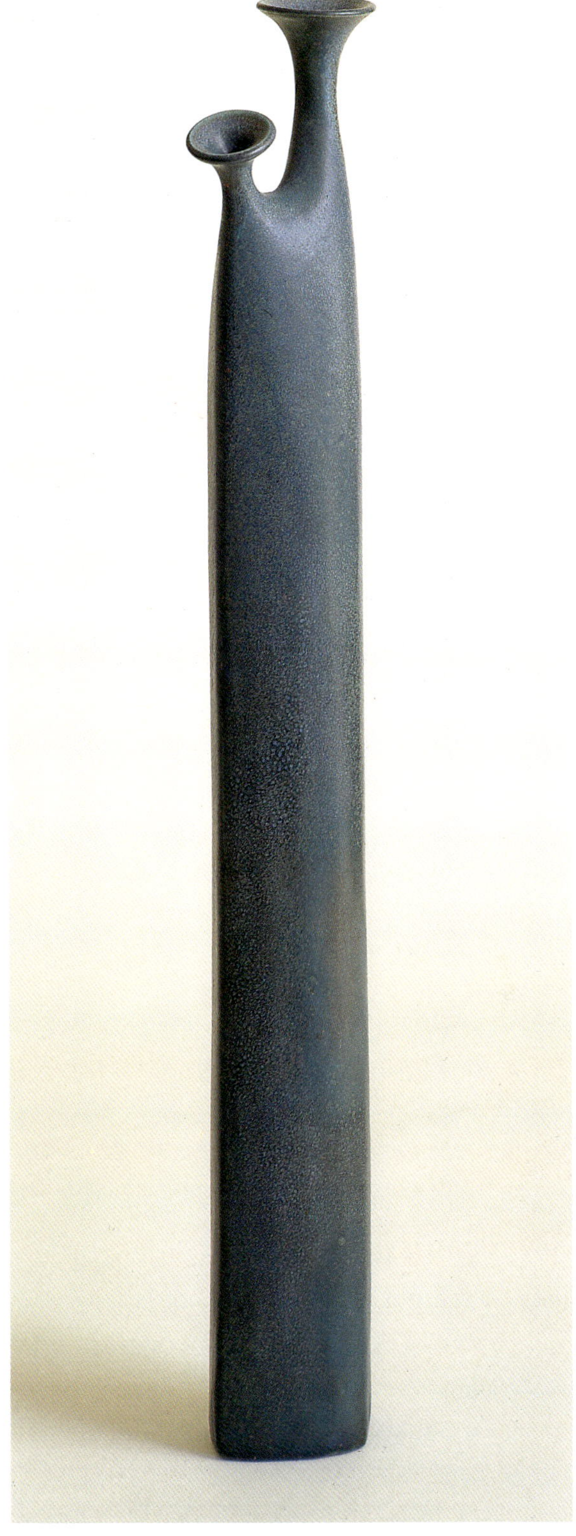

1.22 Multi-spout reed pot in style of Takaezu, 1957. Stoneware, 22 x 3¾

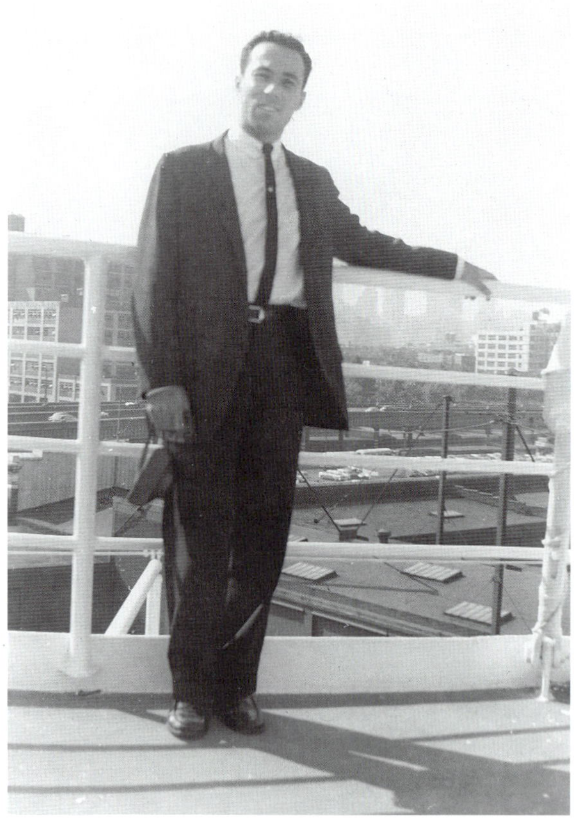

1.23 Sailing for Finland on the Kungholm, 1957

to be totally involved with the clay every step of the way. If it had been possible, I think Grotell would have made every student go out and dig the clay himself. I realized this is a ridiculous approach to take in the twentieth century."[25]

Kottler's tenure at the Arabia Ceramics Factory provided an important technical stimulus for his later work. Touring the production facilities, he studied the creation and application of ceramic decals, a primary method of decorating mass-produced ceramic ware. "There was one major artist at the factory, Kalle Schultz-Köln, who used these factory decals in some of his ceramic reliefs," he recalled. "He worked with linear patterns and cut up the decals into strips, using the decals as colorful collage-bands—without concern for the images. I was never particularly good at drawing . . . so the idea of a possible ready-made appealed to me. My work in Finland involved forms with surfaces that were textural, with no concern for image decoration. And so, although I liked

the decals, I did not find a use for them in my work at that time."[26]

Most of the work Kottler executed in Finland he called "stoneware branch pots." The majority are skinny clay envelopes about twelve inches high with slitlike openings on the top. Their broad, undifferentiated surfaces are pebbly and covered with subtle feldspathic glazes (figs. 1.24, 1.25). Like much of Kottler's mature production, these pots have a strong front-back orientation and bold, crisp silhouettes. The straightforward references to manual process are new: the joining of front and back slabs is undisguised, and the spouts declare themselves as paddled-down rings of clay.[27]

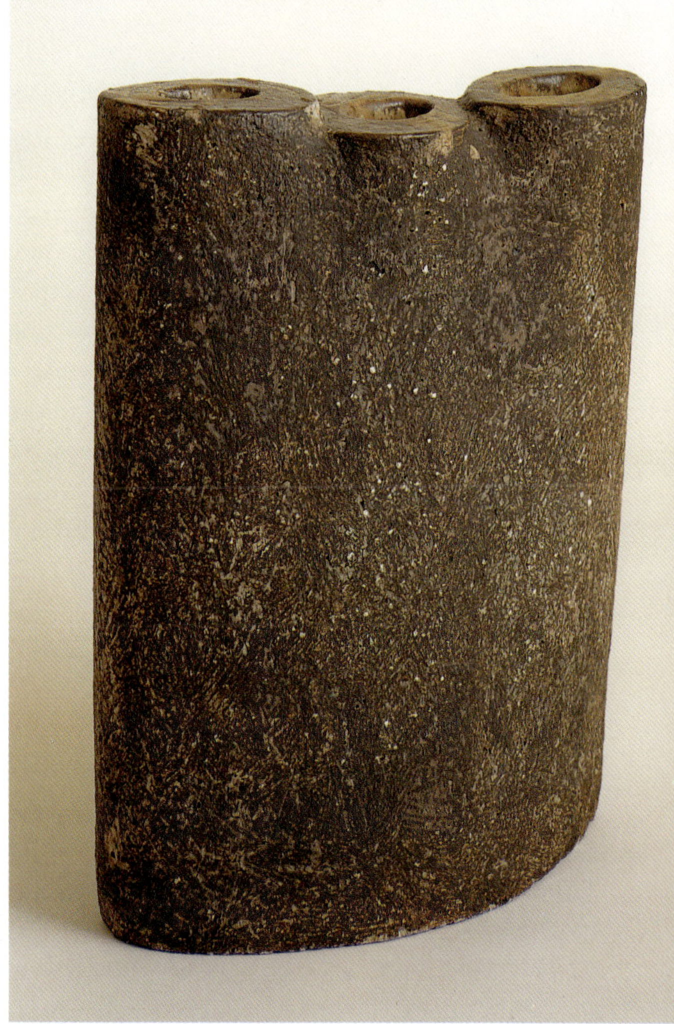

1.24 Envelope pot, 1957-58. Stoneware, 12¾ x 9½

20

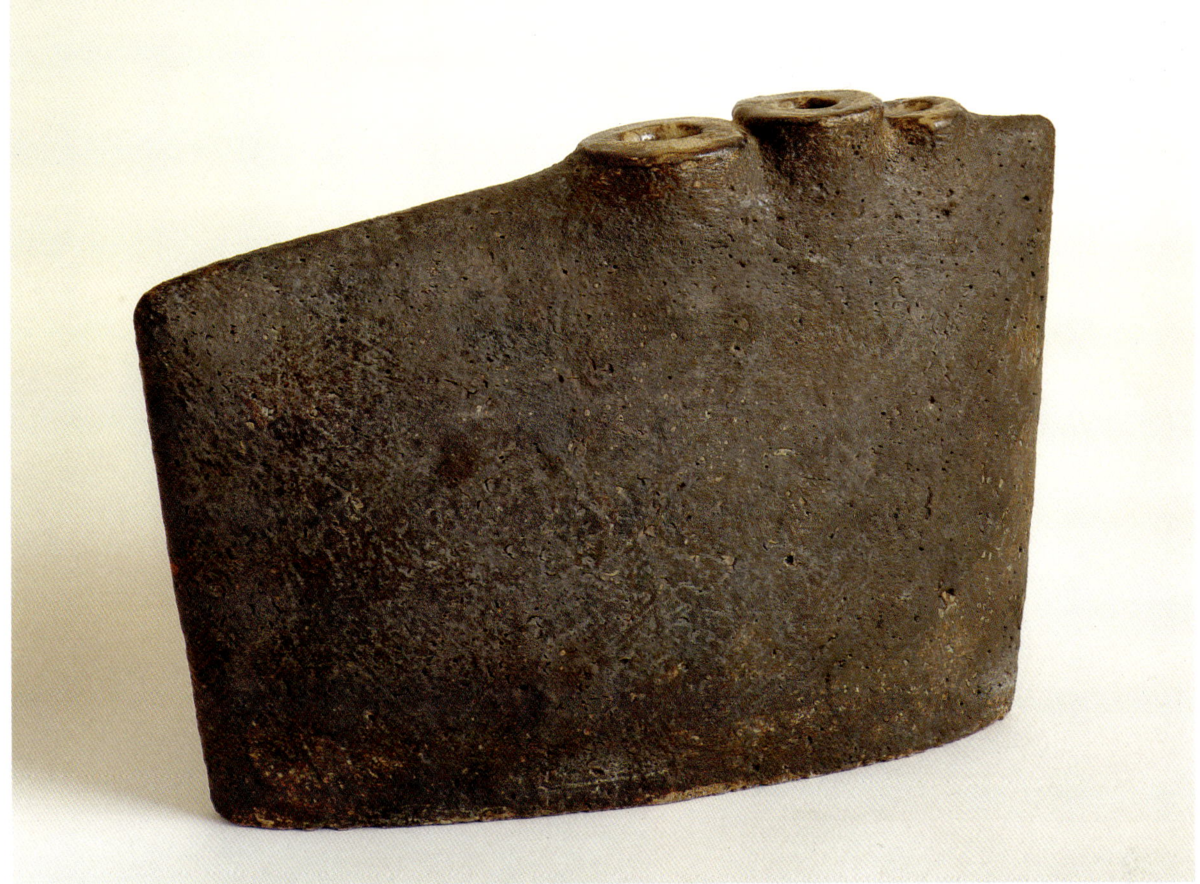

1.25 Envelope pot, 1957-58. Stoneware, 8¾ x 13½

After he left Finland, Kottler joined artist Harry Soviak in Port-au-Prince, Haiti, where Soviak was studying on a Fulbright grant (fig. 1.26). "Harry worked very hard, but I just took it easy," Kottler recalled. "We both came back to the U.S. in 1958; he returned to Cranbrook and I should have started looking for a teaching job—by this time I had two master's degrees. But I decided instead to go back to Ohio State, which was one of the few schools that offered a doctorate in ceramics. I started in March 1958, and it wasn't the wisest thing to do—things hadn't changed at Ohio State. There was still no interest in the Abstract Expressionist direction in ceramics; in fact, the faculty had tightened up even more."[28]

When he returned to OSU, Kottler began imitating the work of Kyllikki Salmenharra, one of the potters he had met at the Arabia Ceramics Factory. "Her work was marvelously thrown, very direct, and I liked both the shapes and the surfaces," he explained. "But I don't know why I was *so* enamored. I got back into throwing, which I was never very good at, and I got trapped for a while. I hated pulling handles too; hers were great, and I couldn't

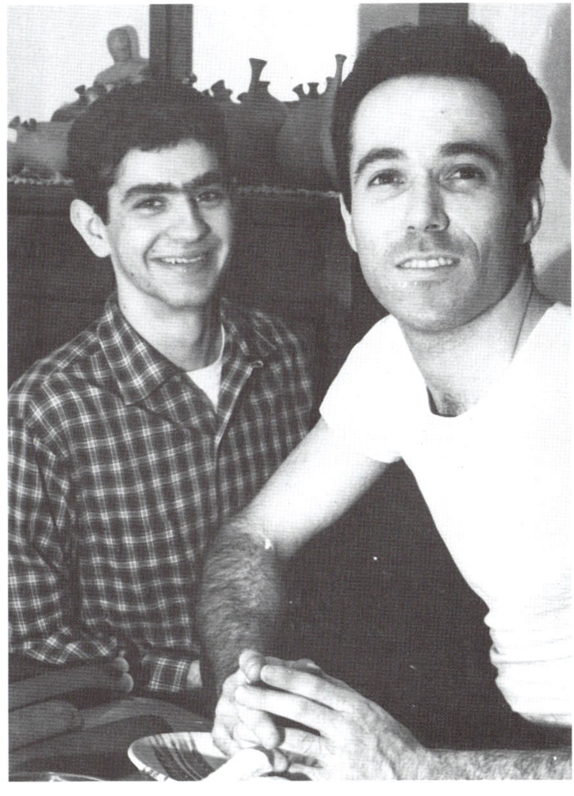

1.26 Howard Kottler (r.) and Harry Soviak, Cranbrook, 1956

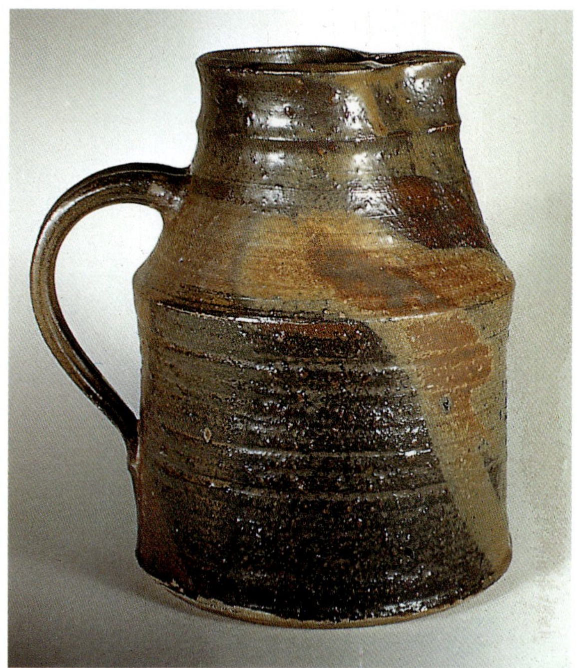

1.27 Stoneware pitcher, 1960. 10 h

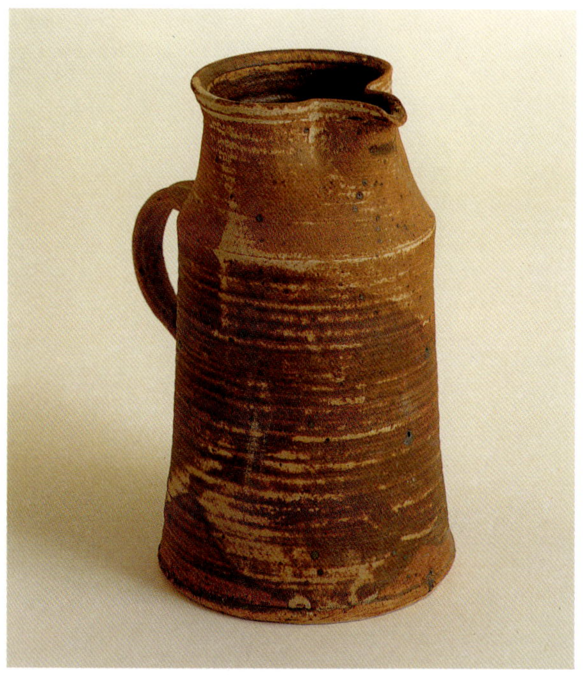

1.28 Stoneware pitcher, 1960. 8½ h

do them as well as she could. It was traditional, functional stoneware, very tight, with poured and layered glazes (figs. 1.27, 1.28). I can't find anything of myself in this work. After an almost wasted period, I did start to go back to hand-building late in 1959, making pots similar to those I did in Finland. But I was not taking any risks."[29]

The Salmenharra-derived cups and pitchers were consistent with the Ohio State outlook on ceramic materials. "There were definite no-no's imbedded in the teaching," Kottler observed. "High-fire clay—stoneware or porcelain—was preferred. I was using stoneware without thinking about why I was using it. We were not taught to think in terms of using a particular material to achieve a particular end. Subtle stoneware glazes were good, but low-fire glazes were not. If red was used, it was permitted only in small areas or used like in Sung dynasty pottery. There was no suggestion that color might be used to elicit emotional response. Voulkos often used color glazes as a dramatic climax point, but we were taught to use glazes primarily to cover the entire piece. These yes's and no's were transmitted to a couple of generations of students who didn't really think about what they were absorbing."[30]

Kottler's Ohio State instructors responded with high praise to his "branch pots" and other stoneware vessels. In a 1960 exhibition flyer, Paul Bogatay observed: "Howard Kottler is a ceramic artist of unusual talent and ability. Strongly motivated in purpose and independent in his thinking, his work reflects a personal quality, restraint and integrity which sets it apart from that of his contemporaries. Devoid of pretense or contrived effect, it is consistent in its total unity and clarity of expression."[31] For another 1960 show, Carlton Atherton wrote: "In this materialistic age it is rewarding to encounter the fine spirit and creative drive shown in the work of Howard Kottler. [Here] is a positive statement rather than the negativism common to much current ware.... The wheel-thrown ware evinces a feeling of freshness which is in part intrinsic to the use of fingers as tools with no mechanical intervention between the artist and his work.... It is refreshing to find a resurgence of expressive power in simple form innocent of virtuosity."[32]

By 1964 Kottler had shown his ceramics in more than fifty regional and national exhibitions. Several museums, including the Detroit Institute of Art and the Cleveland Museum of Art, had acquired his work.[33] He was an accomplished craftsman who worked intuitively, although he had begun to reflect upon the meaning of his forms and the broader rationale for his technique. He was not yet familiar with Robert Arneson's early guerrilla attacks on ceramics tradition—in his view, the work of Peter Voulkos, who gave a workshop at OSU in the early 1960s, represented the field's new frontier. He was not comfortable with Voulkos's spontaneous, expressionistic working methods, yet he began to classify some of his own work as "classical expressionism." In these vessels, the record of physical gesture is more evident, the scale increases, layered glazes are applied in painterly swoops, and surfaces are rough and tactile (one of his OSU instructors reproached him for producing "oven-baked biscuits"). Kottler recognized, however, that his expressionism lacked the intensity that distinguishes memorable Abstract Expressionist ceramics. "I was probably lucky that I wasn't in California working with Pete," he concluded. "I might have given up. I wouldn't have been able to find my personality within that framework. I wish that weren't true, because I love the impact the plasticity of clay can have when it's used in an expressionistic way. My work in 1964 was still unresolved, but I was beginning to see that I needed to find a hybrid position somewhere between expressionism and precision."[34]

Kottler's commentaries in his 1964 Ph.D. dissertation suggest a shift in his professional self-image. He identified himself here as an "artist-potter" rather than a "studio potter" as he had in 1956. Studio pottery, a relatively autonomous field, drew its inspiration primarily from the history of ceramics, while artist-potters, in Kottler's view, aligned themselves with the broader history of modern art. The evolution of the artist-potter in the United States, he wrote, can be traced to the china painters addressed by Adelaide Robineau in her magazine *Keramic Studio*, published from 1899 to 1924. Robineau urged her readers not to rely upon European precedents but to master all phases of ceramic production and to create their own designs. The artist-potter concept gained impetus from 1930 to the end of World War II, he continued, abetted by the growth of university ceramics departments, a new noncommercial support structure that permitted instructors to pursue independent ideas. Although he did not lay out his position systematically, it is clear that Kottler now divided academic ceramists into two groups—studio potters and artist-potters—and that his sympathies were no longer with the former.

The principal argument Kottler develops in his dissertation is that the historical evolution of American ceramics can be linked to alterations in the concept of good craftsmanship. For potters in the eighteenth century, good craftsmanship meant efficient functionalism: there was no room in this art for cups that did not hold liquid or pitchers that did not pour. In the nineteenth century, ceramics factories began supplying functional ware, while a market also developed for hand-painted decorative china. Among early nineteenth-century china painters, good craftsmanship meant successful imitation of European forms of decoration on ready-made plates, vases, cups, and bowls. After the Paris Exposition of 1900, where American entries received little recognition because the ware itself was not the work of the decorator, a new enthusiasm arose (fueled by Robineau) for individual mastery of production techniques. But instruction in the practical craft of ceramics as pioneered at Alfred University and Ohio State, Kottler argued, ultimately exalted technical dexterity as an end in itself. Well-crafted ceramic pottery came to be identified with "clearly defined lyrical contours and an emphasis on the refinement or smoothness of the surface finish. Great admiration is accorded the subtle quality of the glaze which appropriately 'fits' the clay body without evidence of crazing or imperfections, and consideration is given to weight and thickness. . . . Generally speaking, these are the values which derive from an idea of 'flawlessness' or 'perfection' in the use of ceramic processes."[35]

Although Kottler did not use terms with complete consistency throughout his dissertation, the postwar "artist-potter" was represented as a ceramist who "drew close to the other arts in America and came to share with other artists a desire for liberation from convention."[36] Since American art in the 1950s was dominated by Abstract Expressionism, many artist-potters, stimulated by

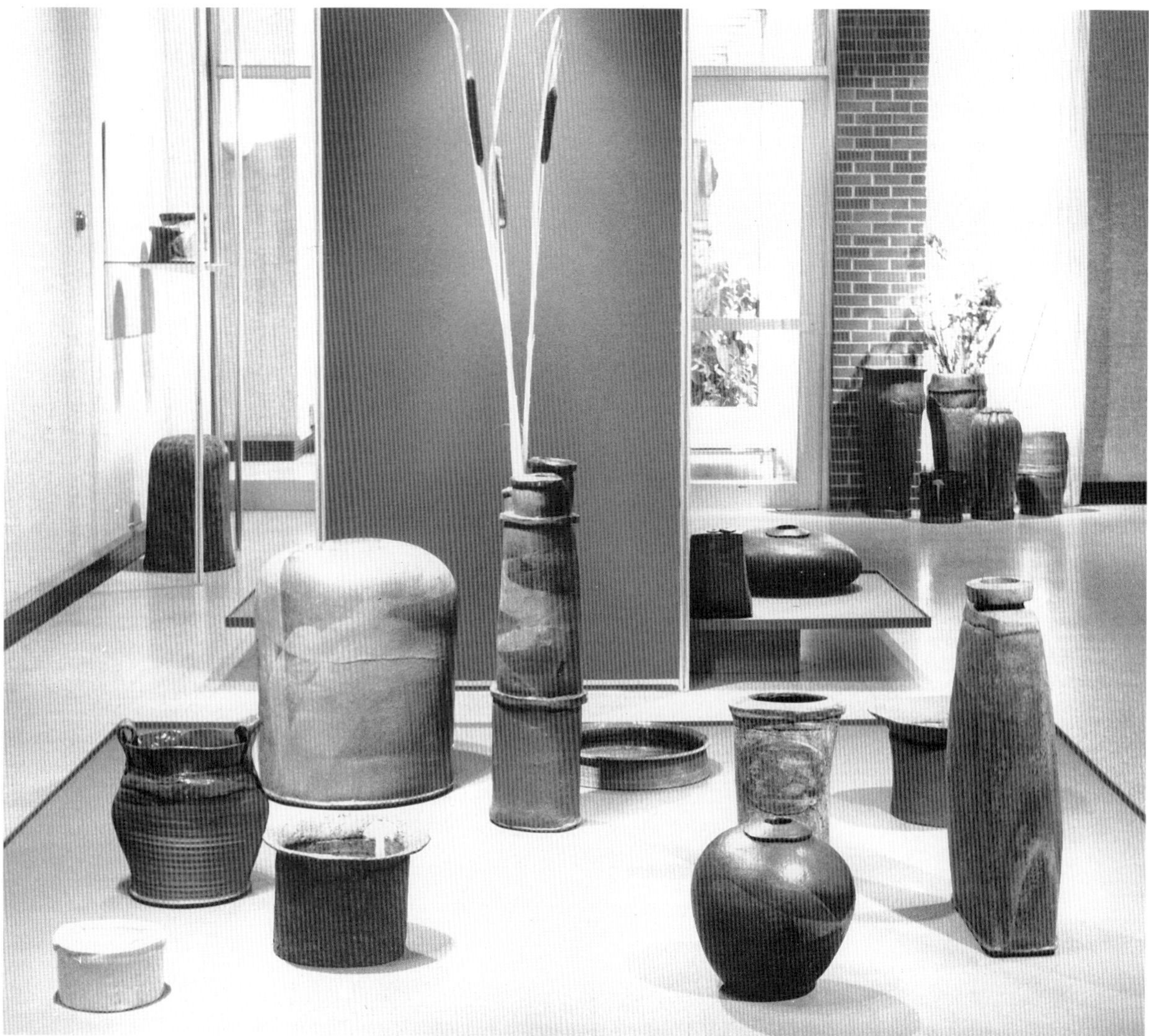

1.29 Howard Kottler, installation view, Ohio State University Ph.D. exhibition, 1964

Voulkos's precedent, began to explore expressionistic approaches to clay. The prevailing academic conception of "flawless" craftsmanship, however, was inconsistent with these new explorations. Kottler quotes ceramist John Mason, who made the following observation in 1957:

> The currently popular mechanistic concept of craftsmanship is a truly alarming concept that is indicative of the influence of our industrial age. This concept has been furthered by teachers looking for a simple ABC way of teaching crafts. It has been passed on from teacher to student not as a concept but as a set of rules and postulates that makes it possible for anyone to be a fine craftsman. But there the line is drawn, fine craftsman—not artist. Craftsmanship separated from art and regulated by rules and postulates can only occur in a crystallized art structure, resulting in the refinement of established form at the expense of vitality and new expression. It should be obvious that craftsmanship and art are part of the same parcel. Craftsmanship is the technical and esthetic structure of an art form. It follows naturally that craftsmanship must change with each new search for form.[37]

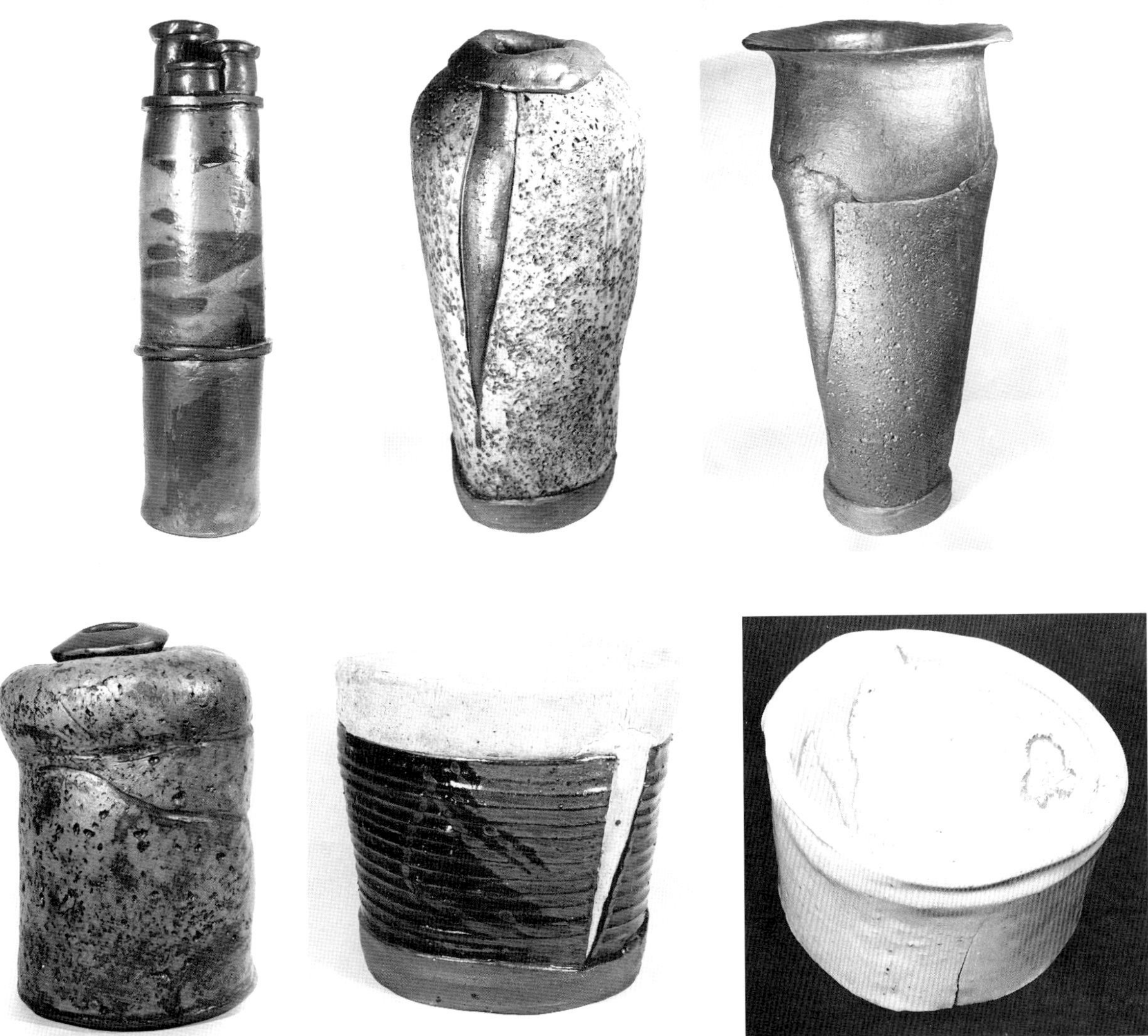

Pots in 1964 Ph.D. exhibition (from left to right): 1.30 Stoneware branch bottle, 24 h; 1.31 Stoneware floor vase, 30 x 12; 1.32 Stoneware floor vase, Ca. 40 h; 1.33 Corncob pot; 1.34 Tear and repair bowl, Porcelain; 1.35 Tear and repair bowl, Porcelain

For the artist-potter, Kottler concludes, "good crafts-manship" means being able to use ceramic materials to express personal ideas that might or might not be related to ceramic tradition. The artist-potter's search "repre-sents a concern for fundamentals and a complete free-dom from historic styles. It constitutes a rediscovery of the basic elements that have always been present but never explored to their fullest potential."[38]

The modernist bravado expressed in the disserta-tion was less evident in Kottler's Ph.D. exhibition (fig. 1.29). Several types of vessels were included: multi-spouted branch bottles and jars; tall (two to three feet high) textured vases; chunky floor-based planters; "corn-cob" pots and early examples of his tear-and-repair series (figs. 1.30-1.36). Most of the pots were hand-built stone-ware, although the tear-and-repair forms were porcelain and included wheel-thrown sections. The corncob and tear-and-repair series represented his most adventure-some productions. To create the former, he rolled crushed corncob into the moist clay; random pockmarks appeared on the surfaces when the corncob was fired out. Kottler relaxed the columnar shapes of these vessels, some based on Japanese water jars, by moving a paddle quickly over the damp surfaces to distort their symmetry.

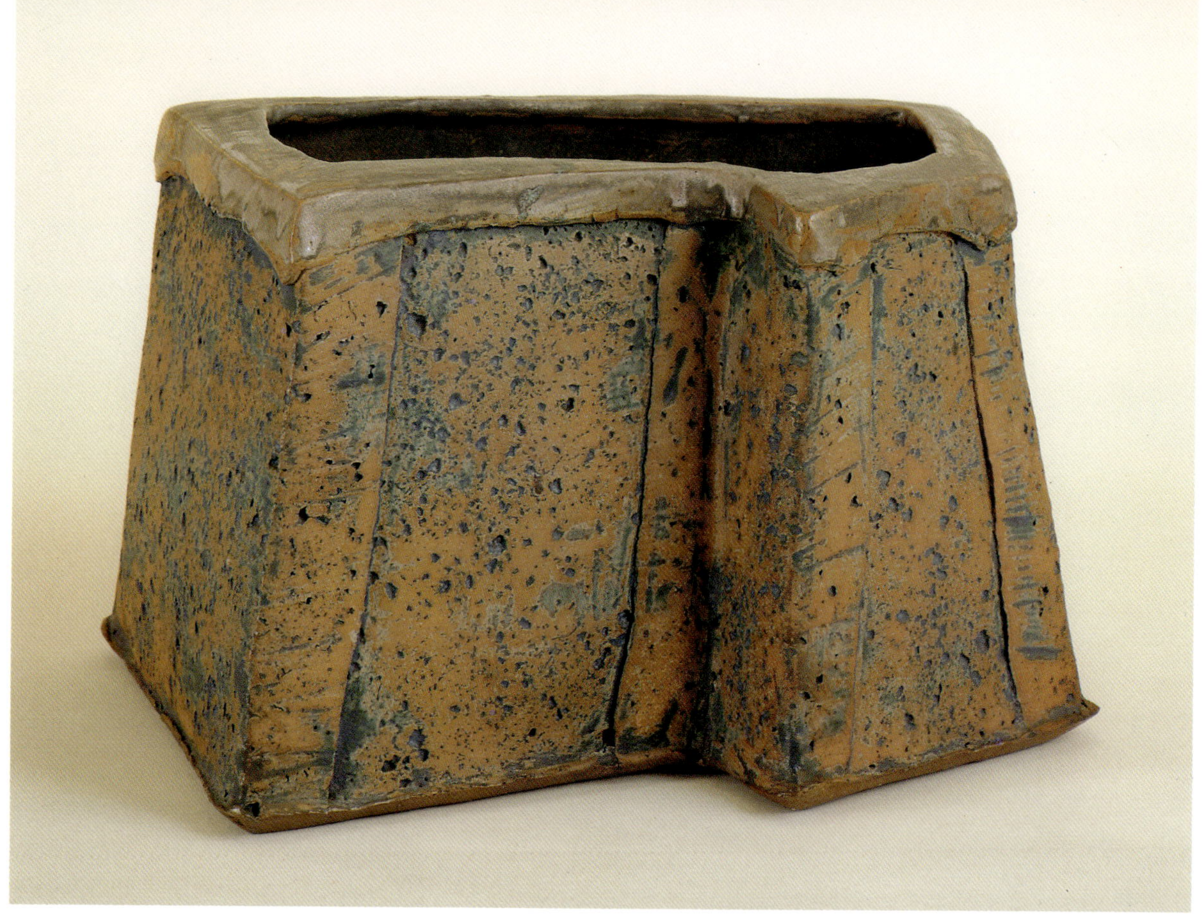

1.36 Stoneware planter, 1963. 11¾ x 16½

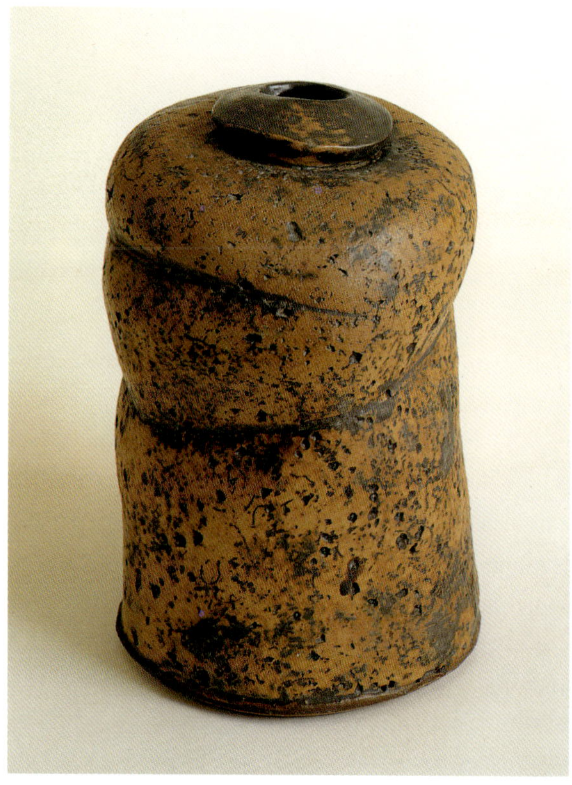

1.37 Corncob bottle, 1962-63. Ca. 8 x 7

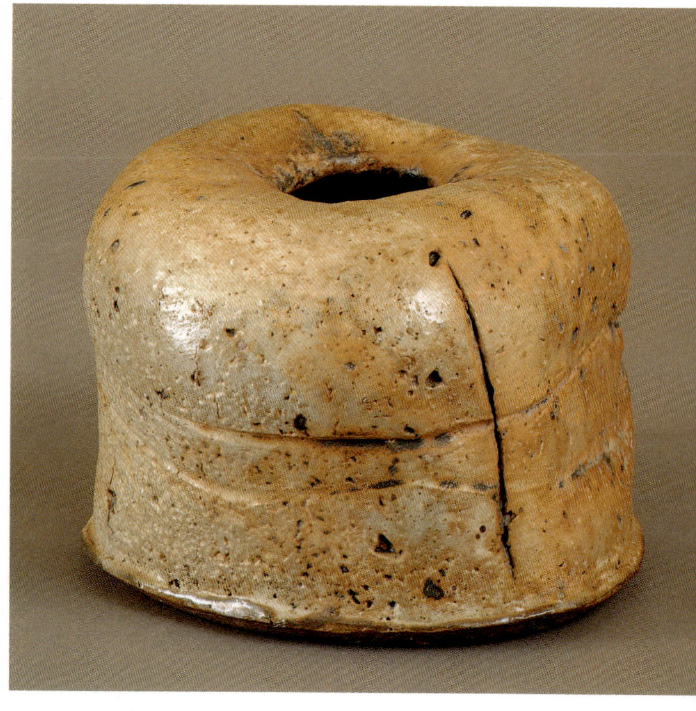

1.38 Corncob bottle, 1963. Ca. 7 x 6

Intermittently pressing the paddle into the clay, he produced linear marks that suggest wrapping or binding or, as Kottler put it, "think what happens when you put a couple of rubber bands around your face" (figs. 1.37, 1.38). Surrounding the openings on the top of these neckless, tumescent pots is a paddled rim of clay that relates the opening to an anatomical orifice. The merger of organic eroticism and clear, bold silhouettes in these vessels illustrates that Kottler had begun to formulate a distinctive hybrid of expressionistic content and formal precision. The tear-and-repair series, inspired by Voulkos, accomplished the same objective. In these compositions Kottler classicized his expressionism by playing violations of a container's physical integrity against the elegant textures of glazed and unglazed porcelain and subtle off-white surfaces (fig. 1.39). "I was definitely influenced by Pete," Kottler emphasized. "The idea of tearing open a vessel, attaching slabs of clay over the tear and leaving the process clearly visible—this is right from Voulkos. For my work I used porcelain because I liked its unctuous quality. Porcelain can have the sensual quality of skin."[39]

Kottler studied ceramics at Ohio State for nearly ten years. During this time he began to find his way among the factions that divided academic ceramists. Unswayed by the anti-industrialist legacy of the Arts and Crafts movement, he envisioned a rapprochement with the factory: he respected the production of good pottery manufacturers and was impressed by the efficiency and collaboration he encountered at Arabia. Studio potters who continued to make functional pottery, he concluded, were technologically obsolete. His allegiances shifted toward the work of artist-potters who, like Voulkos, linked ceramics to the broader context of modern art. In his private life, he gave up the pretext of heterosexuality and immersed himself in gay culture. These decisions, however, were barely reflected in his accomplished but conservative oeuvre of the early 1960s. He considered staying on to teach art history at OSU after his Ph.D. show, but there were no immediate openings. Then in the spring of 1964, an offer to teach ceramics as a visiting faculty member came from the University of Washington. Kottler had never been to the Pacific Northwest, but he was reluctant to stay in Columbus without a teaching job. In the fall of 1964 he moved to Seattle for what was, in his view, a temporary commitment.

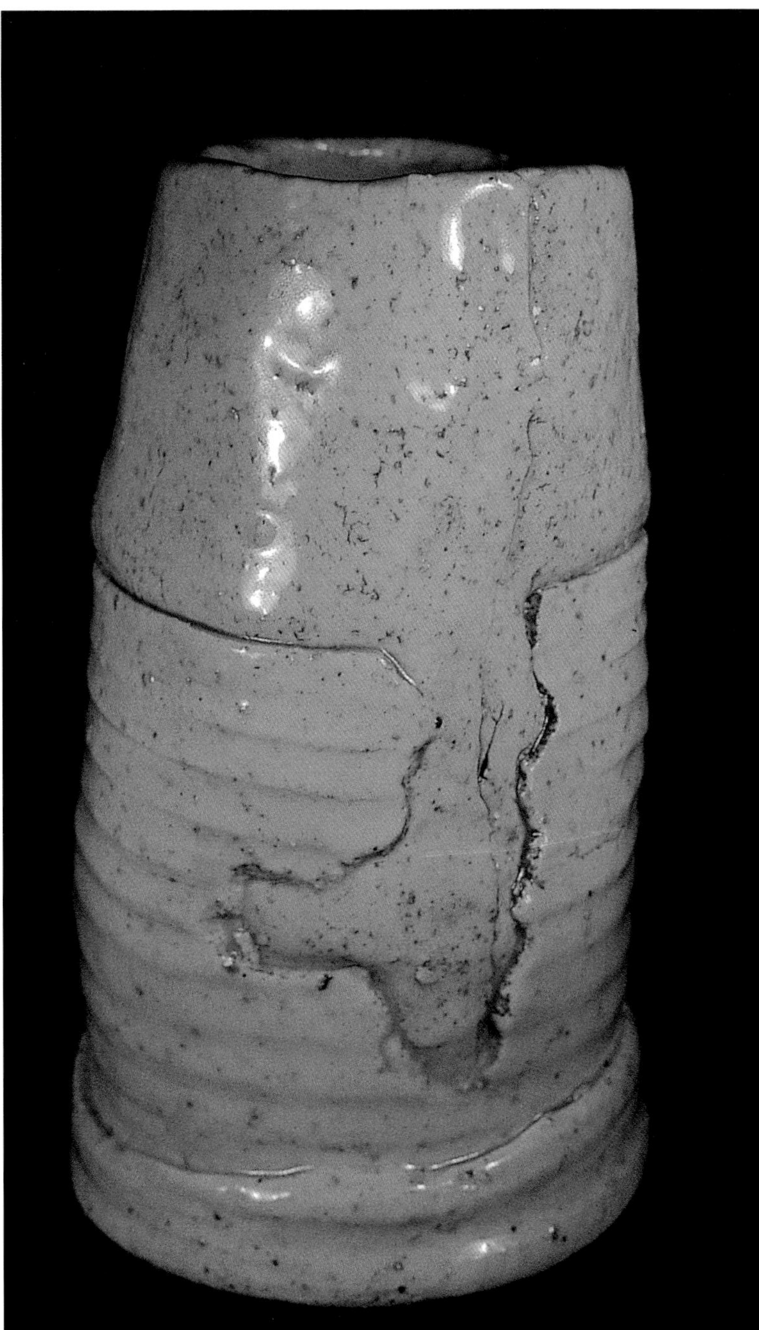

1.39 Tear and repair pot, 1964. Porcelain, 7 h

TWO

Seattle and the 1960s

Kottler lived and worked in Seattle for twenty-five years, but he never felt at home in the outdoor culture of the Pacific Northwest. "I'm not interested in nature *per se*—I even like to keep the drapes closed," he explained. "I don't enjoy things people in Seattle enjoy, like boating and sports. I can't swim and I'm afraid of water. I didn't like most of the Jewish personalities here, either. They were too mellow—they just fit in with everyone else. I had only a few close friends in Seattle. Most of my closest friends lived in other cities. On the plus side, though, Seattle was a very good place for me to work."[1]

He assumed the position of visiting assistant professor of ceramics at the University of Washington in the fall of 1964. Other faculty members in the department, founded by Swiss artist Paul Bonifas in 1946, included Robert Sperry, then on leave in Japan, and Harold W. Myers, who was finishing his last year of teaching at the university. Although he had taught art history for three years, Kottler's previous teaching experience in ceramics was limited to one quarter at Ohio State. Myers, whose nonauthoritarian teaching style appealed to Kottler, became his classroom mentor. Myers joined the University of Washington faculty in 1960 after studying with Peter Voulkos in Berkeley. He was a controversial artist: one of his aggressively thrown and sliced cylindrical vases,

according to Northwest ceramics historian LaMar Harrington, "frightened to tears some visiting schoolchildren." Myers admitted, "It was tough going from the Voulkos atmosphere where students were encouraged to break every possible rule regarding form and surface, to the Northwest, where the emphasis was on traditional functional ware."[2] When the conservative National Conference of American Craftsmans Council was held at the university in 1961, Myers caused an uproar by asserting that "creation should be no different in clay than in painting."[3]

Myers was ignored and misunderstood during his five years at the university, according to Harrington. Given the similarities between his professional outlook and Kottler's views on the role of the artist-potter, Kottler might have suffered a similar fate. Local resistance to new movements in ceramics had eroded by the mid-1960s, however, and fallout from Pop Art and San Francisco Funk had begun to affect the work of younger Seattle artists and University of Washington graduate students such as Patti Warashina and Fred Bauer. In 1963, Warashina was creating full-scale Victorian chairs in clay while Bauer produced hinged boxes three feet high, decorated with cartoóny appliques. Both moved away from Seattle in 1964 to assume teaching positions elsewhere, but they returned in 1968.[4] They joined the Uni-

28

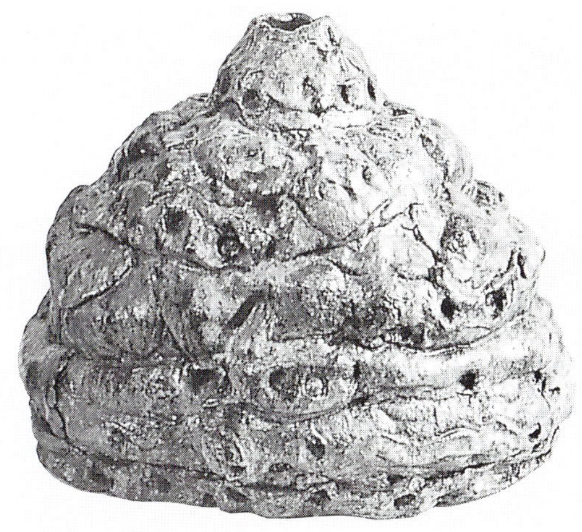

2.1 Harold Myers, Pouch Form, 1963. Stoneware, 18½ x 23

versity of Washington faculty at the end of the 1960s, and Warashina remained to become one of Kottler's closest university colleagues.

Estranged from the Midwest and Ohio State, Kottler soon began to behave professionally as he had not behaved at home. His artistic development after 1965 repudiated, in effect, most of the virtues Atherton and Bogatay had praised in his work. Restraint, lack of contrivance, an absence of mechanical intervention and a "positive attitude" were gradually abandoned in favor of flamboyance, irreverent burlesque, manufactured images and materials, and blatant eroticism. His conservative OSU production, in retrospect, was a screen behind which an exuberant artistic personality had begun to incubate.

When he arrived in Seattle, Kottler was impressed by Myers's "pile" compositions—soft slabs of stoneware built in mounds that unequivocally associated clay and excrement (fig. 2.1). Until he was able to take over a large studio space at the university in June 1965, however, he did relatively little work. He continued his tear-and-repair and corncob pots, but in the summer of 1965 he also began working with raku. In this raku series, which he produced from 1965 to 1967, Kottler merged the excremental sensuality of Myers's organic forms with the urbane, linear biologism and the iridescent surfaces he admired in Art Nouveau. The Art Nouveau style had begun to attract him a few years earlier. "Ohio, as an older

state, was loaded with good things, and in the early 1960s people were getting rid of old junk, calling up Goodwill and the Salvation Army to haul it away," he recalled. "I'd always loved collecting, and then you could go to Goodwill and find really valuable antiques. As I moved on from thrift shops and started going to antique shows with my friends, my eye would always be drawn to the Art Nouveau style and to Tiffany iridescent surfaces. You could buy Tiffany lamps then for $30 to $100. I loved both the craftsmanship and the sensibility."[5] He began collecting Art Nouveau jewelry, particularly gold and silver pieces with different presentations of women's hair, and he ultimately amassed an extensive collection (figs. 2.2, 2.3).

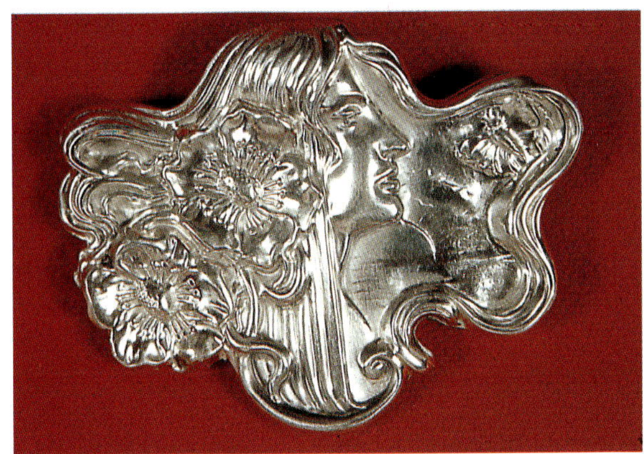

2.2 Art Nouveau jewelry from Kottler collection

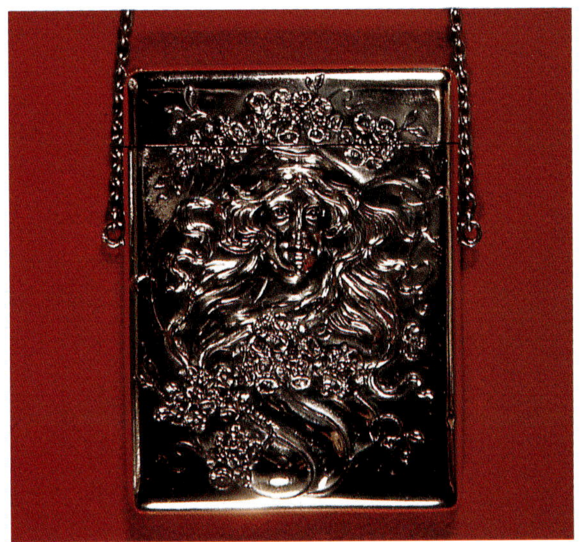

2.3 Art Nouveau jewelry from Kottler collection

Art Nouveau also appealed to Kottler because it was an innovative multimedia art movement in which traditional distinctions between artists and craftsmen were not finely drawn. Art Nouveau produced "palace pottery," as described in Kottler's Ph.D. dissertation. Quoting art historian Meyer Schapiro, Kottler characterized palace pottery as "a system of forms with a quality and a meaningful expression through which the personality of the artist and the broad outlook of the group are visible. This style is a manifestation of the culture as a whole, a visible sign of its unity."[6] Art Nouveau artists who collaborated to produce stylistically unified environmental ensembles thus provided a historical model for Kottler's conception of the artist-potter, the producer of palace ware.

In 1970 Kottler elaborated his concept of palace pottery in *Objects: U.S.A.*, the catalogue of a major traveling exhibition mounted by the Smithsonian Institution. Palace ware, he wrote, has several definitive characteristics: it is (1) "clay ware which exemplifies the style of a

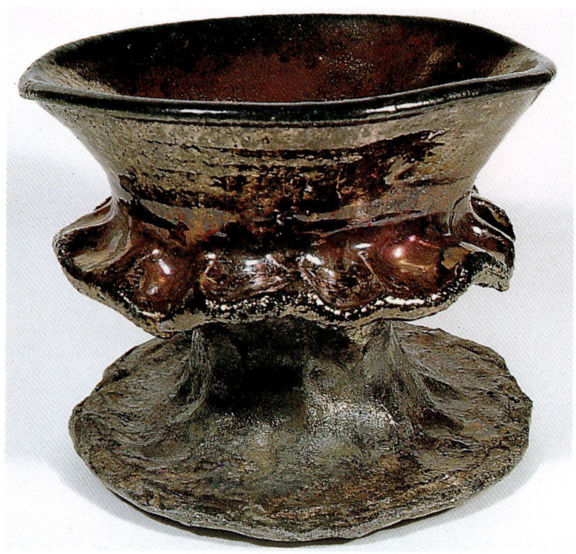
2.5 Raku chalice, 1965

nation, as opposed to folk pottery, where the primary concern is . . . the production of utilitarian objects for everyday use; (2) the stylistic singularities found in the palace ware of any given period are similar to other works of art produced at the same time in that area or national setting; (3) absence of any regimentation imposed by function or utilitarianism, with a shift to individual freedom of expression; (4) ritual objects; (5) experimental research in the development and extension of the possibilities of working with clay; and (6) objects that stimulate the intellect in places that stimulate the body."[7]

Many of Kottler's mid-1960s raku compositions might be more precisely described as objects that stimulate the intellect *about* places that stimulate the body. This series includes biomorphic chalices as well as vases and lidded jars. In several examples, the pinched and twisted handles and lids were based on Myers's work, while the stems fashioned for the chalices were inspired by sinuous floral forms found on the bases of Art Nouveau candlesticks.[8] The pitted and textured raku surfaces provided pockets for small puddles of rainbow-colored glazes, which were also applied to accent the curvilinear movement of the bodies (figs. 2.4, 2.5).

The earlier tear-and-repair and corncob pots frequently evoke anatomical associations, but the raku se-

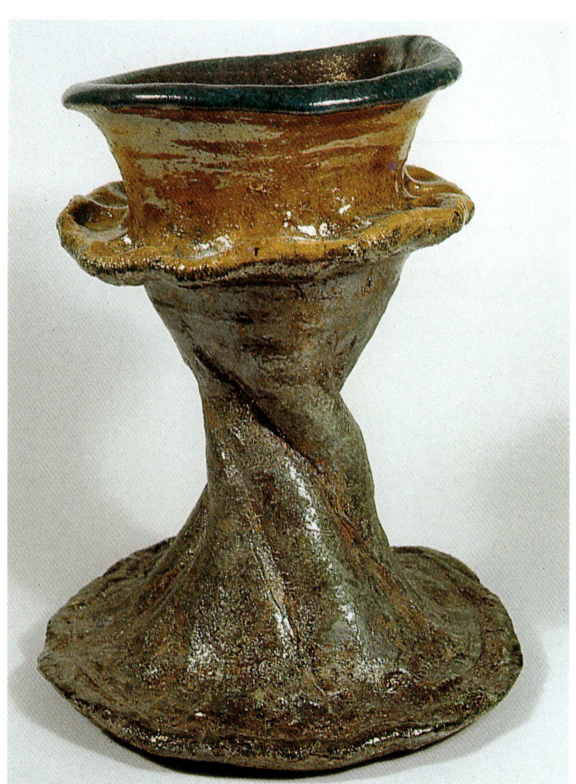
2.4 Raku chalice, 1965. 9½ x 7¼

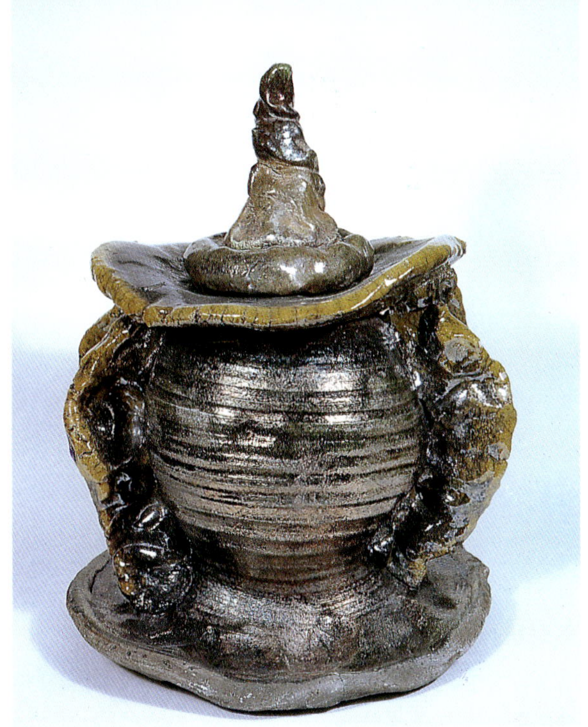

2.6 Raku covered jar, 1966. 15 x 10

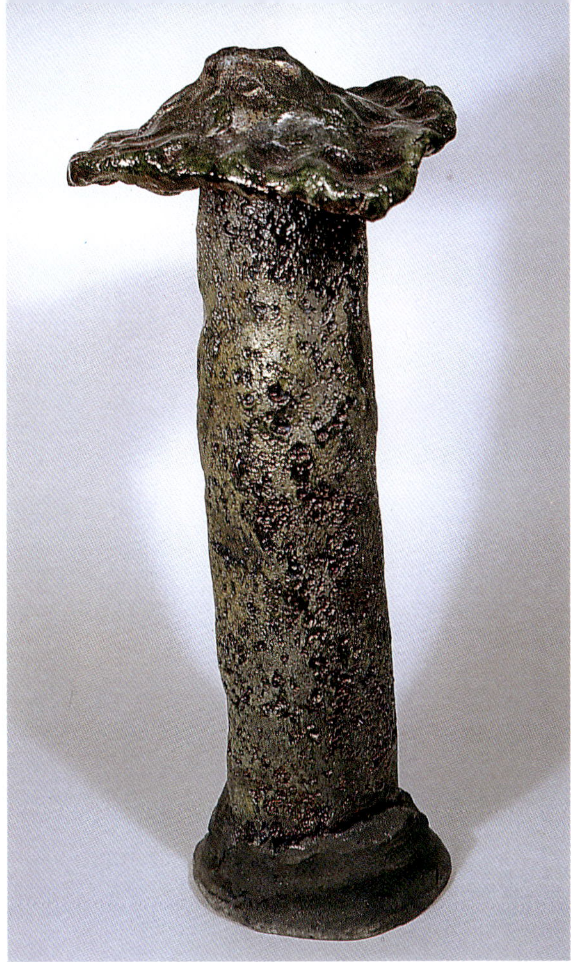

2.7 Raku covered jar, 1965. 13 x 10

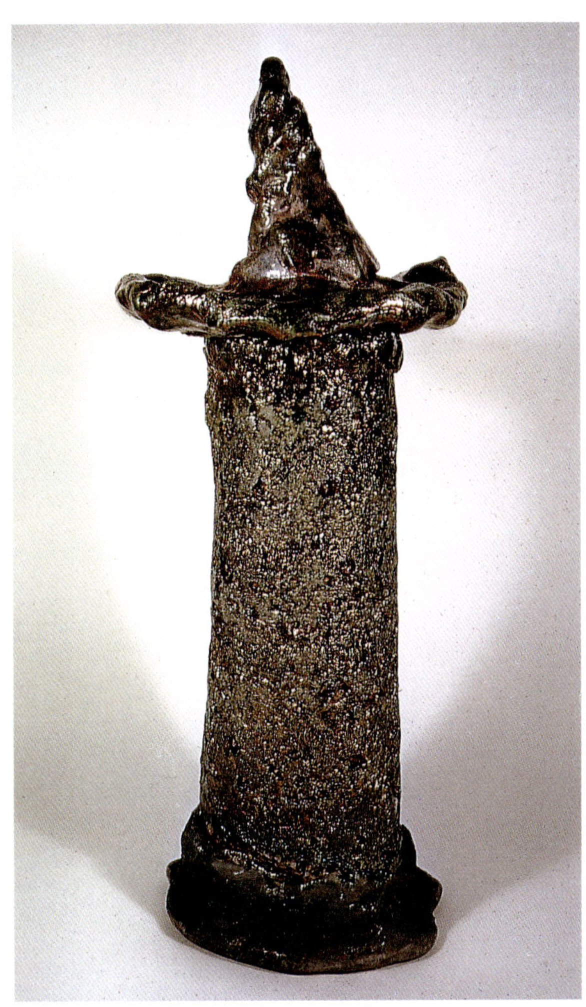

2.8 Raku covered jar, 1965. 18 x 7

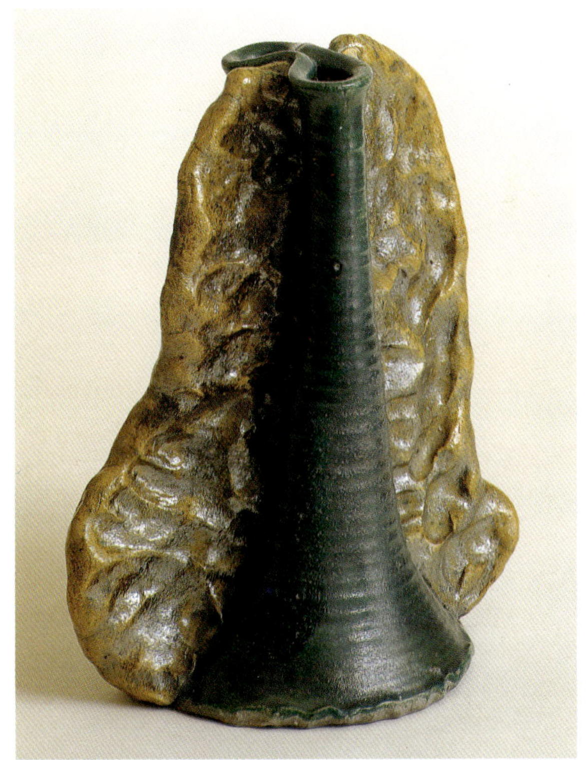

2.9 Raku bottle, 1966. 14 x 12

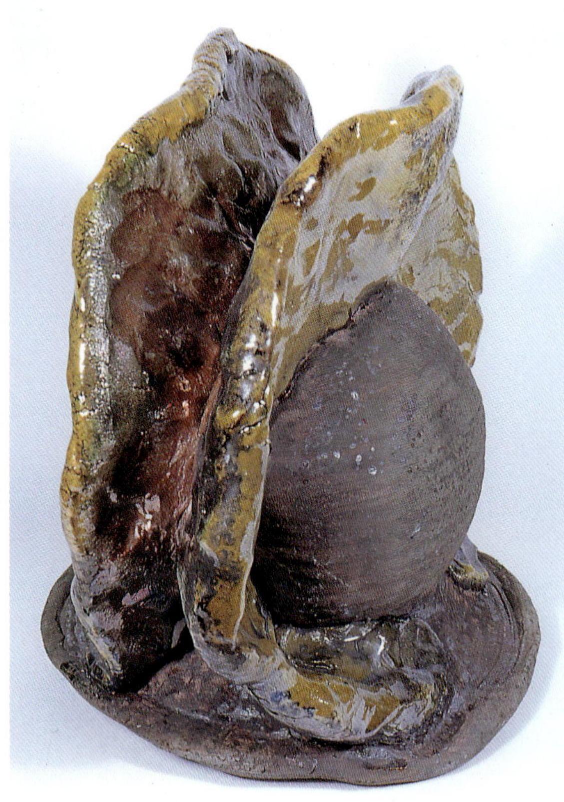

2.10 Raku bottle, 1967. 10 h

ries was the first in which Kottler consistently and self-consciously explored sexually suggestive shapes and gestures.[9] Standing ten to eighteen inches high, topped with mushroomlike stoppers, the columnar bottles are exuberantly phallic; other bottles mounted with labial wings or flanges of pinched clay suggest female anatomy. Wing shapes frequently invade or impinge upon the more precisely articulated thrown forms, distorting their symmetry and silhouettes (figs. 2.6-2.10). In his earlier conceptions of "classical expressionism" such as the tear-and-repair series, Kottler attempted a synthesis of precision and spontaneity, but in the winged raku bottles, he presents both alternatives at the same time. One reviewer compared these pots to "strange barnacles in a grotto,"[10] a vivid analogy that captures the implications of invasion and parasitic growth. By 1967 the wings are positioned to call even greater attention to the openings, which are usually unarticulated, round holes leading into the volumetric body of the pot (figs. 2.11-2.13). Harrington compares the raku series to the irreverent eroticism of George Ohr, whom Kottler later came to admire: Kottler's pots, like Ohr's, she concludes, embody the

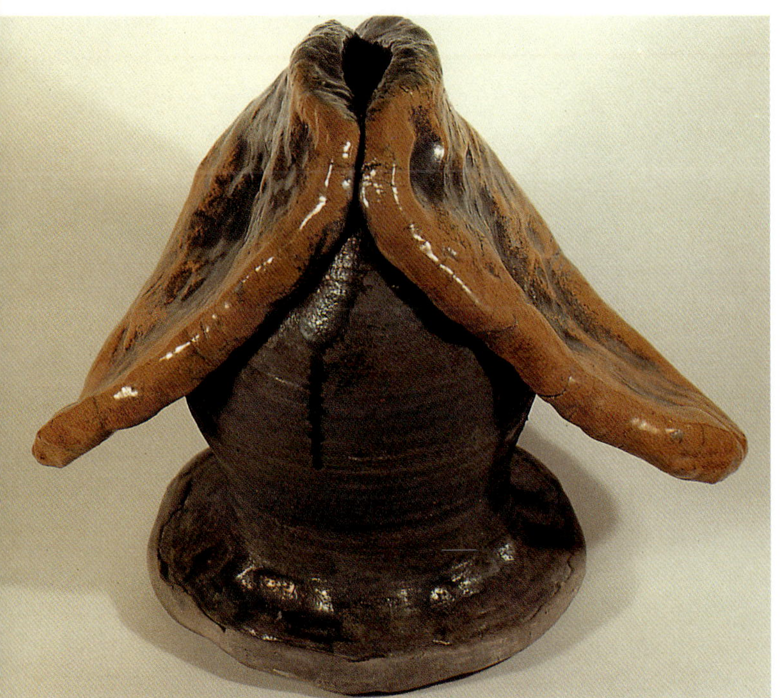

2.11 Raku jar, 1967. 12 h

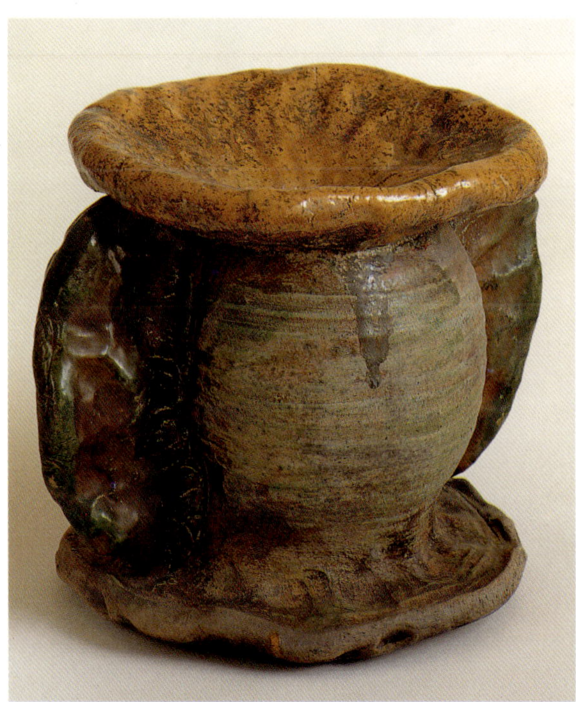

2.12 Raku jar, 1965. 9 x 12

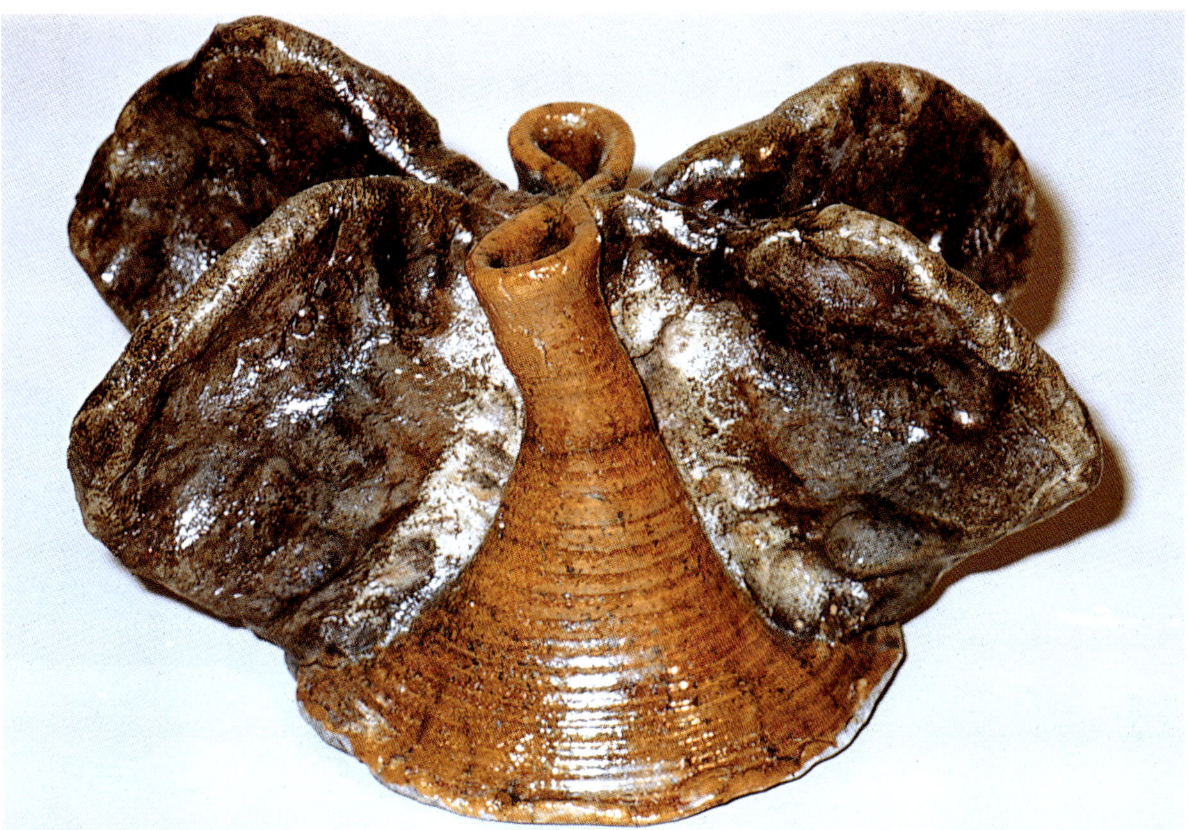

2.13 Winged double bottle, 1967. 10 h

"qualities of Funk Art, a type that has existed throughout history, but was not yet formulated with a title in Ohr's day."[11]

Contrasting Ohr's pottery with that of Peter Voulkos, critic Jeff Perrone points to several subtexts that may have contributed to Kottler's affinity for the former: "Influenced by the form-shattering, paint-slinging abstract expressionists . . . Voulkos' project was a violent, masculinist attack on the metaphorically female vessel form. If Voulkos' violations appeared crazy and anarchic in the 1950s they nevertheless had embedded in them a traditional psychological premise: the mastery, dominance and power of the (male) creator over the (female) materials." The sexuality of Ohr's undulant pottery is more complex: Ohr's forms suggest "cross-gender slippage . . . the male succumbing to his own femininity." It was the feminine morphology and sexuality of Ohr's pots, he concludes, that was especially disruptive. "For it is never aggressive male sexuality that comes as a shock,

but female sensuality unleashed, aroused, no longer repressed." Kottler's raku series is similarly disturbing: slipping back and forth between signs of male and female eroticism, these compositions allude to a range of desires that resist classification as strictly masculine or feminine.[12]

The raku series also included rectangular slab-built platters reminiscent of sixteenth and seventeenth-century Bizen-ware imitations of wooden plaques found in imperial residences (figs. 2.14, 2.15).[13] "These trays were related to the tear-and-repair technique and they emphasized the triangle—a female form," Kottler said. "The female forms are flat and related to the frame, whereas the male forms have a more three-dimensional character. Some of these ideas came from Lucio Fontana's sliced canvases, which influenced Voulkos too."[14] The references to female sexuality in these compositions also received a more literal presentation. In 1967 Kottler made several porcelain platters topped with rear-view casts of

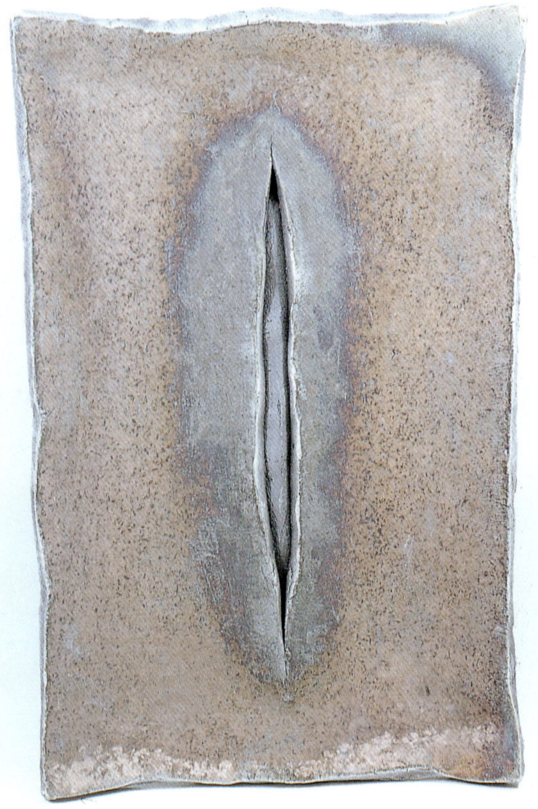

2.14 Raku tray, 1966-67

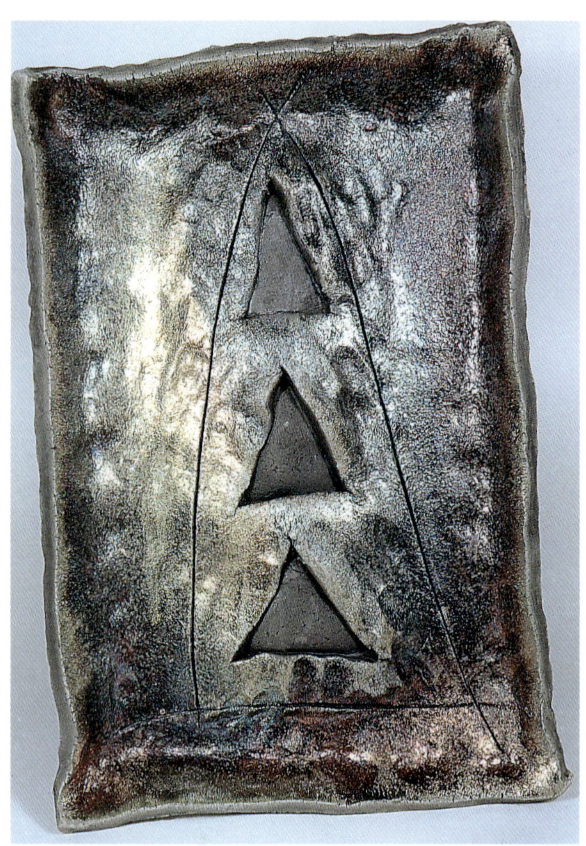

2.15 Soft triangle tray, 1967. 16 h

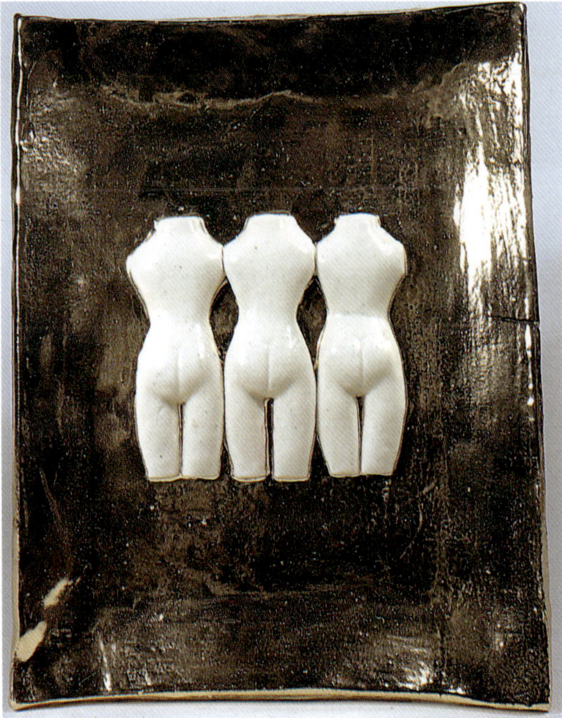

2.16 *The Three Graces,* 1967. Porcelain, 10

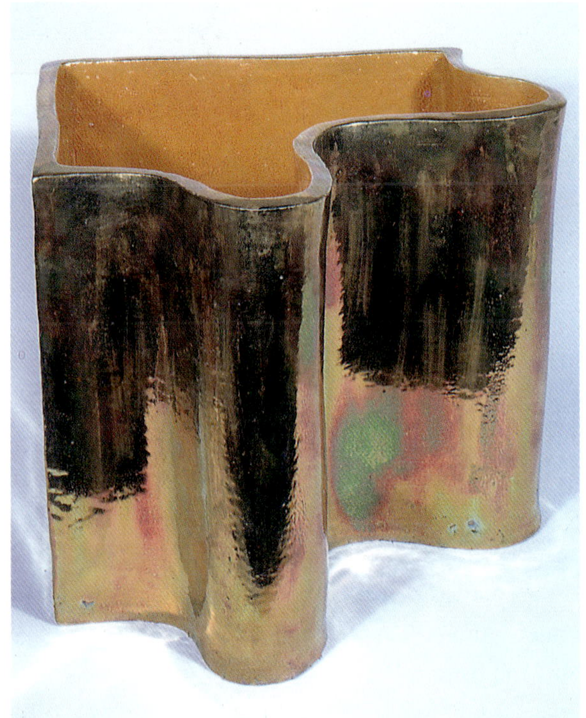

2.17 *Cool Hot Box,* 1966. Earthenware, 10 h

Barbie-doll torsos (fig. 2.16); some of these have punning titles, which Kottler first used in 1966 for pots such as *Cool Hot Box*, a vase based on Alvar Aalto's well-known design (fig. 2.17).

Shortly after his move to Seattle, Kottler began collaborating with Warren Maruhashi, the first of several University of Washington graduate students who significantly influenced his work. In addition to developing his raku series, he began investigating Egyptian paste with Maruhashi. Egyptian paste, a brightly colored self-glazing clay, lacks the requisite plasticity for large-scale construction and was traditionally used for small forms such as beads. Mixing the paste with finely ground ball clay and building their forms in sections, Kottler and Maruhashi were able to create objects several inches high. "I really wanted to work with brighter colors," Kottler explained. "This was the Pop Art era and I was looking at artists like Tom Wesselmann and Roy Lichtenstein, who were using a brilliant color range. Some of these colors had begun to show up in Arneson's work of the mid-1960s too, when he began using low-fire glazes and clays. But I took a circuitous path and went back to Egyptian paste. I came [to Seattle] from Ohio State with some formulas and recipes for the paste, and I knew how to work with it. It's hard to manipulate—every time you change color you have to use another body of clay. But this came easily for me after all the work I did at Cranbrook with inlaid glazes."[15]

The bright palette of Egyptian paste was especially attractive to Kottler because the colors are acidic. "I really had an affinity for acidic colors," he said. "That's one of the reasons I began collecting old Hawaiian shirts. They were made from printed or silk-screened rayon, and the acid colors are glorious—they just glow."[16] Kottler's Egyptian paste pots also resembled Hawaiian shirts in their bold graphic patterns and playful excessiveness: like the garments, the pots are positioned on the borders of polite taste, tweaking the prescriptions of the Bernard Leach aesthetic.

In their strong front-back orientation, the Egyptian paste compositions often resemble the stoneware branch pots Kottler executed in Finland and Ohio in the late 1950s. Also, like many of the contemporary raku vessels, the paste pots are additive constructions, put together as a sequence of formal zones: foot, body, and opening receive different treatments that preserve their regional identity. The foot or base often commands as much visual attention as the body; in other examples the body is essentially a support structure for appendages that accentuate the opening (figs. 2.18-2.21). "I was looking for a very personal presentation of a classical bottle form," Kottler explained. "I wanted to redefine the parts; for example, I took the idea of the lip of a bottle literally and made openings bracketed with 'real' lips" (figs. 2.22, 2.23).[17] These lip brackets shift the meaning of the spout by identifying the opening as an anatomical reference point. Many titles in this series, such as *Blue Nibble Tips Pot, Yellow Lemon Lips, Red Hot Blue Cross Buns,* and *Kool Green Kookie Keeper*, refer to oral sensations and reinforce the opening/orifice duality. In vessels such as *Madame Chiquita Pot*, where the opening is simply a hole in the top of the body, serpentine lines and biomorphic comma-shapes spurt from or into the mouth, engaging the invisible interior in a multilayered physical analogy.

Well known among his colleagues for his sarcastic wit, Kottler opened up a new arena for personal commentary in 1966 when he began titling his work. "I don't really know why I started to use titles," he remarked. "I do know I liked the way the words braced the forms. I always wanted to incorporate the title in some way directly into the surface. Titles add another way of looking: they can be a means to get into the piece, and at the same time the work can have another dimension because of the way the title relates to it, directly or indirectly."[18] The verbal-visual puns of René Magritte were an early inspiration for Kottler, whose titles are typically humorous or ironic. Often they would be suggested by his students or friends; he enjoyed collaborative wordplay and felt no hesitation about incorporating ideas contributed by students and colleagues. The onset of naming also suggests that the content of his work was beginning to occupy more of Kottler's attention: in his OSU pottery he concentrated on formal relationships, but by 1966-67 he had also begun to approach the medium of ceramics as a forum for

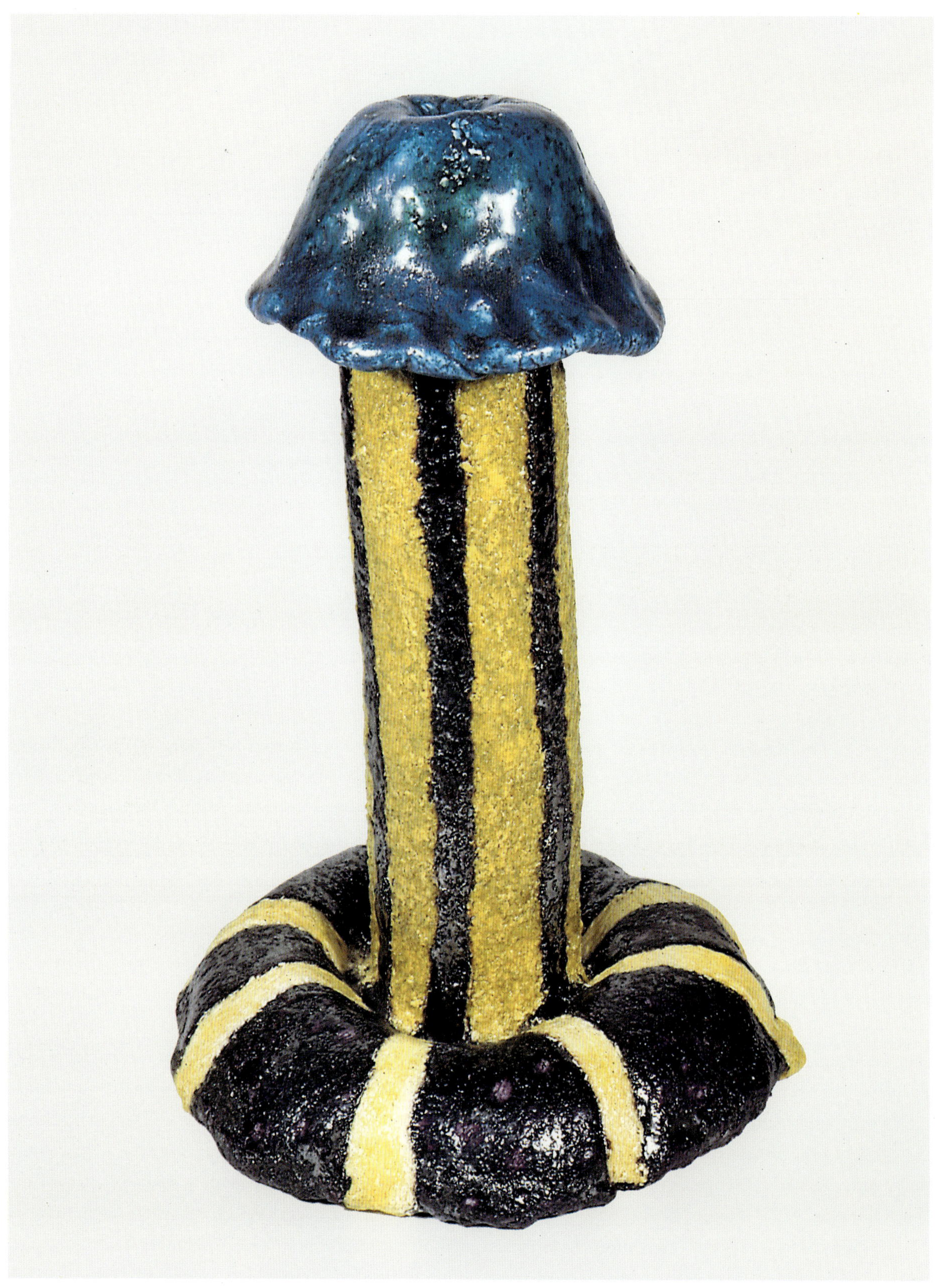

2.18 *Fairy Lamp Pot,* 1966. Egyptian paste, 9 h

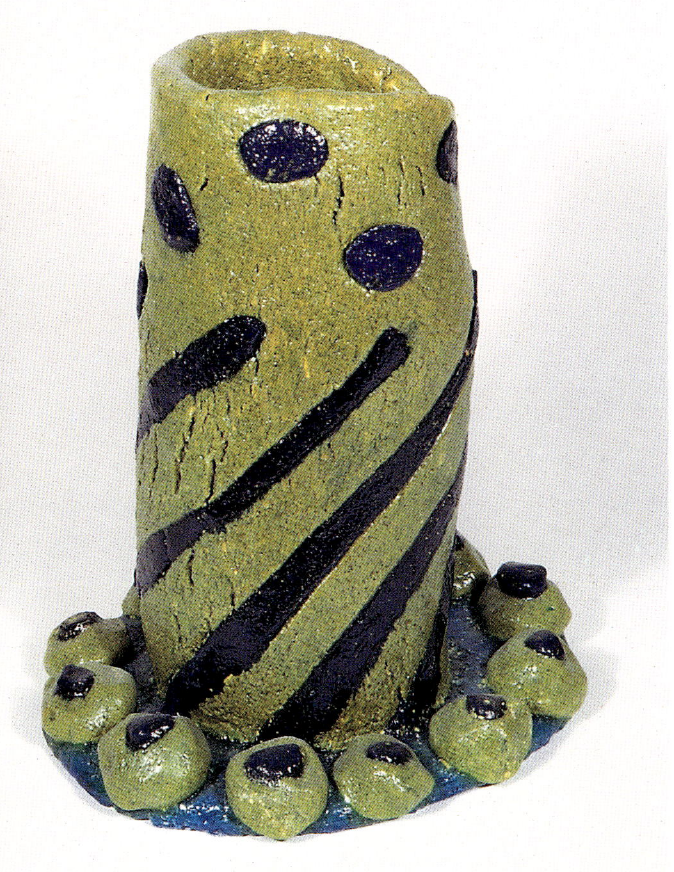

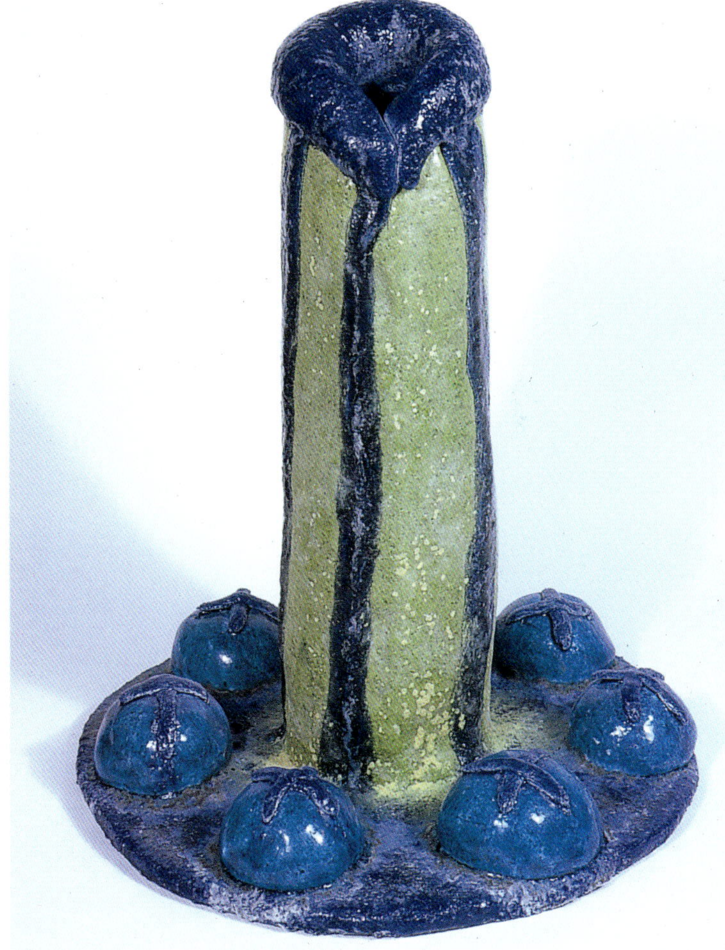

2.19 *Kool Green Kookie Keeper,* 1967. Egyptian paste, 10 h. Collection Seattle Art Museum. Gift of Howard Kottler Testamentary Trust

conveying eroticism along with commentary on the conventions of academic ceramics.

The more expansive conception of form and content in Kottler's work of the mid- and late-1960s was indebted both to New York Pop Art and to San Francisco Funk ceramics. By 1966 Kottler was familiar with Arneson's work, and the following year Arneson was invited to present a workshop at the University of Washington. Kottler also began traveling frequently to the San Francisco Bay Area. "I saw some important shows," he recalled, "but what was even more important to me was the costuming of the people. There you could be a living character by defining yourself through what you wore. It wasn't that people didn't give a damn, but you could live whatever lifestyle you wanted to. These ideas didn't hit Seattle until sometime later. I remember going to a faculty meeting in 1967 wearing a sparkling vinyl vest and

2.20 *Red Hot Blue Cross Buns,* 1966. Egyptian paste, 10 h

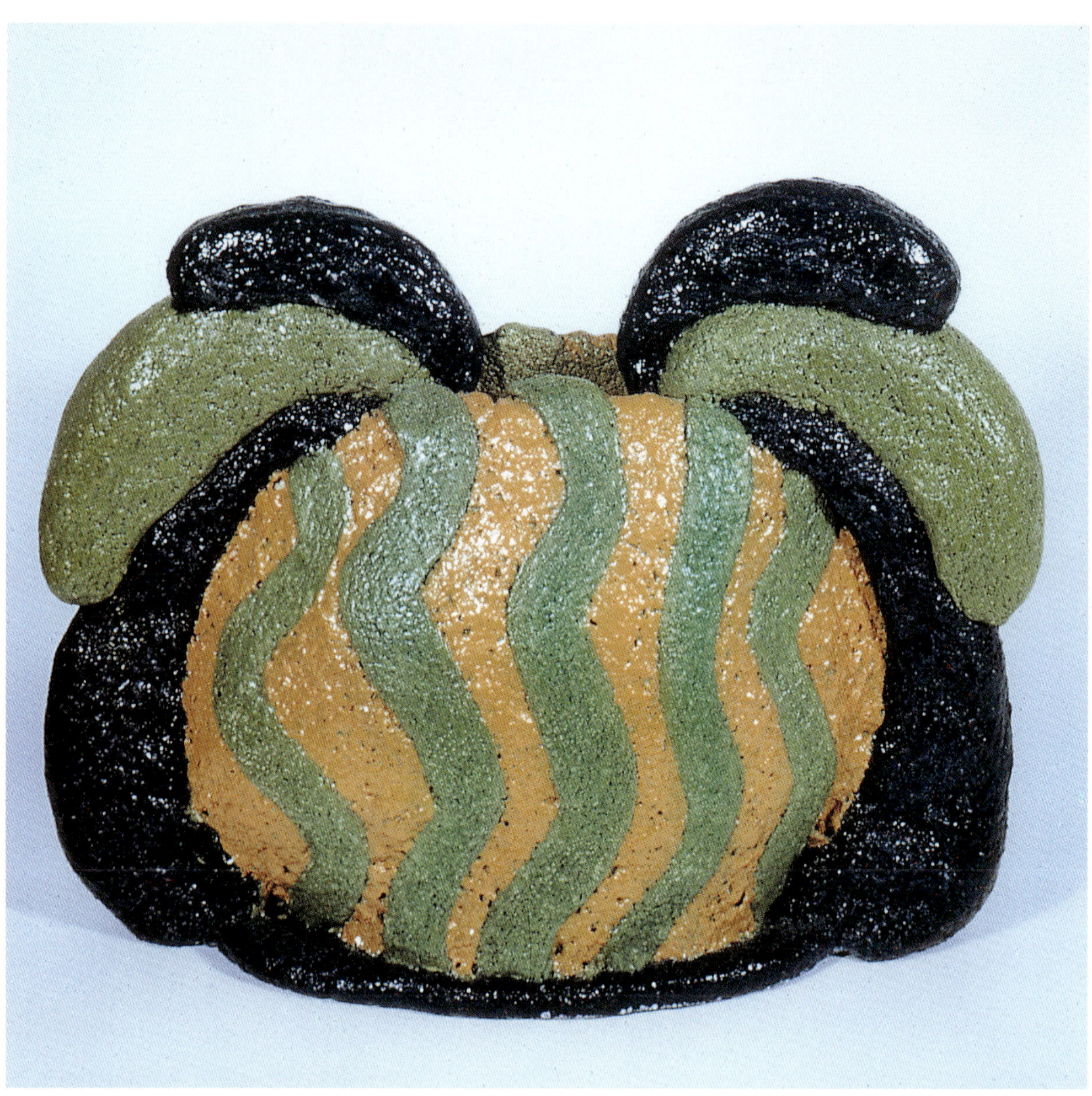

2.21 *Madame Chiquita Pot*, 1966. Egyptian paste, 10 x 13

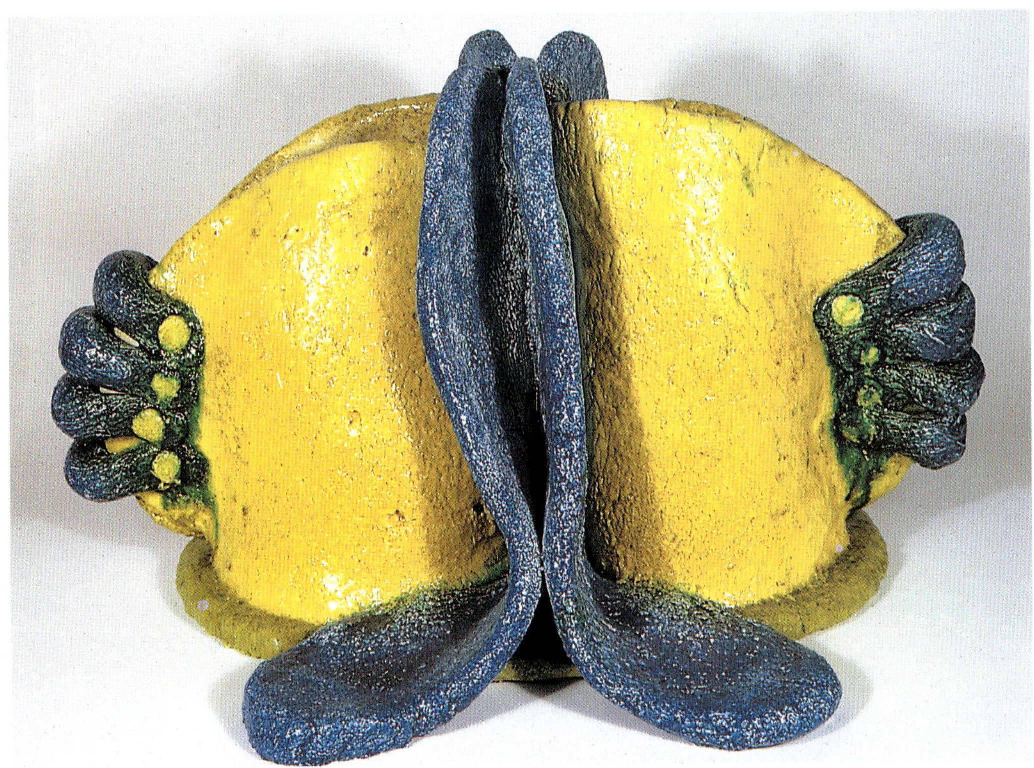

2.22 *Double Vase*, 1966. Egyptian paste, 11 x 16

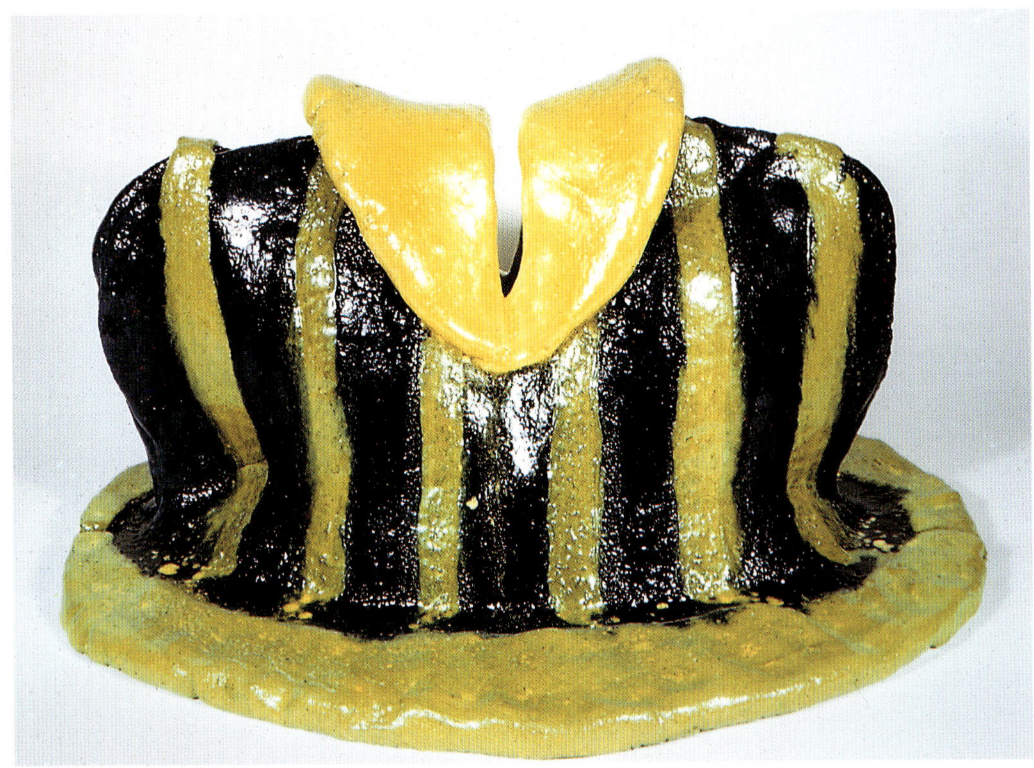

2.23 *Yellow Lemon Lips Pot*, 1966. Egyptian paste

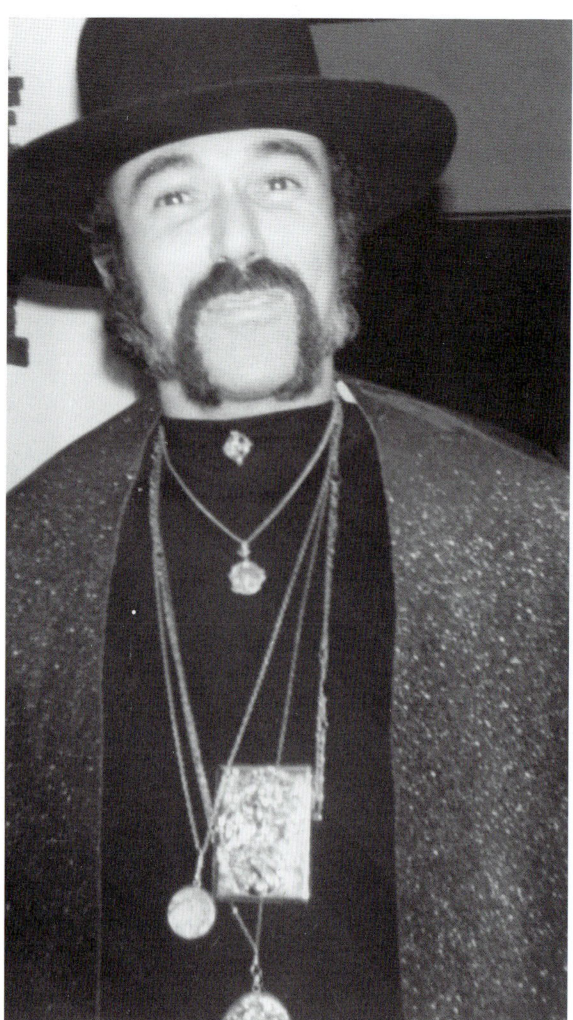

2.24 Howard Kottler wearing selections from his Art Nouveau jewelry collection, 1967

five or six different necklaces. At first people stared at me with their mouths open and then the comments really started to flow (fig. 2.24)."[19]

This affinity for theatrical surfaces is reflected in Kottler's raku and Egyptian-paste work of the mid-1960s, and also in a series of porcelain pot and basket forms he began in 1964-65. An extension of the tear-and-repair series, these porcelain vessels represent a fluid counterpoint to the grittier textures of raku and Egyptian paste. Kottler acknowledged that he "owed a lot to Ann Stockton, who used porcelain in a very gutsy way. There are also references to Sung dynasty pots in the way volume is thrown above the center line, which tends to

give the work a more elegant, more feminine, thrust."[20] This porcelain series combines wheel-thrown lower sections with slab inserts that are usually patched in above the center of the pot (fig. 2.25). The group includes Kottler's first multimedia compositions: some of the

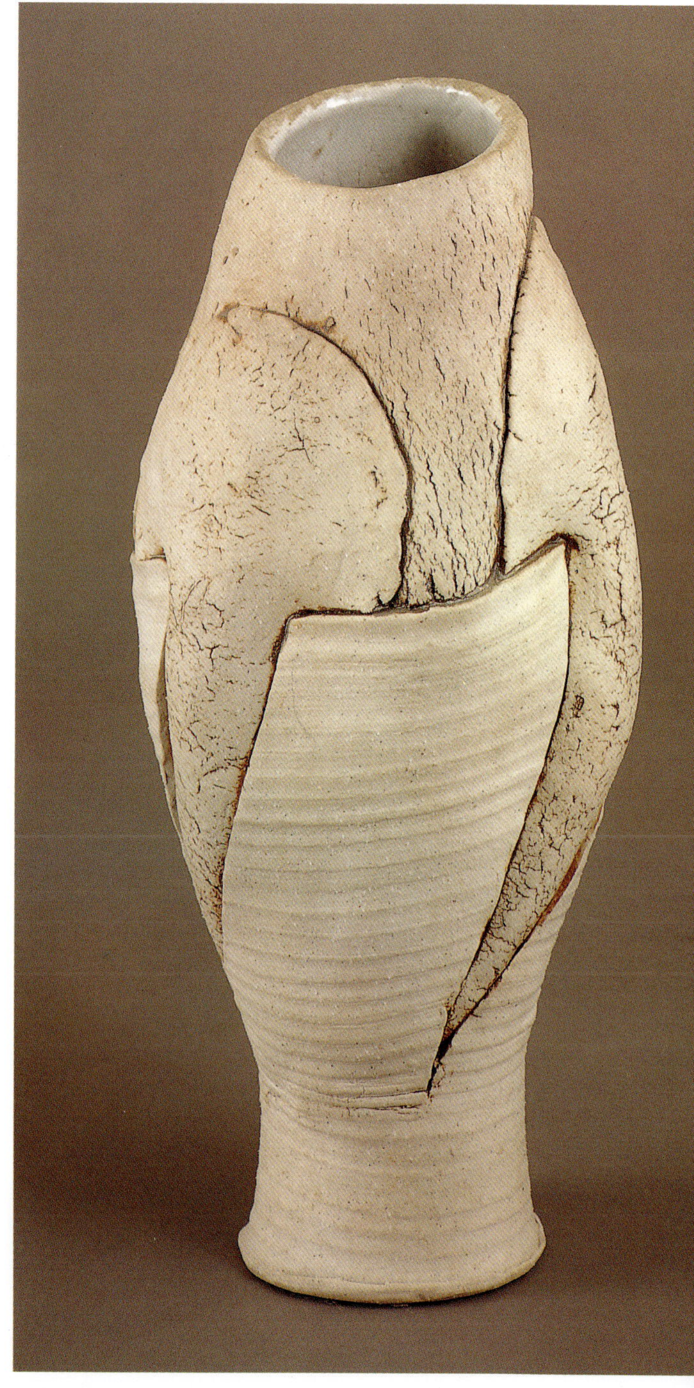

2.25 *Grand Twist Pot*, 1965. Porcelain, 14¼ x 5¾

vases are upholstered with gold or silver lamé fabric, accenting the lush metallic glazes (figs. 2.26, 2.27).

In 1967 and 1968 the porcelain series evolved into a group of basket forms with handles that illustrate the physical process of attaching the handle to the body.

Most of the baskets are covered with glittering metallic lusters that play up the undisguised records of pinching and slicing in the slabs and handles (figs. 2.28, 2.29). This conjunction of contradictory visual codes—the expressionistic informality of the construction process and the

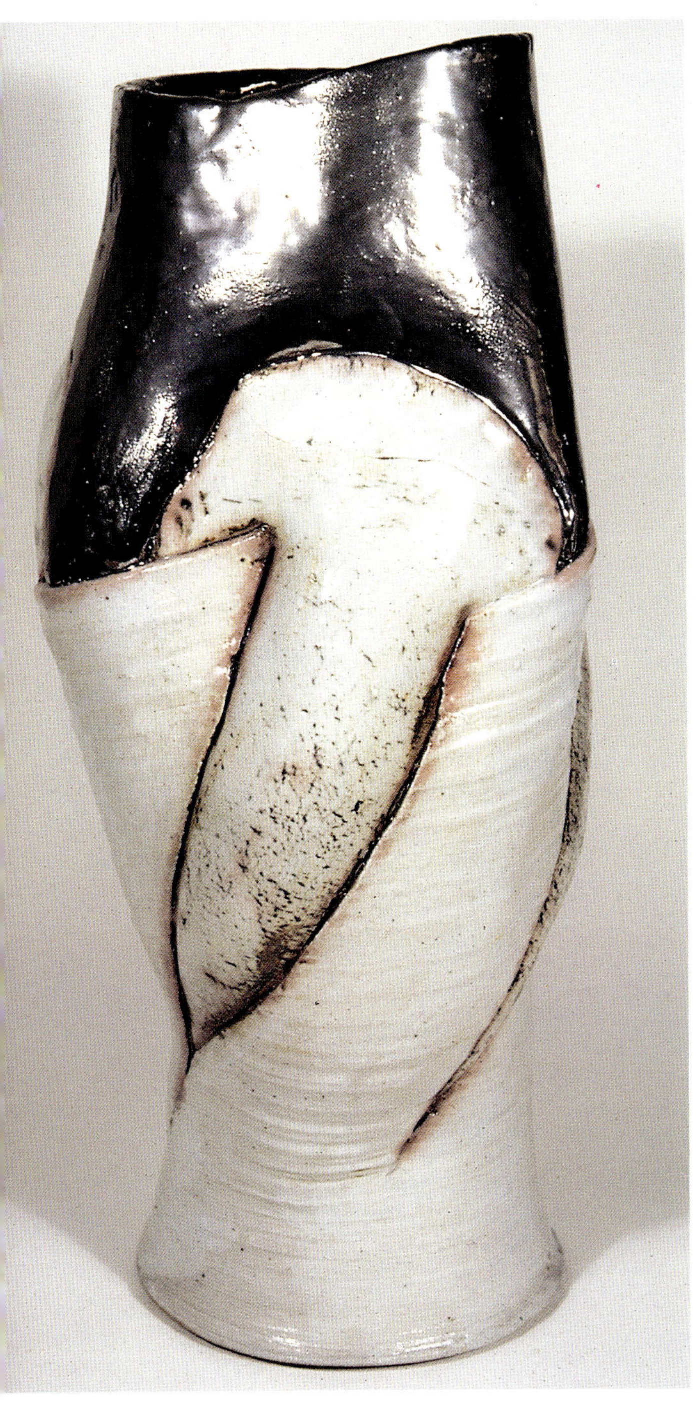

2.26 Jar, 1965. Porcelain, 10 h

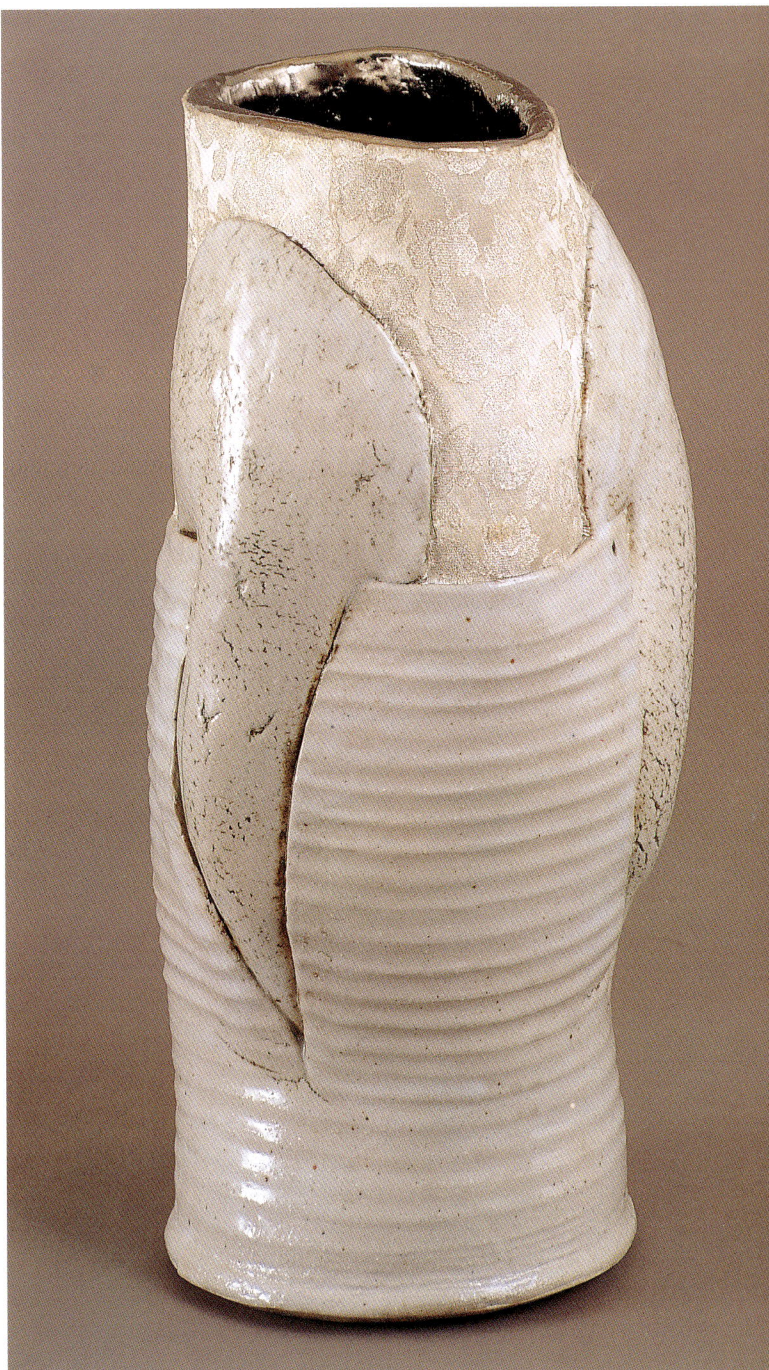

2.27 *Twist Fabric Pot*, 1965. Porcelain and fabric, 15 h

jewel-like preciousness of the lustered surfaces—was another strategy Kottler began to employ in the late 1960s to snub the authority of the ceramics academy. "Lusters were used during great periods in the history of ceramics," Kottler pointed out, "but they were not part of the university ceramics studio programs in the U.S. At OSU, lusters were put down. I remember one of my instructors went out and got a bottle of luster and let me use it just for the border of a cuff link—if lusters were to be used at all, it was just for small touches. By 1967 I was using lusters to cover the entire piece, and I knew that would be frowned upon."[21]

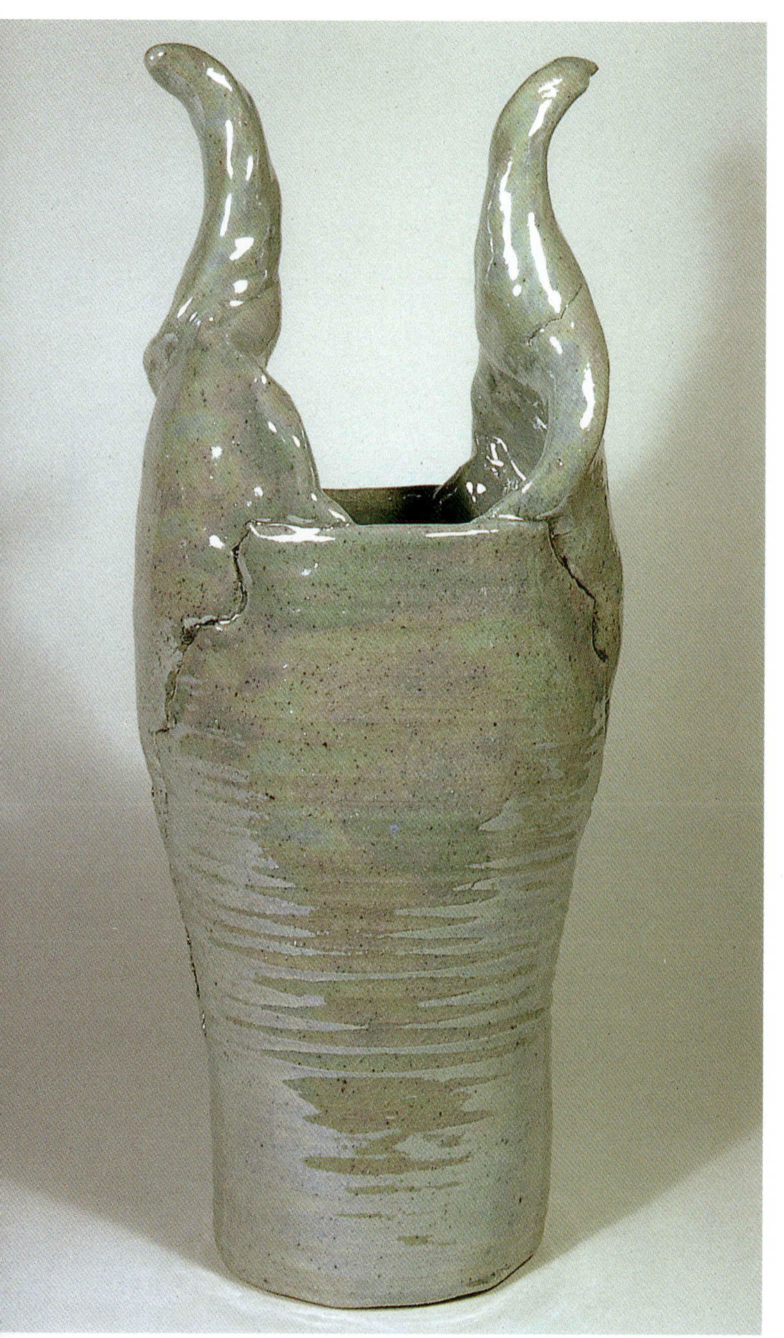

2.28 *Pearly Peaked Pot,* 1967. Porcelain, 14 h

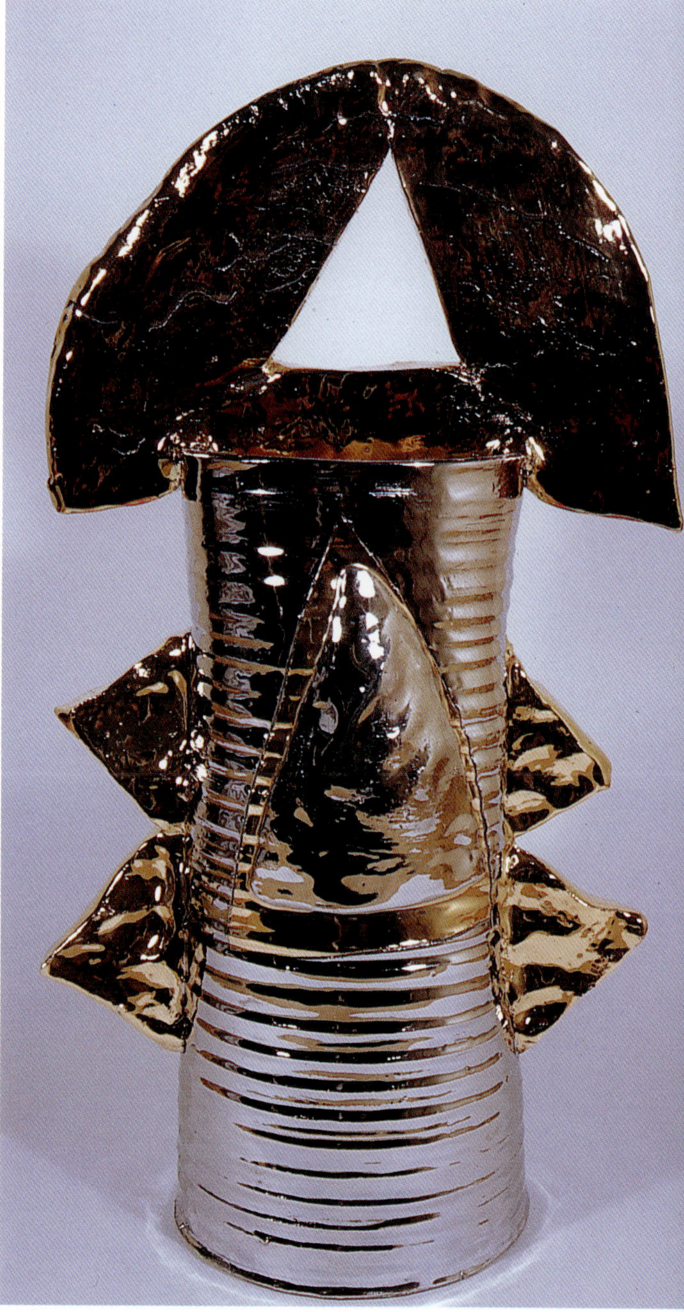

2.29 *Aztec Blaze Basket,* 1968. Porcelain, 15 h

Kottler's views on the semiotics of lusters, however, were by no means confined to academic teaching practices. "I also used them because of their connotations of richness and status. I liked the fact that lusters looked like real gold and silver, but weren't. I think this was the beginning of my interest in simulated materials—materials one step down from, or more than one step down from—the real thing, and yet so satisfying to people. Some of the later pieces were almost gaudy. There's a fine line between richness and gaudiness—rich is OK; gaudy is a no-no. I wanted to put the work right on the edge. On a formal level, I was attracted by the reflective qualities— by the way lusters tend to dematerialize a surface. They bring in another layer of questions about reality and unreality—surface appearances that may or may not be reliable."[22]

By the end of 1966 Kottler became dissatisfied with the size limitations of Egyptian paste and began translating some of the paste forms into variations in stoneware. For this new series Kottler used bright low-fire glazes purchased from ceramic hobby shops. "Arneson and other Bay Area ceramists were using hobby-shop glazes then, too—they were so well controlled and there are manufactured colors that are difficult to make yourself, especially reds and oranges," he explained. "But this was frowned upon too, because a REAL artist-potter, a REAL craftsman, was supposed to make everything himself. This antitechnology attitude is a part of the academic sensibility that goes all the way back to the Arts and Crafts movement of the nineteenth century. It's ridiculous."[23]

Kottler's receptivity to hobby-shop materials was also consistent with the high art/low art inversions of Pop Art. Hobby shops, the province of the semiskilled amateur, served a lower caste of ceramists. The priestly caste of artist-potters insulated within academia was set apart by, among other factors, its command of glaze technologies. Paralleling Andy Warhol's paint-by-number paintings, the appearance of hobby-shop materials in the work of artist-potters disrupted the social order. Established canons of ceramic craftsmanship, as Kottler pointed out in his Ph.D. dissertation, began to disinte-

grate when the range of content in ceramics expanded in the 1950s and 1960s. The ironic references to the professional taboos and hierarchies of the field that proliferated among Bay Area ceramists influenced by Pop Art not only widened the range of subject matter in American ceramics but also shifted the meanings of certain methods and materials. Like Arneson, Kottler deliberately involved himself with what was frowned upon, first in the realm of technique and then in his subject matter.

In his new stoneware series, Bright Color Pots, he continued to celebrate the hole at the top of the vessel. The surface treatment becomes more hard edged, graphic, and cartoony than in the mealy textured Egyptian-paste predecessors. Like *Madame Chiquita Pot*, the decorated bodies of these containers function as support structures for phallic or serpentine forms that converge upon the opening. The orange-and-green-chevroned *Hustler's Delight Pot*, for example, is framed by shiny black and silver phallic tubes stretching to penetrate the orifice at the top. In *Lemon Punch Pot*, the body is a bright yellow field that showcases silver, snakelike appliqués of clay flowing down from the top of the pot into a shiny pool at the base. Apostrophe-shaped flanges that first appeared in *Madame Chiquita Pot* reoccur frequently in this series, which includes some of the first compositions Kottler decorated with ceramic decals (figs. 2.30-2.32). Also part of this group is the exuberant *Radio City Pot* (fig. 2.33), one of Kottler's early homages to Art Deco, a major source of inspiration for his later work.

The years 1966 and 1967 were among Kottler's most productive: during this period he initiated or elaborated his raku and Egyptian-paste series, his porcelain baskets, Bright Color Pots, Barbie-doll trays, and Alvar Aalto-style vases. "The group of pieces from this time I enjoyed the most, though, was one of the most personal series I ever did," Kottler observed. "This was a series of about ten pieces with fur, which I started at the end of 1966. I don't know why I started to use fur then, but I often went to Salvation Army and Goodwill stores where the furs were incredibly cheap—vintage monkey-fur coats for five dollars. Later my students started to bring me furs—

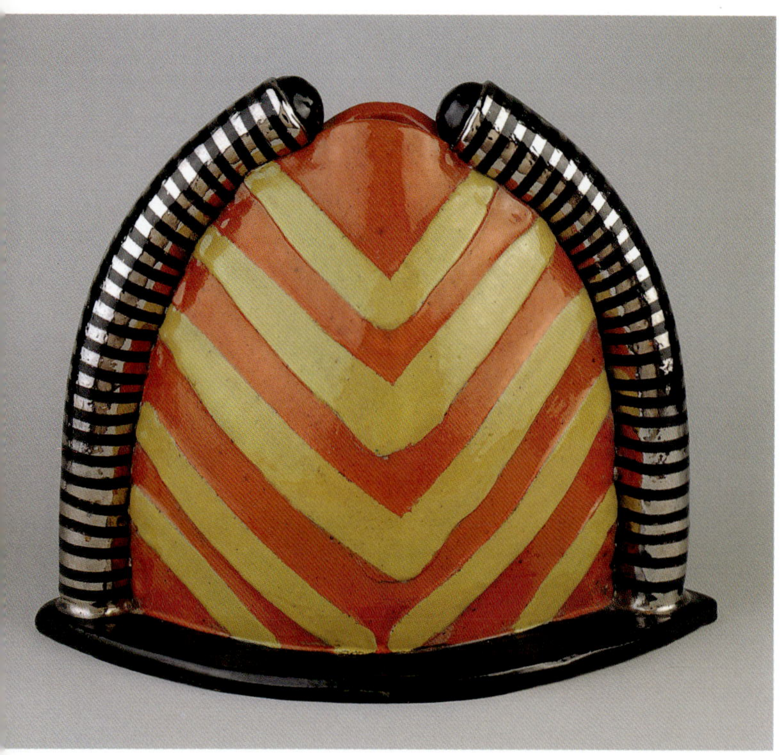

2.30 *Hustler's Delight Pot*, 1967. Stoneware, 12 x 15

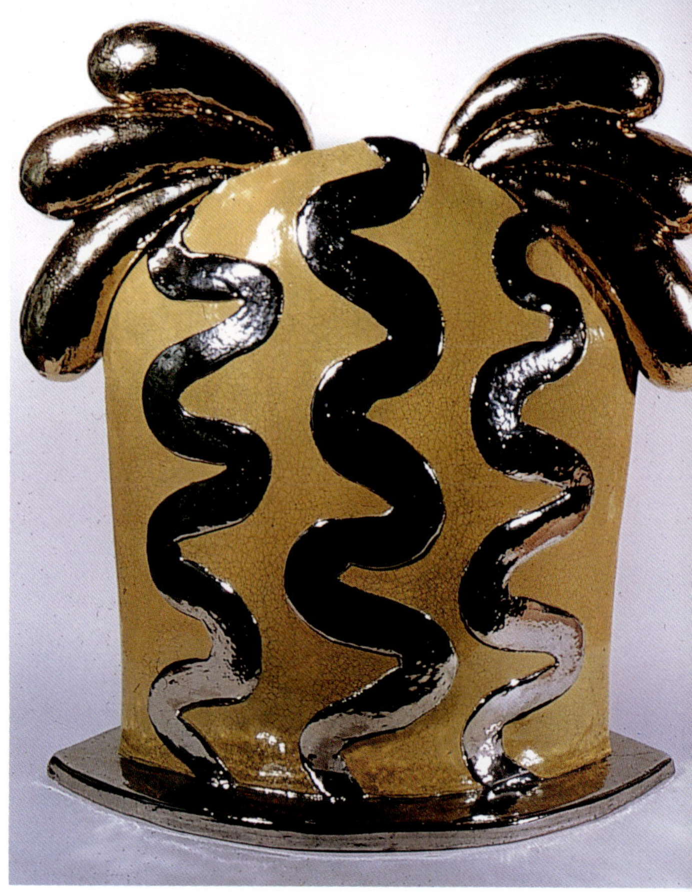

2.31 *Lemon Punch Pot*, 1967. Earthenware, 17¼ x 16¼

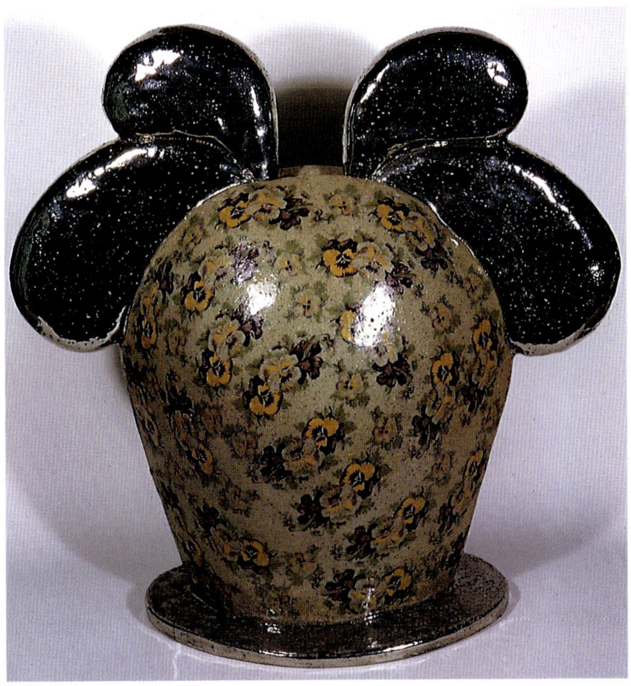

2.32 *Pansy Pot*, 1967. Stoneware, decals

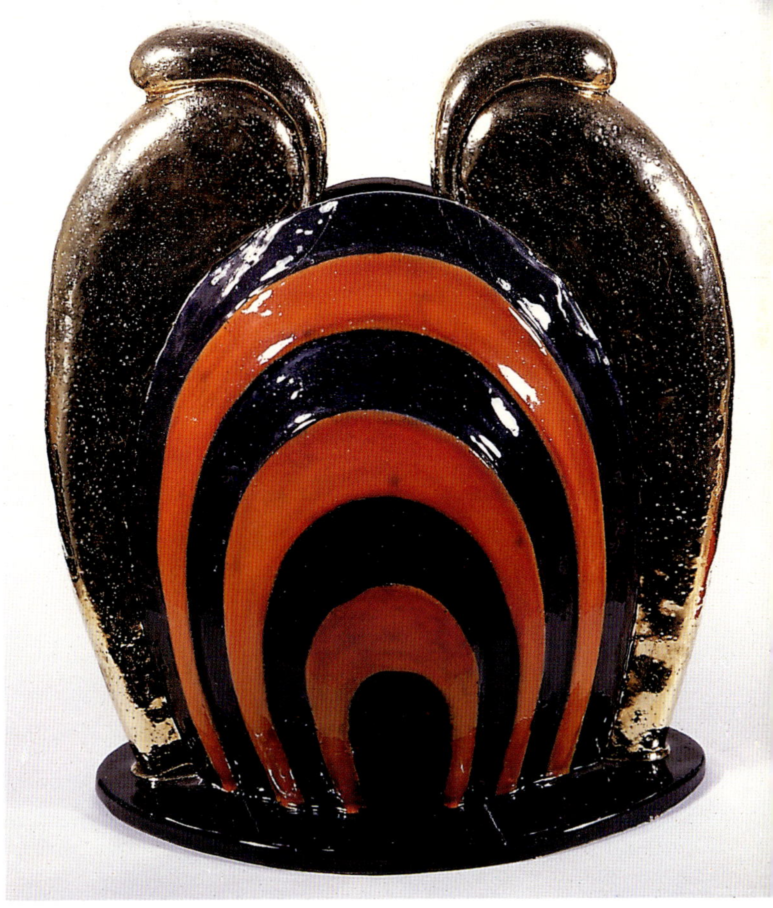

2.33 *Radio City Pot*, 1967. Stoneware, 17 x 14

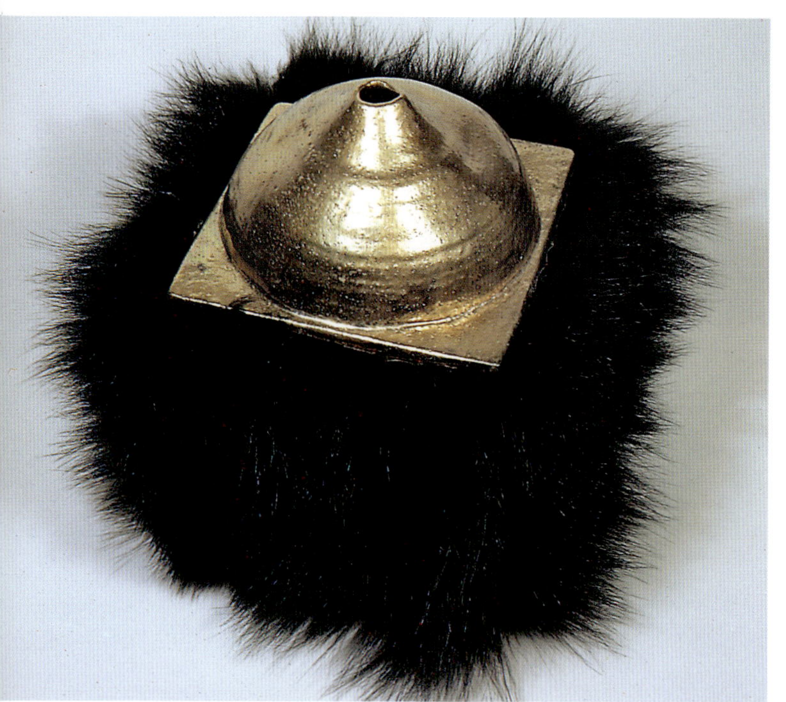

2.34 *Charged Box,* 1967. Stoneware, fur, 9 h

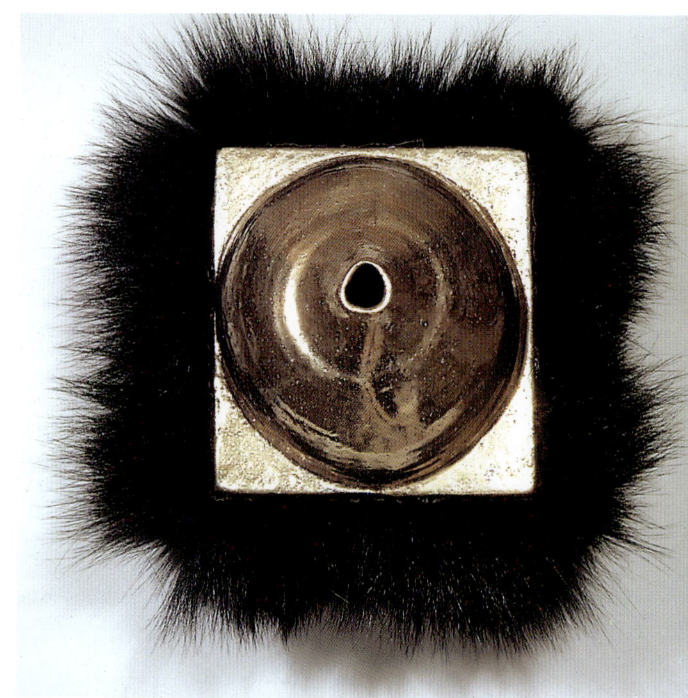

2.35 *Charged Box,* 1967. Top view

fox, mink, and phony fur. It was the relationship between fur and hair that really attracted me, and combining hard, shiny ceramics with soft, organic material. David Gilhooly had done some pieces with fur too, but I didn't know about those until later."[24]

The fur compositions all have punning titles—*Guilt Feeler, Muff Pot, Booby Trap, Mommy Volcano,* and *Geisha Garden,* for example. Most involve a columnar bottle-form of silver or gold, circled with a collar of fur that exposes the opening and neck. In *Charged Box,* the fur surrounds a breast-shaped mound; others, like *Guilt Feeler,* are emphatically phallic (figs. 2.34-2.36). The *pièce de résistance* of this series is *Hole Grabbing Bud Vase* (1967), later titled *Hole Grabber* (fig. 2.37). From the circular base decorated with rosebud ceramic decals rises an erect tube wrapped in fox fur. Reaching across a horizontal gilded disc positioned at the tip of the tube are casts of Barbie-doll arms, radiating like the petals of a flower. The fingers touch and reach into the edge of the opening, also lined with fur.

The neo-Surrealist eroticism, irreverent humor, and unconventional materials in these pots align them

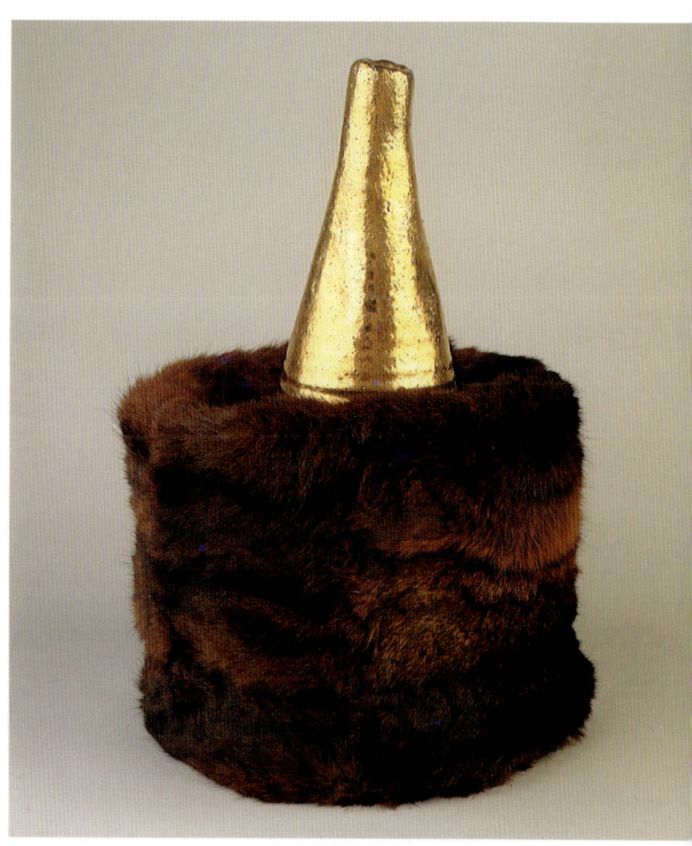

2.36 *Guilt Feeler,* 1966-67. Stoneware, fur, 16 x 10

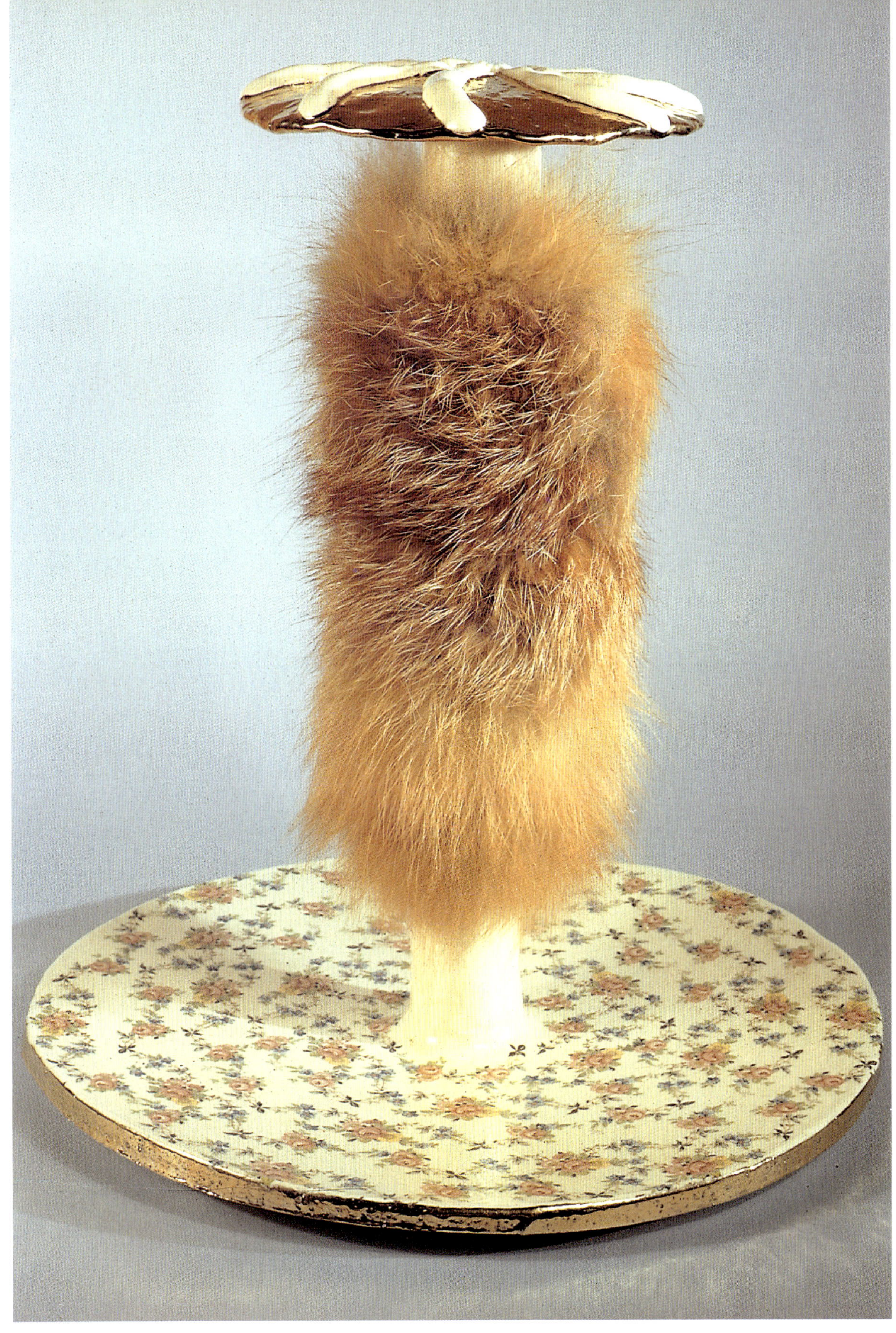

2.37 *Hole Grabber,* 1967. Stoneware, decals, fox fur, 16 x 14. Collection National Museum of American Art, Smithsonian Institution. Bequest of the artist

with work shown in Peter Selz's legendary 1967 Funk Art exhibition, which Kottler visited shortly after he began his fur series.[25] The fur pots also represent another variation on "classical expressionism"—cold, clean, hard bottle-forms played against the warm sensuality of the fur. As in the raku series, Kottler established a binary play of references in the fur pots rather than attempting an integrated synthesis: starting in the mid-1960s, similar forms of doublespeak become an important factor in the evolution of his distinctive compositional voice.

In 1967 an exhibition reviewing Kottler's work of the 1960s originated at the University of Washington's Henry Art Gallery and traveled to the Cranbrook Academy and the Museum of Contemporary Crafts in New York. Included were examples of the porcelain tear-and-repair series, raku ware, Egyptian-paste pots, and Bright Color Pots, compositions with fur, and ceramic-decal plates. Painter Fred Mitchell provided the notes for the Contemporary Crafts Museum. "Kottler's work has the iridescent gleam of an organic kingdom of surprise and elegance," he wrote. "When pottery becomes expressive beyond the skill of creative function, we find ourselves challenged by fantasy and visionary qualities evoked by the artist, as he tests the question of extension of meanings in his medium. Howard Kottler manages very well to contain his realm of suggestion within the act of making, so that his brusque poetry of combinations becomes a unity expressing great durability. He not only celebrates the object as a startling and even obsessive form, but also shows how geometric continuities can have organic rightness. These works are thus rich in idea and performance, intimate and sturdy, signaling to all their special garden of delight."[26] Reviewing the Henry Gallery show, LaMar Harrington composed a more vivid summary: "The gallery was filled with garish subtleties. It was like walking into Kottler's private cache of ceremonial vessels—vessels for rites to the gods of humor, of satire, of energy, of joy, of sex, of life, of another universe."[27]

In 1968 Kottler also turned his attention briefly to the medium of glass. While a graduate student at OSU, Kottler participated in historic glass workshops at the Toledo Museum of Art conducted by artist Harvey Littleton and Dominick Labino, research vice-president of the Johns-Manville Fiber Glass Corporation.[28] "About fifteen people from all over the country, most of them Harvey's friends, came to this workshop," Kottler recalled. "They brought in the last remaining glass blower at Libby-Owens, and we learned from him how to use the blowpipe. It was all pretty disorganized and technically primitive: they didn't have an annealing oven, for example, and without this oven it's hard to cool things properly and they crack. I wasn't happy with what I did there, but I was still very interested in Tiffany glass and wanted to learn more about the medium. Then in the mid-1960s I stopped in to see Marvin Lipofsky, who had been at that first workshop, when I was on a trip to San Francisco. I did a few pieces with him and began to get the feel of it again. Later one of my students, Clair Colquitt, got interested in glass and in 1968 we set up a glass furnace at the University of Washington."[29]

For several months Kottler worked with the furnace, creating a series of bottle forms that celebrate the taffylike consistency of molten glass. Often he began with a base blown in a mold; the glass at the top was then pulled and stretched into loopy horizontal projections (figs. 2.38, 2.39). In some compositions, the glass was encased in ceramic jackets covered with gold or silver lusters. "I was basically working with formal ideas Harvey Littleton had popularized earlier in the 1960s," Kottler observed. "My addition was to use lusters that were painted on and then fired into the glass, so that I could get a changeable iridescent surface. The best in the group were very liquid and tonguelike (fig. 2.40). I wish I had continued, but I really hated the heat and the fact that you have to work so quickly and there's no chance to work things out. What I needed was a master glass blower, like Dale Chihuly has, who could do whatever I asked him to do. That kind of collaboration really appeals to me, even though it bothers people with traditional ideas about craft."[30]

Kottler's work was exhibited frequently in the Northwest and in Ohio during the late 1960s. Most reviewers admired his virtuosity and enjoyed his humor, although some, like Katherine White, who reviewed his

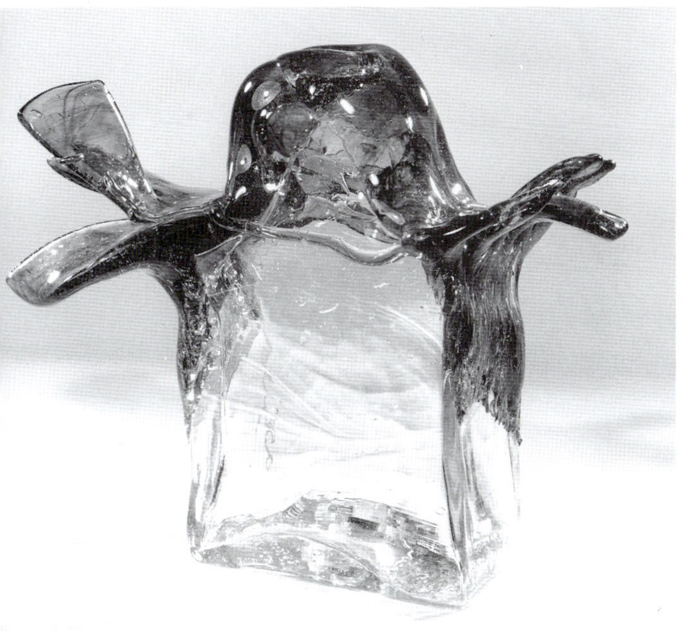

2.38 *Winged Bottle,* 1968. Glass, lusters

one-person exhibition at the Cleveland Institute of Art in 1968, were offended by his "disrespect." "Howard Kottler displayed his new line of sarcastic ceramics in this show," she reported. "Always prolific, he turned out loud half-pots, half-propaganda objects which, like some Pop Art, flung mud at accepted standards. . . . Kottler's inventions may arise from a colossal boredom with the usual aesthetic attitude. These excursions into anti-art—this search for a new sublime in the slime—may well pay off. The ennui may be interior, however; there may be no more tricks worth the name. These pots and objects are rare for their total impersonality, their undercurrent of generalized despair."[31]

Although he was motivated more by exuberance than despair in the late 1960s, White correctly identified Kottler's boredom with the "usual aesthetic attitude." His self-image as an artist-potter drew him to Pop and Funk,

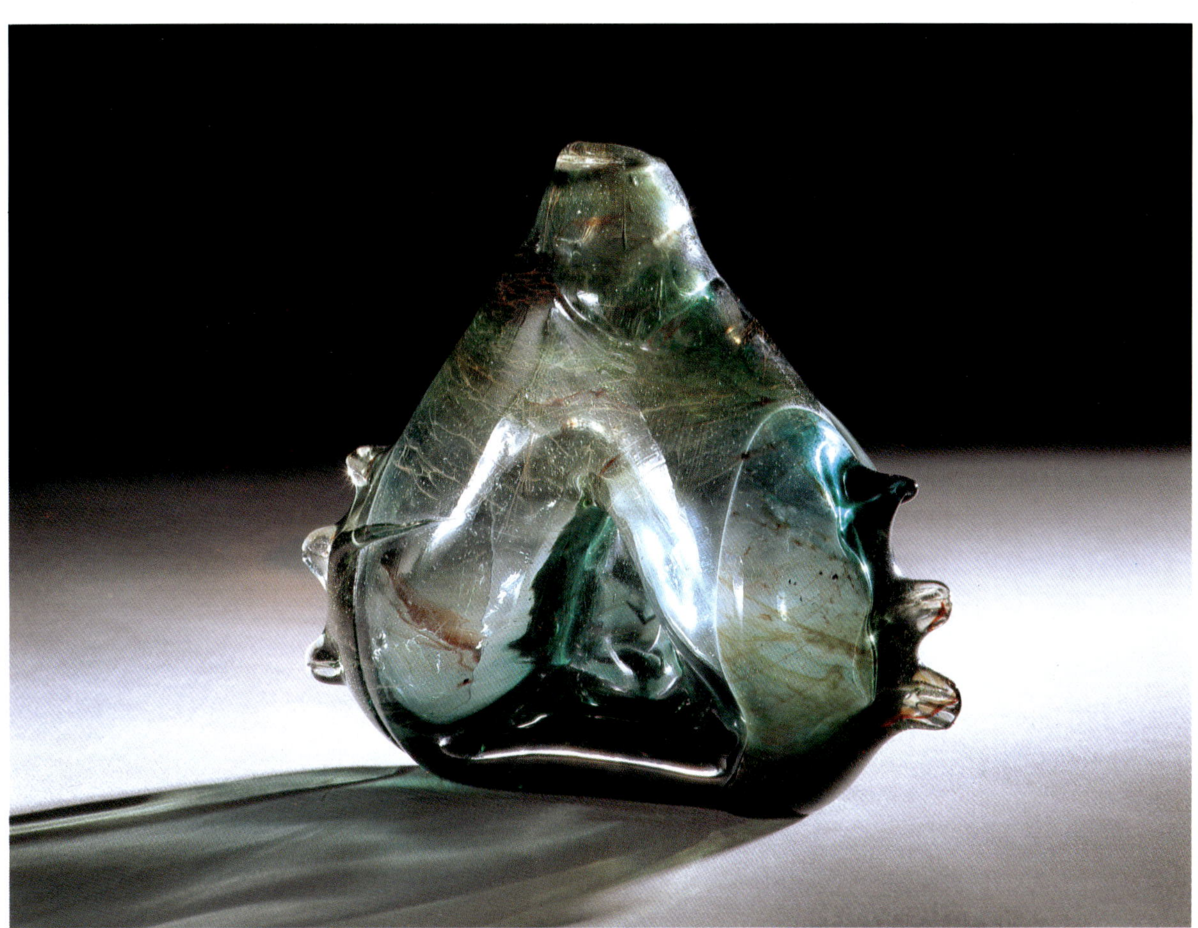

2.39 *Nibble Tips Double Bottle,* 1968–69

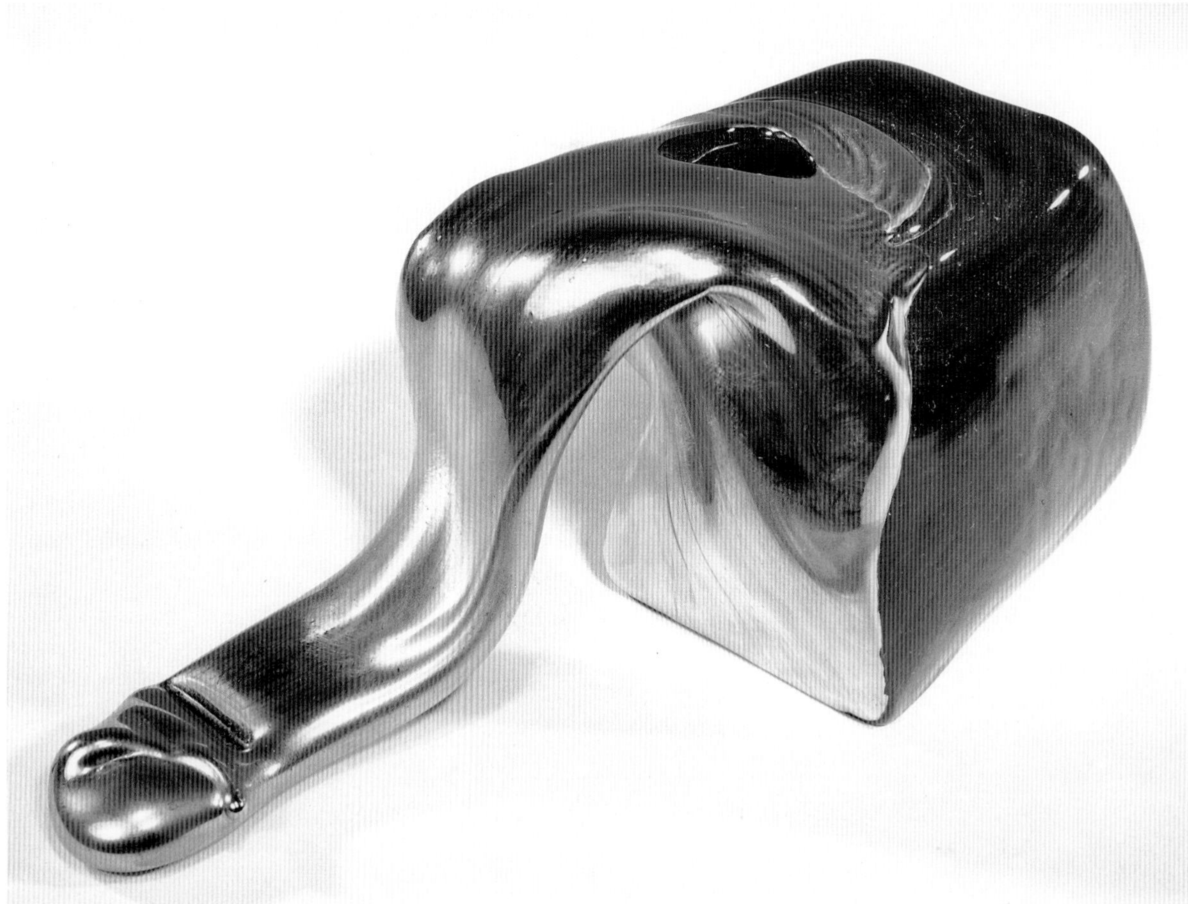

2.40 *Silver Butter Bottle,* 1968. Glass, lusters

which he appreciated not only in formal terms but also for the irony, chutzpah, and double entendres that extended the literal content of the work. Compared with Funk icons such as Arneson's penis teapots, however, Kottler's production gravitated toward more indirect sexual references, aligning it with certain practices of gay culture. In the 1982 New York writers' symposium "Extended Sensibilities: The Impact of Homosexual Sensibilities on Contemporary Culture," one participant observed that contemporary gay life in the United States is distinguished by the "use of verbal and non-verbal communication to mean more than it usually does. Double meanings in verbal communication, the whole art of non-verbal communication to get across messages the straight world will not pick up on—this is something we are always involved in."[32]

Beginning in the mid-1960s, Kottler developed a repertoire of visual forms, particularly holes and phallic shafts, in which the meaning shifts with the complexion of viewer desire. Punning and coded titles like *Hustler's Delight* extend the associative shifts of the visual forms by linking the images with subcultural patois. He had also begun to explore a range of formal and art-historical coding to convey special meanings to ceramics insiders. In this respect his work was consistent with Pop and Bay Area Funk Art; with compositions like *Hole Grabber,* however, Kottler began diverting the strategies of Pop and Funk to establish the foundations of a truly personal art.

THREE

Vessels and Sculpture of the 1970s

Most of the 1970s, in Kottler's view, was an anticlimactic period in his professional development. "This was a mixed-up time for me, both in terms of my personal life and my work," he said. "I worked erratically. I was spending a lot of time socializing in San Francisco. Then, in 1973, my father became ill, and for several years I went back to Ohio for long periods of time. I often spent my sabbaticals there (fig. 3.1). My mother had suffered from severe depression starting in the mid-1940s, and by the 1970s the length of these periods increased. My father could attend to her until his health started to decline. He needed moral support and I served that purpose for him." His parents relied on him more and more, Kottler recalled, "because my sister had married and had her own life. My mother, who died in 1985, was always anxious for me to marry. She believed I didn't marry because I was devoted to taking care of them. I don't think it occurred to them that there might be another explanation. At a certain point I became part of a fantasy world for my parents," he continued. "They didn't really understand that I had a job or work I really wanted to do. The impact of all this on my work was very bad. I usually work in a series, and I really need to see a finished piece before I can go on to the next one. I could always go back to something I did earlier and pick up from there. But every time I took off for San Francisco or Ohio, the momentum was broken."[1]

Despite these interruptions, Kottler produced a significant body of new work in the 1970s. Pots made in 1969 and the early 1970s reflect his burgeoning enthusiasm for Art Deco, another modernist movement that produced palace ware. In the late 1960s Kottler began a study of the Art Deco architecture in Seattle, where a surge in downtown and residential development in the 1920s and 1930s coincided with the height of enthusiasm for Deco styles. In the early 1970s he also researched and photographed scores of Deco buildings in the San Francisco Bay Area, particularly structures with elaborate ceramic detailing. He was especially fond of the Marine Building in Vancouver, British Columbia, where the ceramic façade extends for several stories (fig. 3.2). Later he began collecting Deco furniture and design. "I think my interest shifted from Art Nouveau to Art Deco at this point partly because I began to realize that my potential was really in hard-edged, nonvolumetric form," Kottler concluded.[2]

By 1969, Deco fountain or waterfall motifs and a typically Deco play of symmetry against asymmetry had begun to appear regularly in his work. In compositions such as *Fountain Fun Pot*, Kottler adapted a phallic Deco waterfall design to frame the opening and the left and

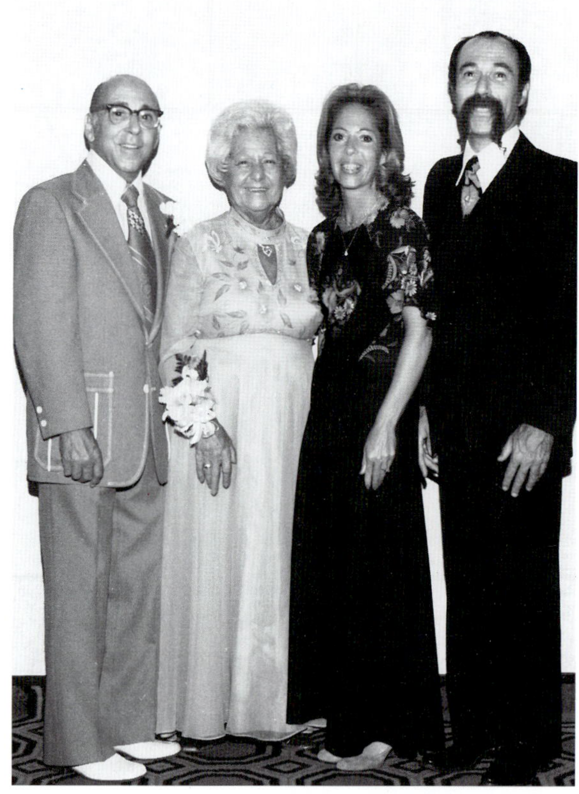

3.1 Howard Kottler with his sister, Shirley Shoenberg, at their parent's fiftieth wedding anniversary, l976

right perimeters of a rectangular vase, underscoring the vessel's sexual coding with the title. Like most Deco architecture, this militantly symmetrical composition has a strong frontal orientation and bold juxtapositions of geometric and organic form. In several related vases from 1969-70, among them *Spirit Rose Pot*, Kottler combined Deco motifs with atmospheric color surfaces not unlike some of Jules Olitski's canvases of the same period (figs. 3.3, 3.4). In these vessels the layers of glazes and lusters create an illusion of physical depth, slightly dematerializing the edges of the geometric forms.

Other Deco-inspired pots from the early 1970s were "wallpapered" with sheets of commercially manufactured paisley ceramic decals. Placed over colored glazes or opaque lusters to create luxurious patterns, the wallpaper decals not only embellished the surfaces but expanded their visual depth (figs. 3.5, 3.6). Kottler had been introduced to decal techniques at Ohio State and the Arabia Ceramics Factory in Helsinki, but he rediscovered these ready-made images in the mid-1960s when he began patronizing hobby shops to buy low-fire glazes. In a statement on decals, he reported: "At the shops the

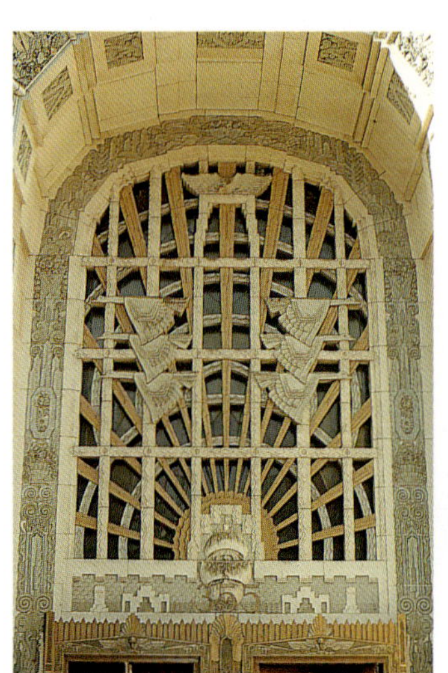

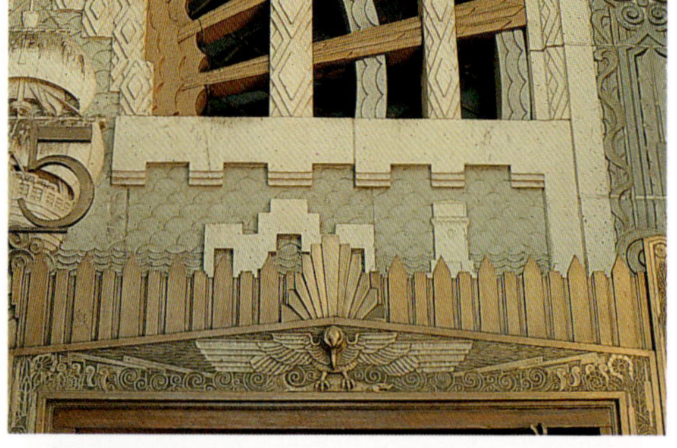

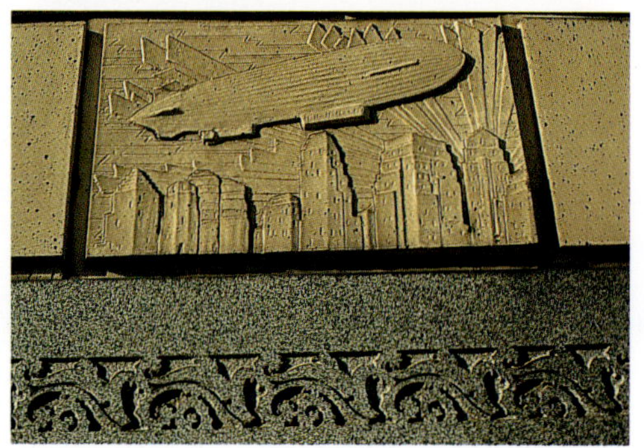

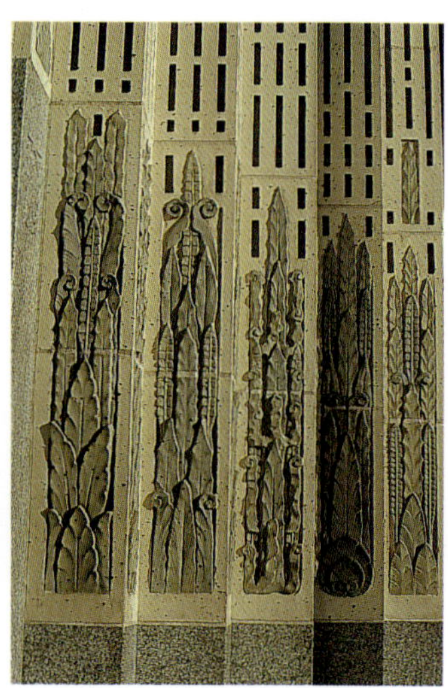

3.2 Marine Building facade, Vancouver, British Columbia. Howard Kottler photographs

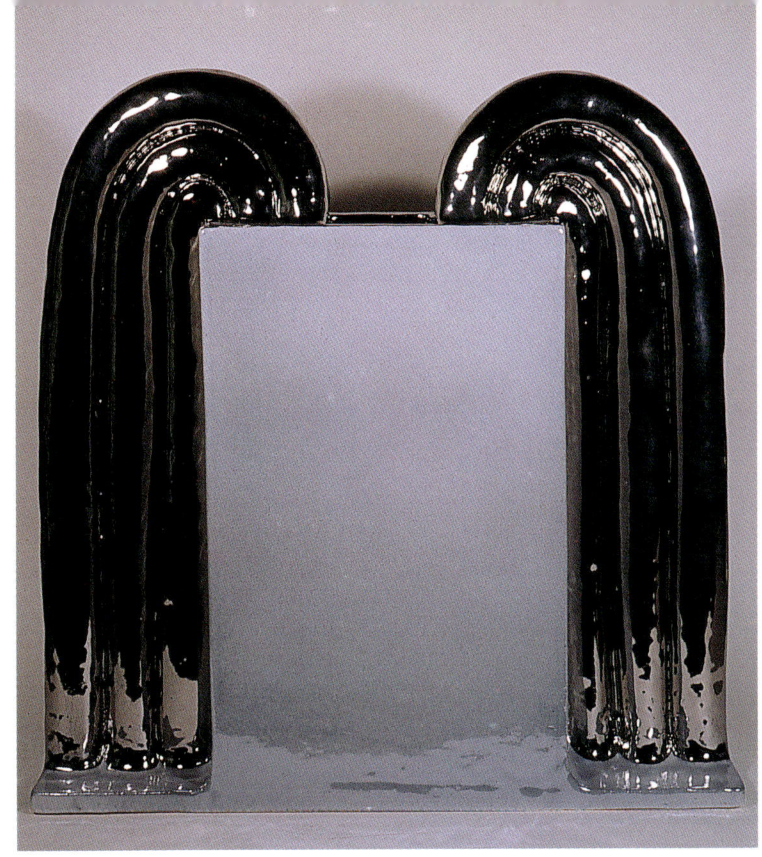

3.3 *Fountain Fun Pot*, 1969. Earthenware

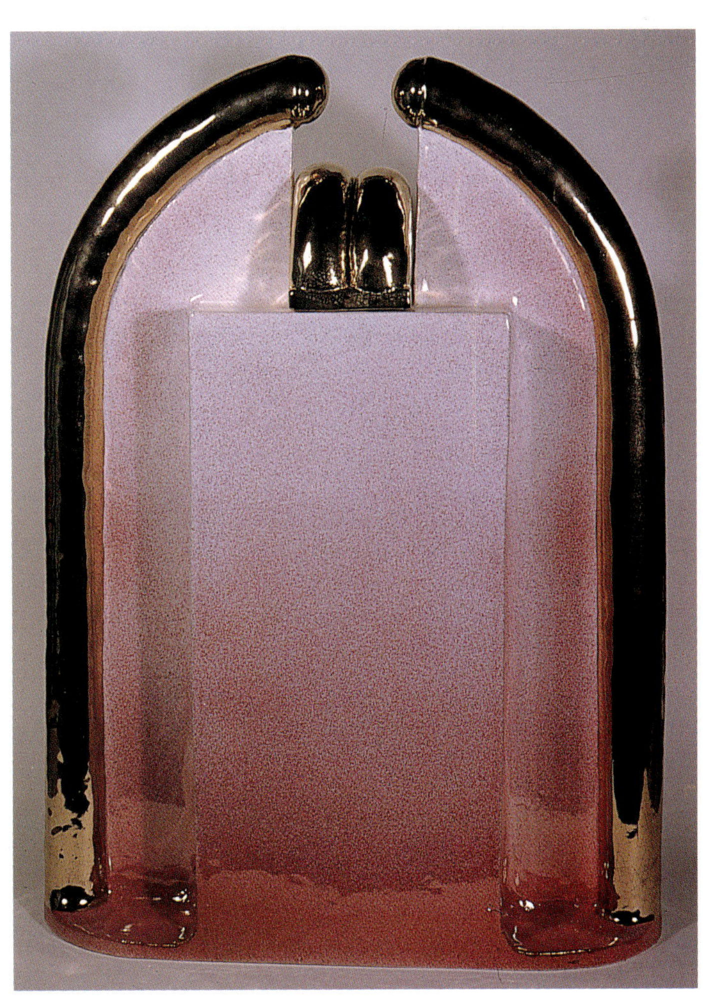

3.4 *Spirit Rose Pot*, 1970. Earthenware, 18 h

53

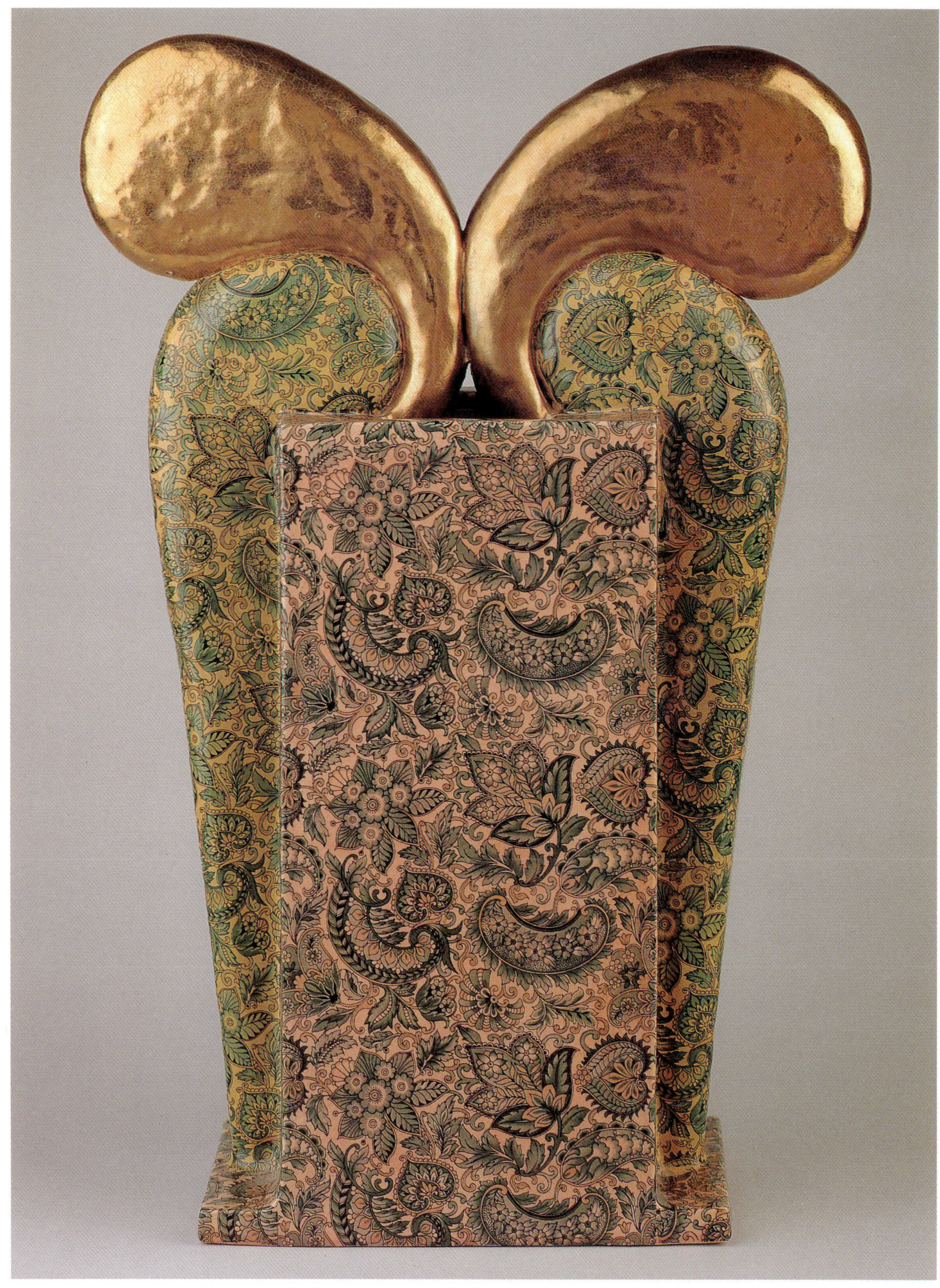

3.5 *Bunny Hop Pot,* 1970. Earthenware, decals, 20 h

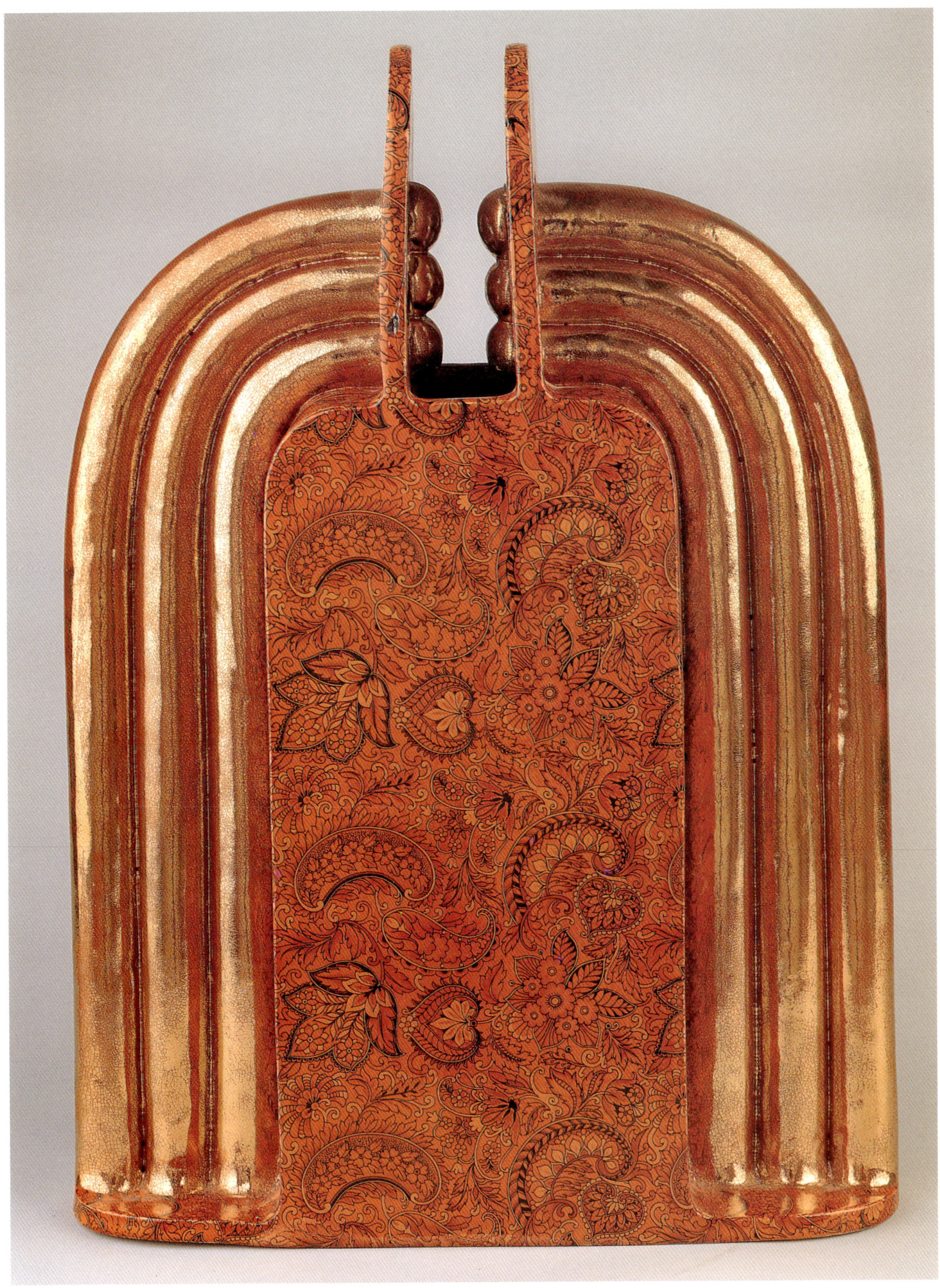

3.6 *Message Gestures Pot,* 1970. Earthenware, decals, 20 h

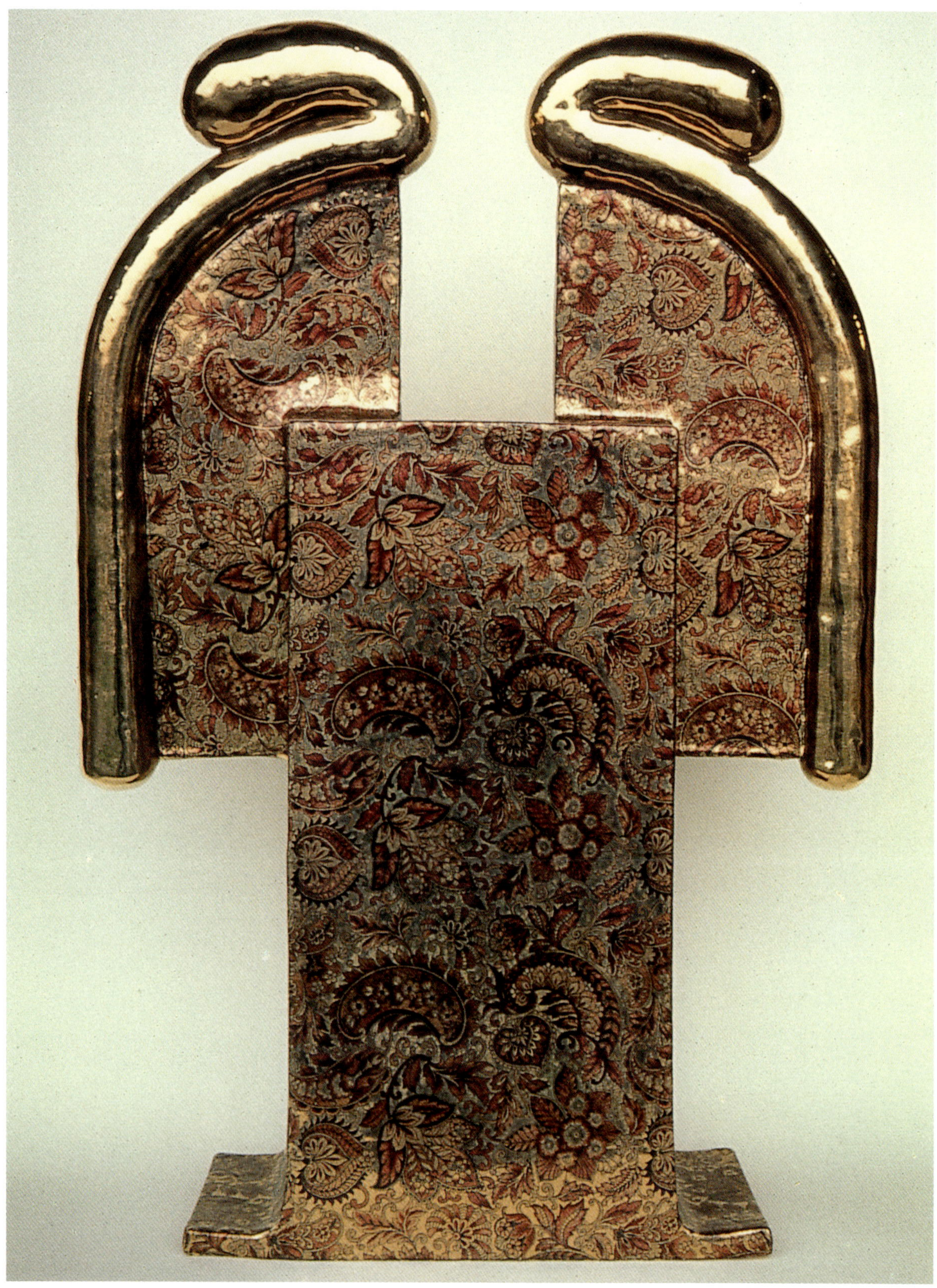

3.7 *Rich Paisley Pot*, 1970. Earthenware, decals, 22 h

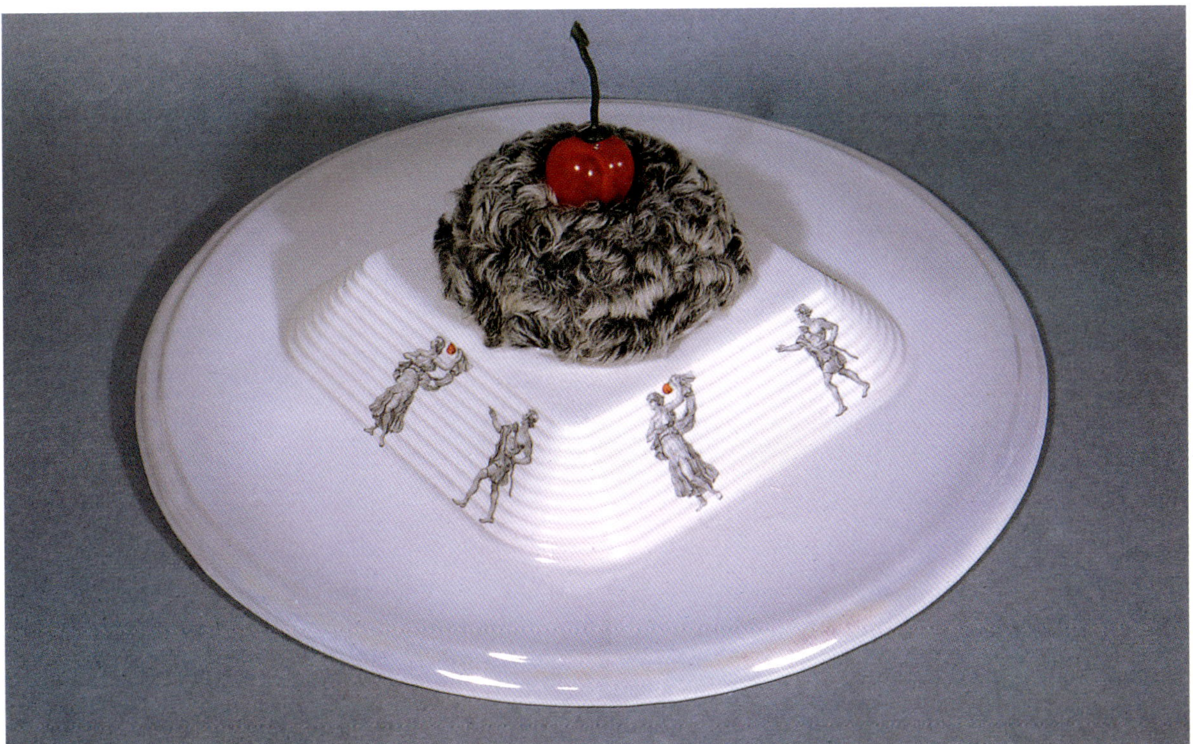

3.8 *Ode to a Cherry,* 1970. Slipcast earthenware, decals, fur, 6 h

decals were sold one or two at a time and were rather expensive. I decided to write directly to the large ceramic-decal suppliers and manufacturers. They sent me their catalogues with a range of decals that surpassed the few images being sold in the hobby shops. However, a purchase from the manufacturer necessitated buying the decals in large quantities. . . . I made my purchase and found myself with hundreds of the same image. I immediately set out to find ways of using repeated images."[3]

Kottler covered several of the paisley pots entirely with gold (then $37 an ounce) before he wallpapered them with decals (fig. 3.7). The paisley patterns appear to float on the gold surfaces, creating a spatial ambiguity that disrupts the architectonic precision of the container. "There's an interesting contrast here with Arneson's work," Kottler pointed out. "He told me he didn't like these pieces because the lusters tended to destroy the form. He was using lusters then to do just the opposite— to enhance the experience of volume. But in my case, I *wanted* to create uncertainty about whether the surfaces were volumetric or flat."[4]

Contemporary with the Deco-inspired pots of 1969-70 was Kottler's first ceramic sculpture series. Based on casts of ordinary household objects such as Jell-O molds and lamp bases, these compositions are technically related to the 1967 Barbie-doll platters. The new series was inspired in part by the work of University of Washington graduate student Irvin Tepper, who received his M.F.A. in 1971. Tepper used casting to create irreverent ceramic assemblages based on the format of a T.V. dinner, while Kottler combined cast forms into symmetrical phallic shrines and illustrations of adolescent sexual humor. In *Ode to a Cherry* (1970), for example, ceramic-decal male figures pursue females around a stepped pyramid cast from a lamp base. On top of the pyramid is a dome of fur topped with a long-stemmed, bright-red cherry.[5] A tall phallic column rises from a similar base in the nine-inch-high *Properly Pisces*, where the pattern of the steps is replayed in Deco fountain-motif lustered tubing (figs. 3.8, 3.9). The title is autobiographical; Kottler's birthday fell under the sign of Pisces. He correctly assessed most of this series, which included

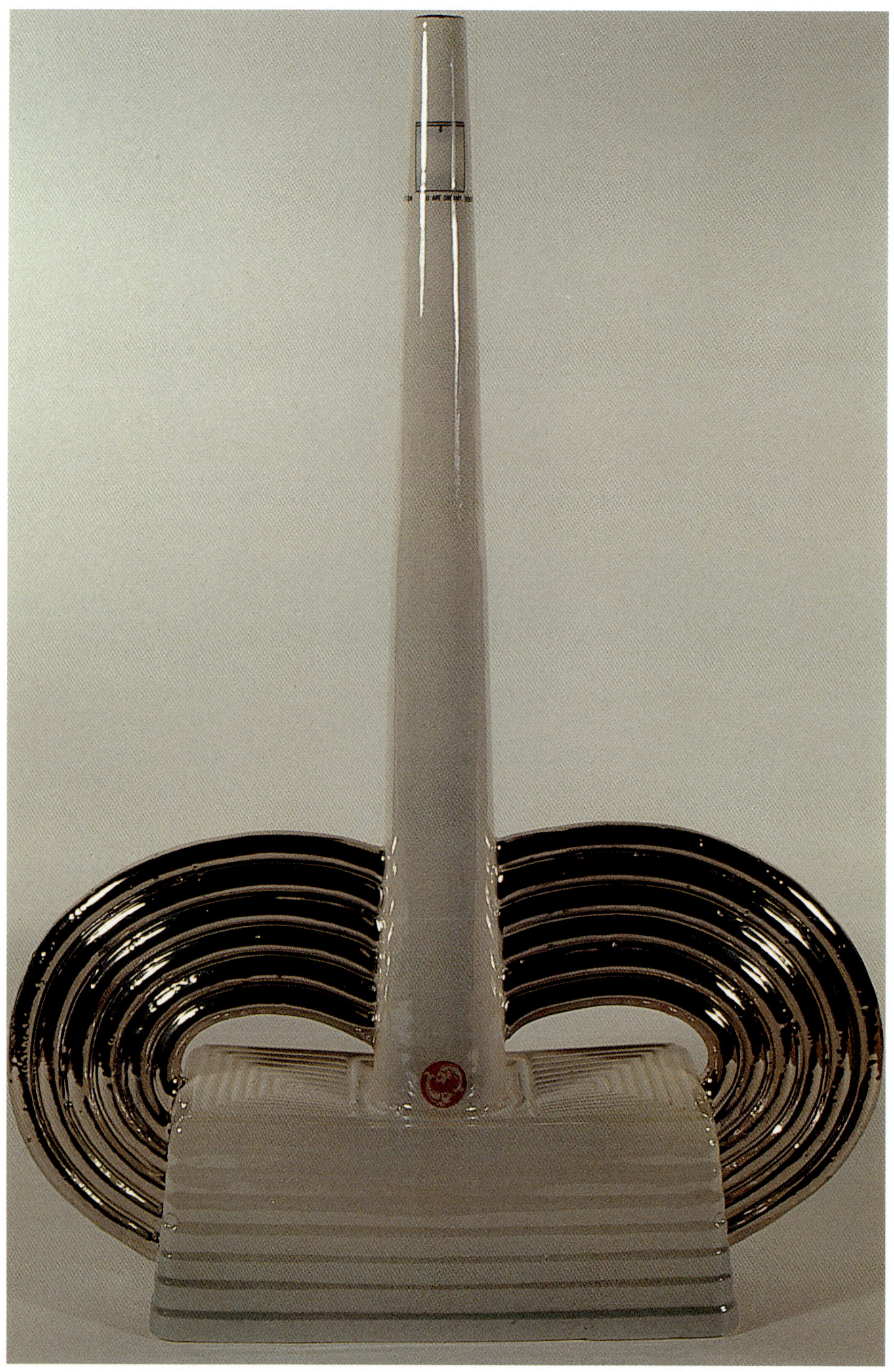

3.9 *Properly Pisces,* 1970. Slipcast earthenware, 9 h

several variations on the cherry theme and the *Properly Pisces* compositional format, as "not dreadful, but pretty close."[6] This experience was instrumental, nevertheless, in drawing him toward more challenging investigations of slip-cast iconography.

In 1972 and 1973 Kottler turned to the manufactured ceramic cup as a vehicle for conceptual commentary and burlesque. He had been invited to participate in a 1970 Museum of Contemporary Crafts cup exhibition surveying "individual approaches to the classic container," which included cups by Robert Arneson, Irvin Tepper, David Gilhooly, Richard Shaw, Clayton Bailey, James Melchert, Patrick Siler, and Ron Nagle. Kottler's contribution was a teacup and saucer decorated with collaged decals.[7] This cup exhibition, among others, exposed him to newly expanded definitions of a familiar vessel form, and in 1972 he challenged himself and his students to design new presentations of the essence of "cup." He was subsequently invited to participate in an influential Japanese exhibition, the "Thinking, Touching, Drinking Cup," which opened in 1973. Further stimulus for his cup series was the much-discussed 1973 joint exhibition of cast ceramics by Richard Shaw and Robert Hudson at the San Francisco Museum of Modern Art.

"This kind of re-thinking of functional forms took off in the mid-1960s with artists like Ken Price and Roy Lichtenstein, and later, Ron Nagle—artists whose work was popularized in *Ceramics Monthly* and *Craft Horizons*," Kottler observed. "But there was a big difference between Price and Lichtenstein. At first Price's cups were still fairly functional elaborations of form. With Lichtenstein, the cup was a format to present an idea—it was a more conceptual approach."[8] As Lichtenstein himself explained, discussing his 1965 stacked cup series, "I liked the idea of a sculpture of a cup done in the material and size of a cup, so there is no difference between the cup and the sculpture of the cup."[9] In the early 1970s, Kottler too approached the standard shape and size of a manufactured cup as an intellectual structure; for him, however, the form of the ready-made cup was primarily an occasion for raising questions about actuality and illusion, or for visualizing a verbal pun.

Most of Kottler's cup compositions of the early 1970s involved a ceramic cast of a plaster mold used to manufacture slip-cast cups. *Portrait of a Cup*, Kottler's contribution to the "Thinking, Touching, Drinking Cup" exhibition, for example, is a cast of an empty slip-casting mold mounted on a base and encased in a Plexiglas box. In *Paisley Cup* (1973), a fully three-dimensional cup is trapped on one side within the negative space of the mold. The surfaces of mold and cup are united with an all-over paisley pattern, and the trapped cup is presented in a Plexiglas case covered with the same paisley decal (figs. 3.10, 3.11). As in the Deco paisley pots, the patterning creates spatial ambiguity, heightening the paradoxical byplay of negative and positive form. *Cup of Light* (1973) is a cast of a half-cup mold turned upside down and enclosed in a Plexiglas case lighted from below (fig. 3.12). "If you turn a cup upside down, you normally don't get to see the interior," Kottler commented. "In this piece the cup is upside down but you can still see what's inside. It reminded me of the kid who wants to know if the light really goes off when the refrigerator door is closed."[10] In the catalogue for the 1987 traveling exhibition "Clay Revisions: Plate, Cup and Vase," Seattle Art Museum curator Vicki Halper grouped *Cup of Light* with the work of other ceramists who "concentrate on the empty space of an unfilled cup and focus our attention on the void itself by dematerializing the bowl." In *Cup of Light*," she observes, "Kottler reverses light and dark, positive and negative.... The shell is filled with light and the cup's skin becomes simply a frame to catch it."[11]

Other cup compositions from this group literalize verbal cliches. *Mug Shot*, for example, combines a toy gun with a three-dimensional cup trapped in a mold like *Paisley Cup*. "*Mug Shot* makes a play between a three-dimensional ceramic gun juxtaposed with similar [two dimensional] ceramic decals," Kottler wrote in 1982. "The gun decals form a camouflaged pattern over the cup/mold and accentuate the scale shift between the guns. A bullet is passing through the Plexiglas base and yet there is no bullet hole in the cup, which helps promote the ambiguity of the work."[12] A more complex double entendre inspired *Hand Jive*: on one side of the composi-

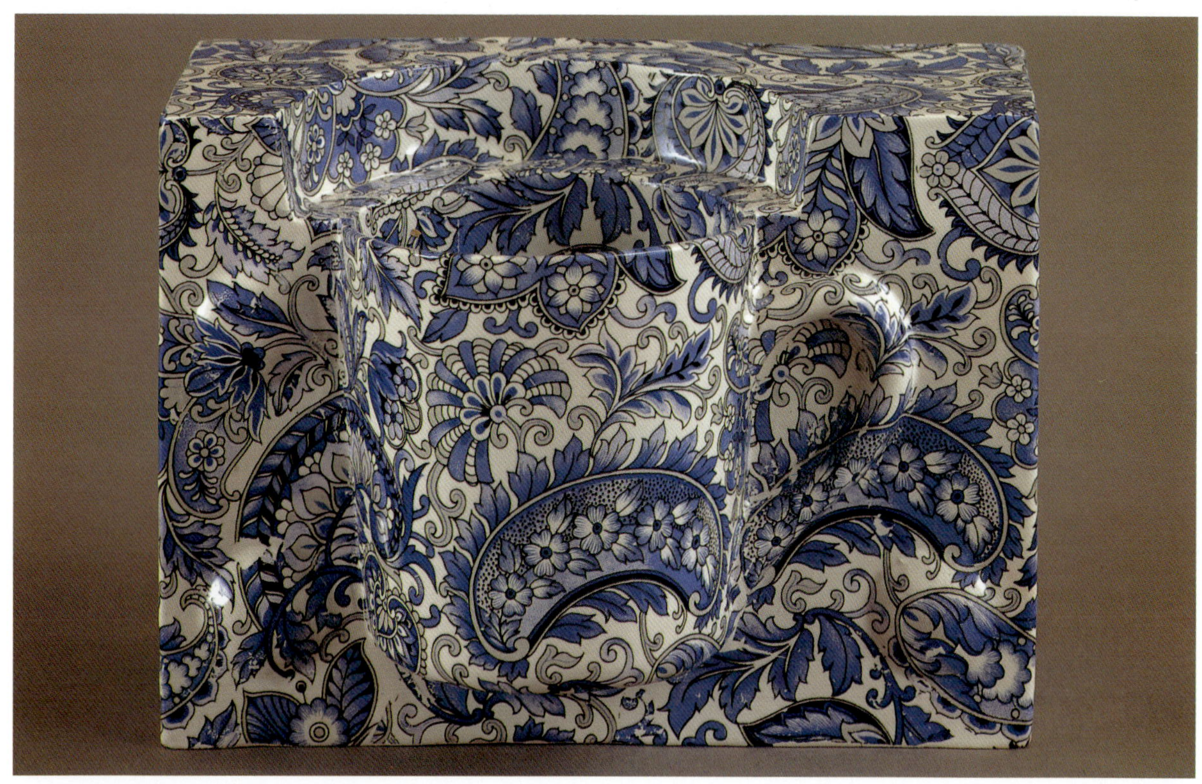

3.10 *Paisley Cup,* 1973. Slipcast earthenware, decals, 4½ x 6½

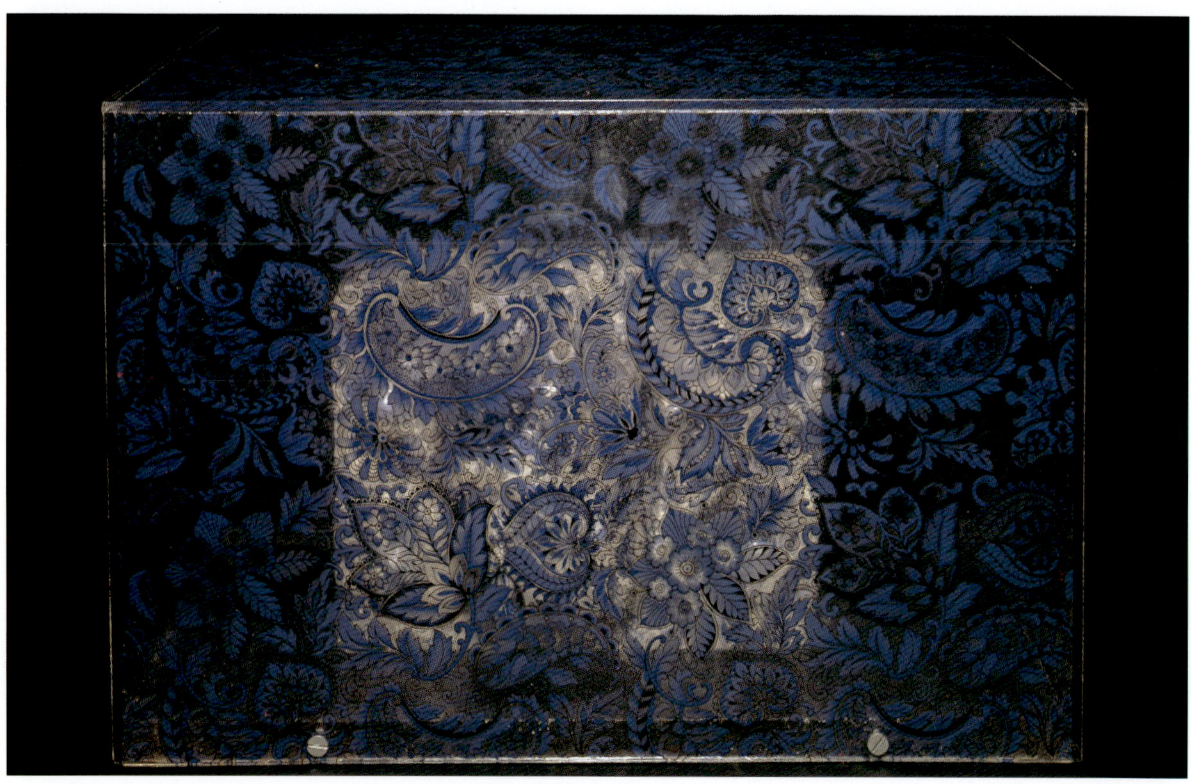

3.11 *Paisley Cup Box,* 1973. Slipcast earthenware, decals, Plexiglas, 8 x 12

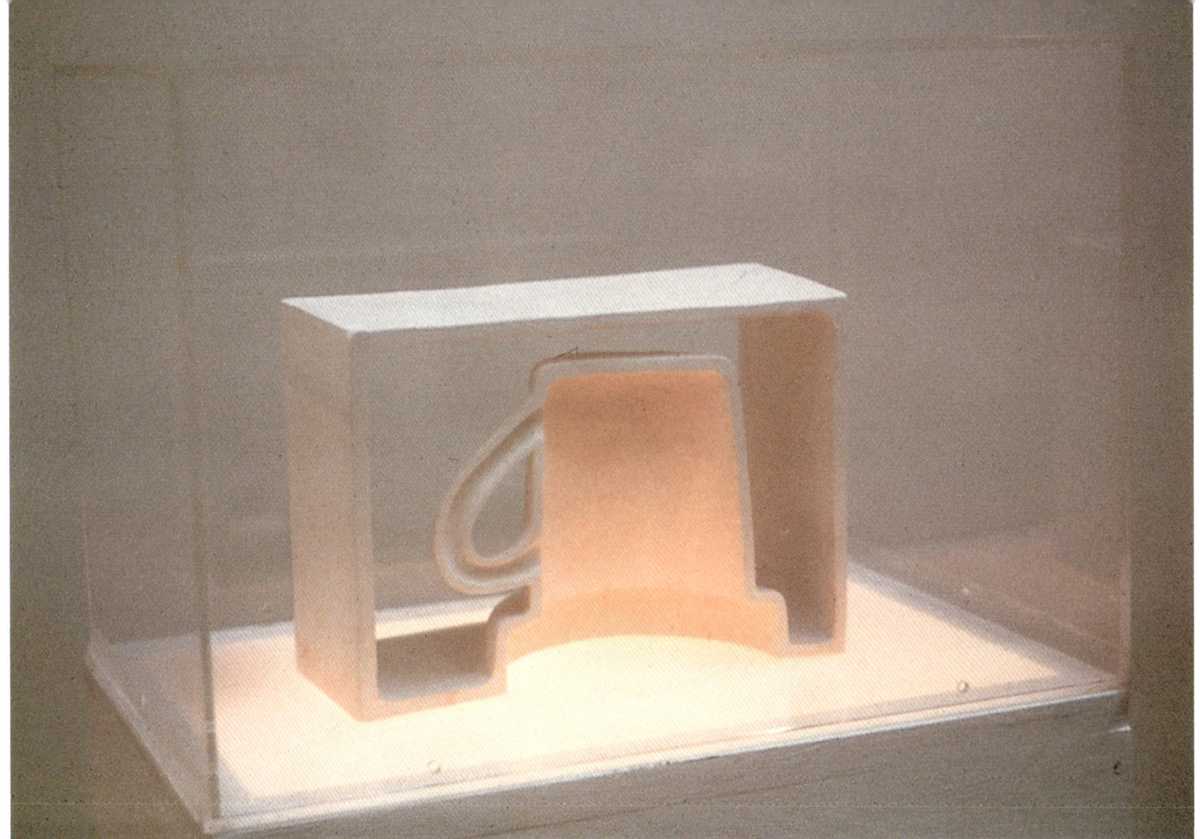

3.12 *Cup of Light,* 1973. Slipcast earthenware, 8 h

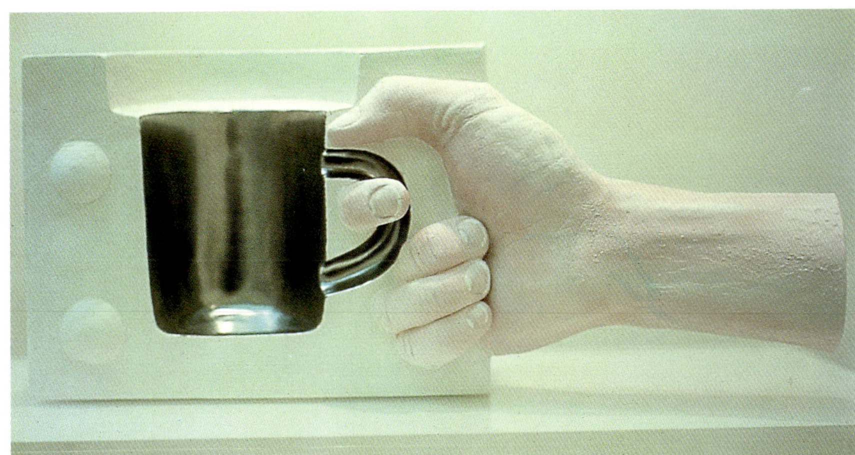

3.13 *Hand Jive,* 1973. Earthenware, 5½ x 11

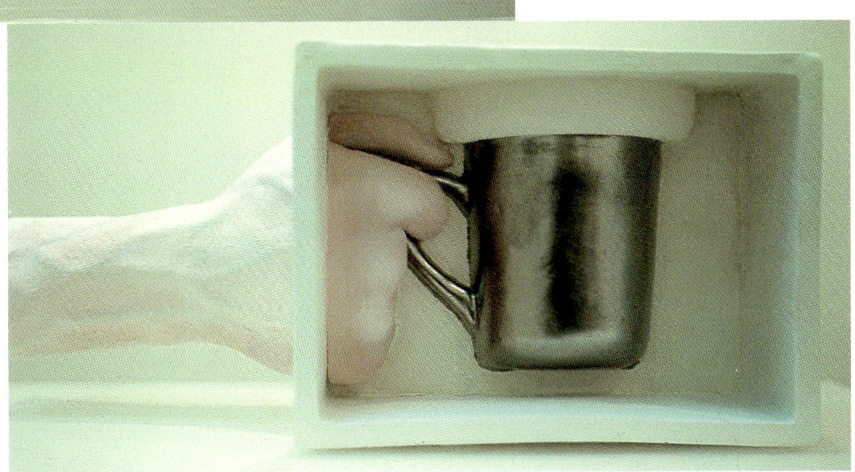

3.14 *Hand Jive,* 1973. Rear view

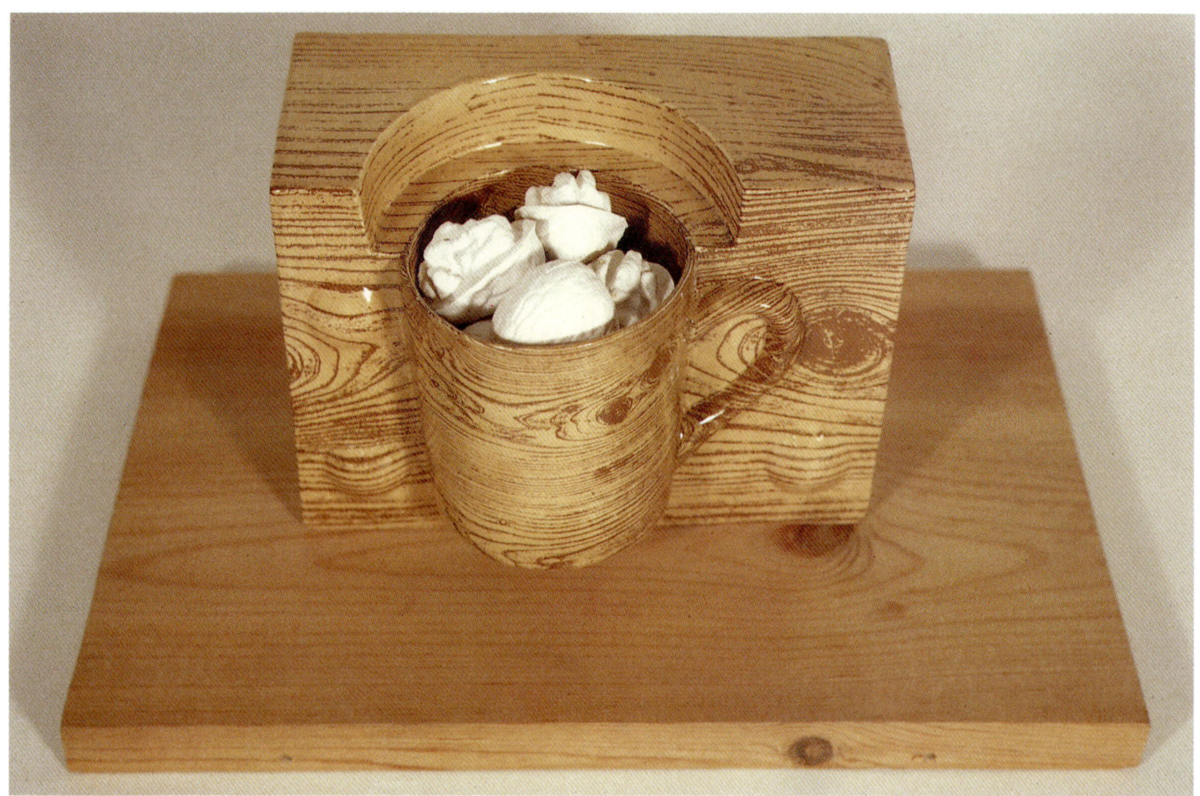

3.15 *Walnut Cup,* 1973. Slipcast earthenware, decals, 5 x 6 ½

tion a life-size, three-dimensional hand grips the negative form of a cup; from the back, the hand appears to
enter the empty frame of the mold to grasp the convex
side of the same vessel (figs. 3.13, 3.14). *Hand Jive* was
executed in collaboration with Mark Burns, another
University of Washington M.F.A. student who influenced
the development of Kottler's work. Burns painted the
trompe l'oeil hand and wrist, which Kottler integrated
into another statement about the flimsiness of polar op-
positions such as "reality" and "illusion."

True/false and real/fake polarities were further cor-
rupted in earthenware cups and molds covered with
wood-grain decals, such as *Walnut Cup* and *Bushel and a
Peck*, both 1973 (figs. 3.15, 3.16). Kottler made the decals
himself from a photograph of fake wood grain. ("A photo
of real wood grain is pretty dull," he explained. "The reproduction gives a more graphic representation of what
wood grain really is.")[13] Describing *Walnut Cup*, Kottler
reported: "Both the mold and the cup are covered with a

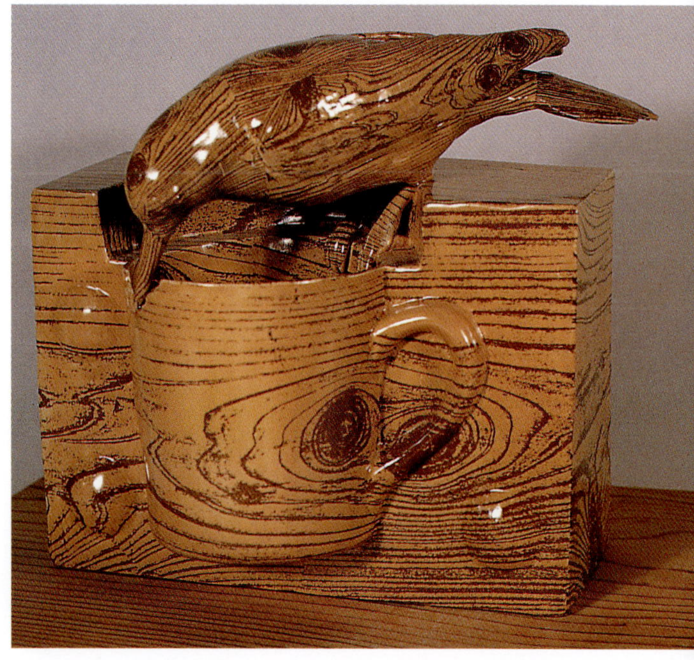

3.16 *Bushel and a Peck,* 1973. Slipcast earthenware, decals,
6 x 6. Collection Seattle Art Museum. Gift of Howard Kottler
Testamentary Trust

62

simulated wood-grain ceramic decal, which gives an illusionistic camouflage effect to the cup/mold. The cup is filled with slip-cast white walnuts and rendered nonfunctional in a Surrealist byplay between the walnut wood-grain ceramic mold, cup, and white walnuts, which act as ghost images."[14]

A ceramic bird nibbles away the cup in *Bushel and a Peck*, a composition covered entirely, except for the actual wooden base,[15] with simulated wood-grain decals. These explorations of simulationism were inspired in part by Kottler's aversion to truth-to-materials, clay-as-clay partisanship within the field of ceramics. As he emphasized in a later pronouncement, "I am not concerned with revealing clay as clay or to glorify ceramic processes. My concerns are to use the material of clay in any way that answers my needs. I refuse to let the materials or tradition dominate my direction."[16] As the 1970s progressed, he also became increasingly intrigued by middle America's satisfaction with simulated surfaces, such as imitation chrome detailing on automobiles or marble-pattern bathroom Formica.[17] More an ironic observer than a social critic, he began to view these cultural phenomena in metaphorical terms: the multiplication of fake materials and surface disguises in American life, he ultimately concluded, had its analogue in various forms of human relationships. Compositions such as *Bushel and a Peck* represent an exploratory encounter with this theme, which he picked up again and developed in his sculpture of the 1980s.

Initially the cup-series translations of verbal puns or clichés, like *Mug Shot*, were indebted to precedents such as Robert Arneson's *Call Girl* (1967), a female telephone figure, and to the verbal-visual conundrums of Marcel Duchamp and René Magritte. The ancestry of *Bushel and a Peck* also includes the incongruous appearance of wood-grain patterns in the canvases of René Magritte. In another series reminiscent of Magritte from the mid-1970s, Kottler reversed the strategy of *Bushel and a Peck* by concretion of the verbal signifier itself. These new compositions were based on free-standing three-dimensional block letters spelling the words "wood" and "brick." Kottler was familiar with James

Melchert's letter "a" series, in which the same three-dimensional letter shifted its meaning according to surface treatment and title. He also knew Arneson's trompe l'oeil ceramic bricks stamped with stenciled letters, as well as the work of Jasper Johns and Pop artists who incorporated stenciled lettering in their paintings. In his own letter compositions Kottler sought a layered interplay of verbal-visual commentary; the objective was a cumulative experience of meaning, based on oscillations between the connotative and denotative references of the verbal sign.

In the catalogue for a 1977 exhibition at the Laguna Beach Museum of Art, Kottler's 1974 letter sculpture, *Acapulco Plywood*, was paired with two of Arneson's trompe l'oeil terra-cotta bricks, one stamped with the word "meat," the other with "milk." In *Acapulco Plywood*, three-dimensional ceramic block letters covered in front with wood-grain ceramic decals spell the word "brick." The backs of the letters, mounted on a thick plywood base, are colored brick-red (figs. 3.17, 3.18). Curator Elaine Levin links the brick compositions of Kottler and Arneson first to Marcel Duchamp; she then suggests that Kottler's work plays off Arneson's precedent.[18]

These art-historical preludes played a role in the conception of *Acapulco Plywood*, but Kottler had other, more immediate objectives in presenting linguistic signs as physical objects. With the coded title, for example, he bypassed straight culture to address viewers who knew that Acapulco Gold marijuana was sold in bricks.[19] The title thus linked the word "brick" with its subcultural connotations, while the surface treatment of the letters played upon its denotation. The "correct" denotative correspondence—brick red—is retained in the back of the letters, while the wood-grain decal in front disrupts the material correspondence between sign and denoted object. The decal also functions as a disguise or camouflage, apropos both of dope culture and of Kottler's disavowal of the truth-to-materials morality in ceramics.

Another work in this series, *Layed Back* (1974), preserves the denotative references of the verbal sign: here the three-dimensional letters spelling "wood" are covered with wood-grain decal, and they rest on a two-tiered

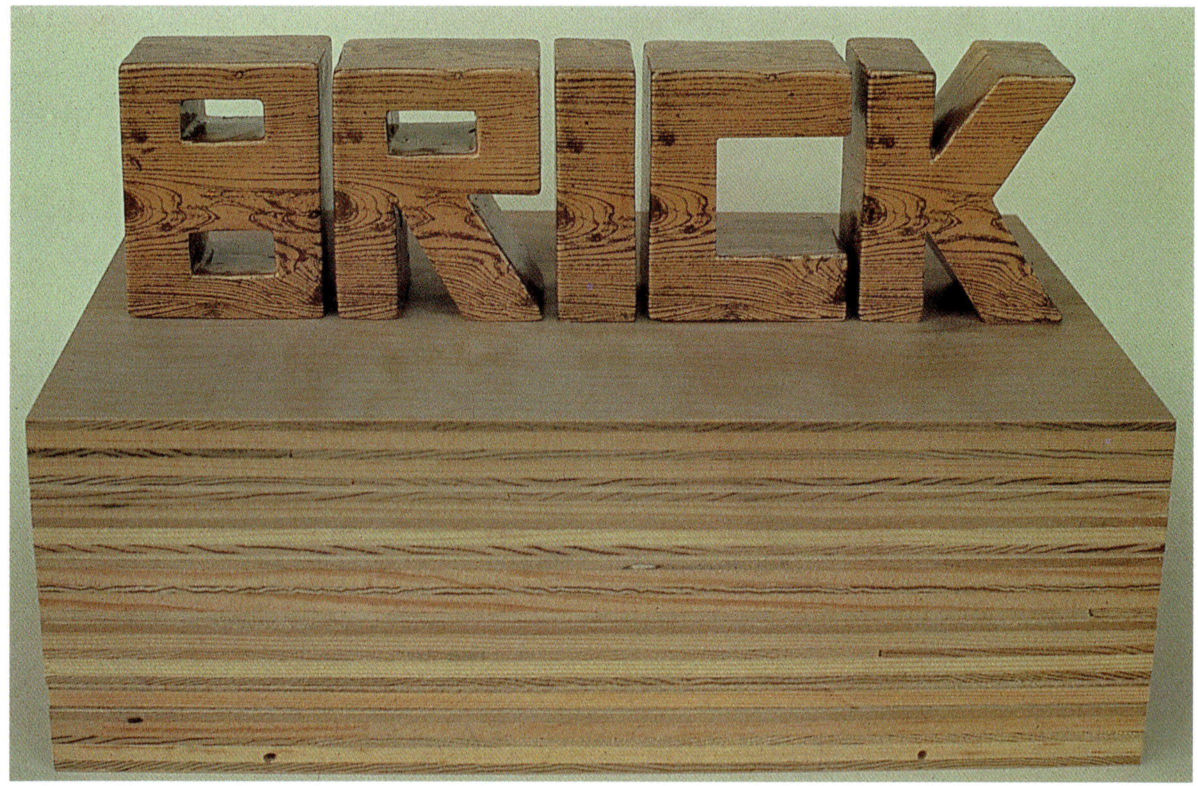

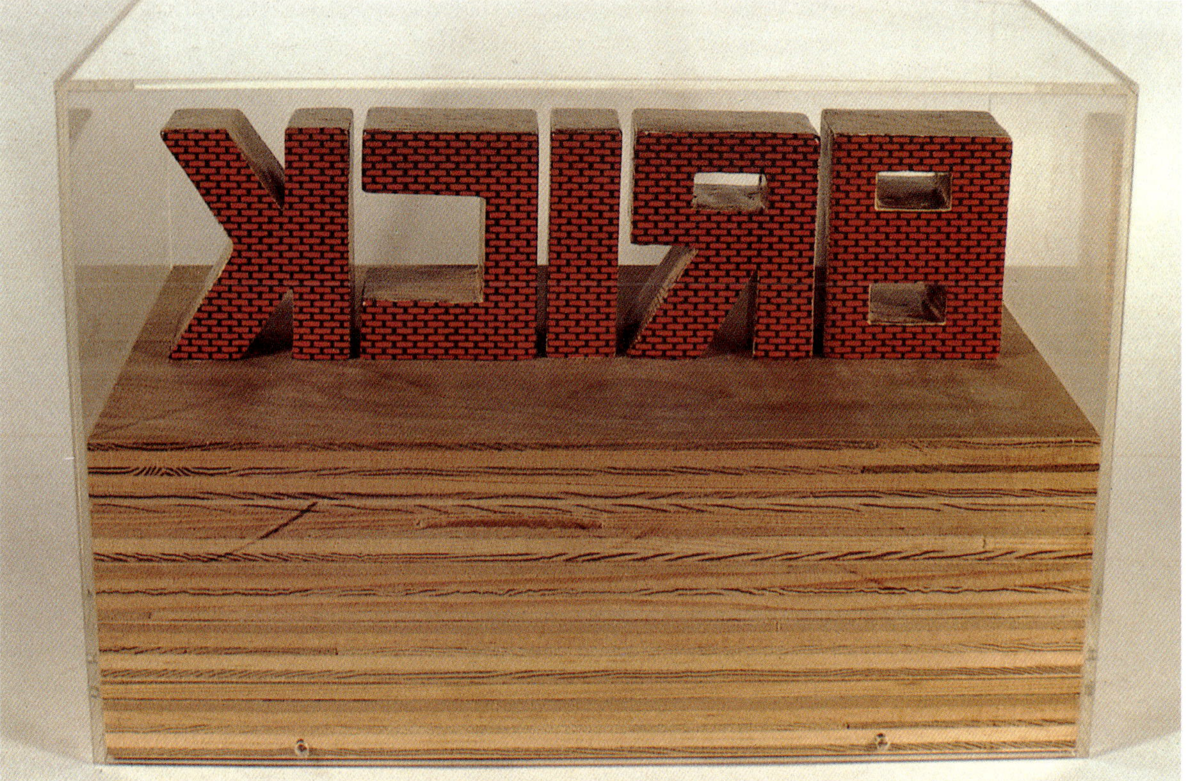

(Top) 3.17 *Acapulco Plywood*, 1974, mixed media, 8 x 12. Collection American Craft Museum, New York. Gift of Howard Kottler Testamentary Trust; (Bottom) 3.18 *Acapulco Plywood*, 1974. Rear view

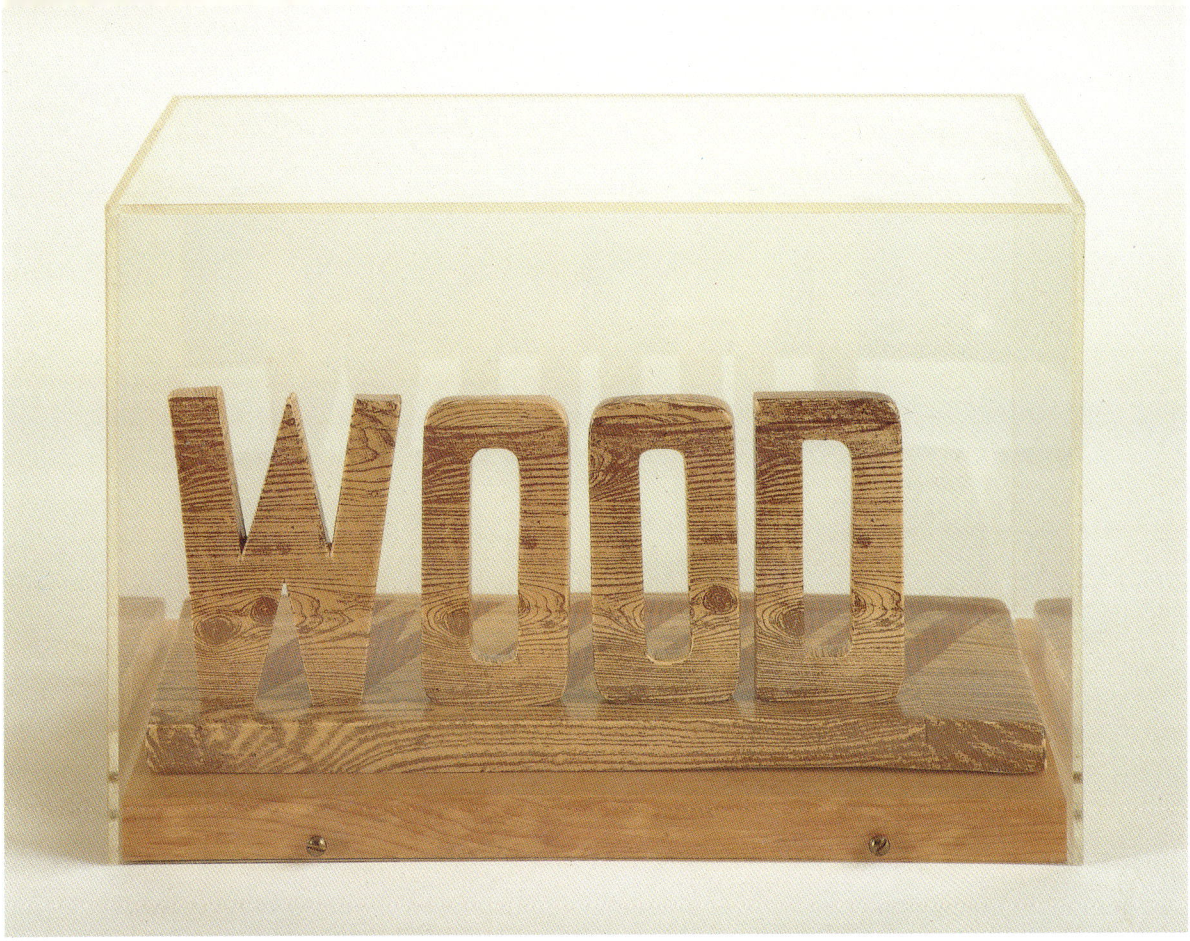

3.19 *Layed Back*, 1973. Mixed media, 8 x 12

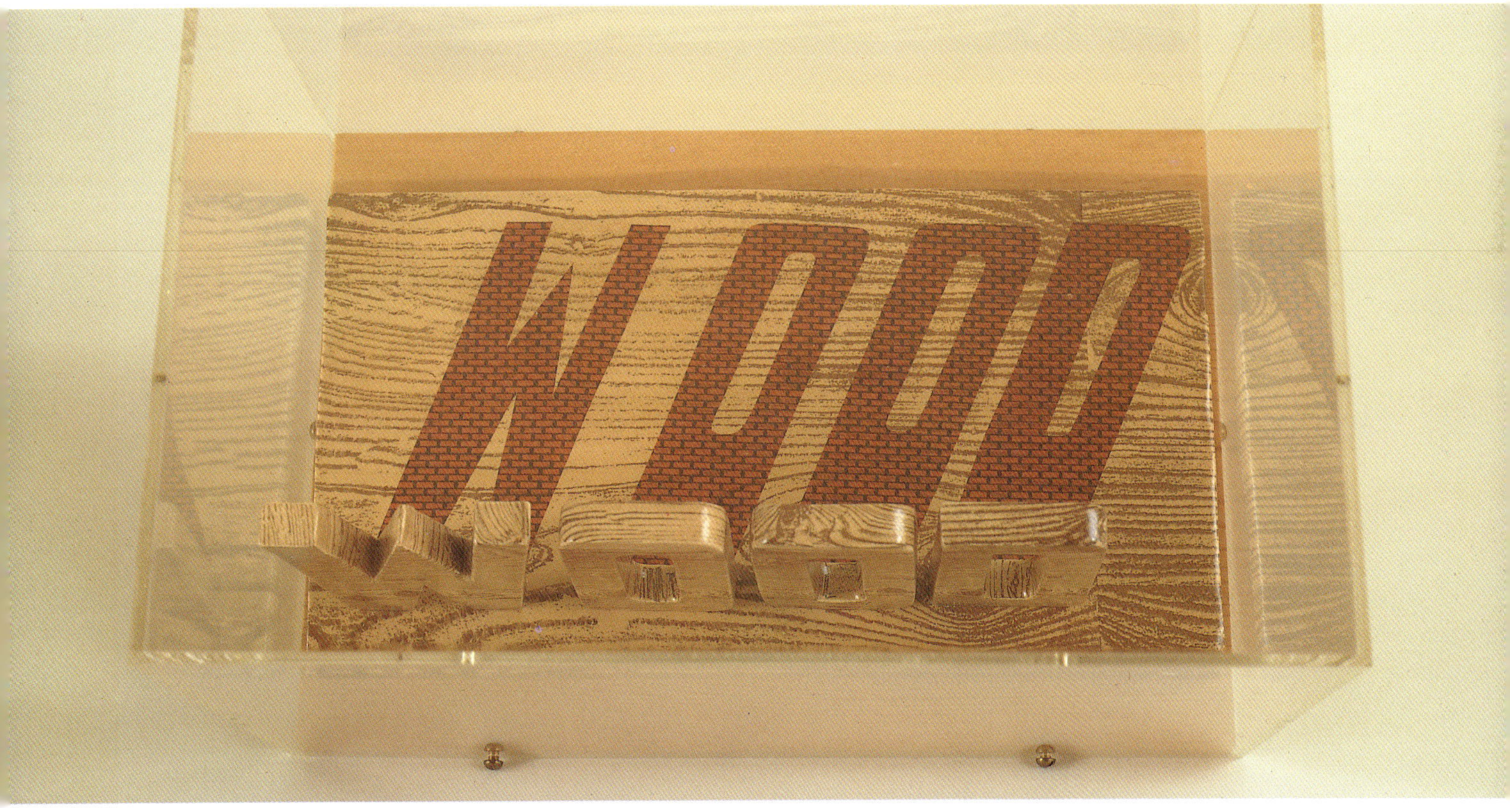

3.20 *Layed Back*, 1973. Top view

real- and fake-wooden base. In this composition Kottler accentuated the physicality of the letters by simulating their cast shadows, permanently inscribed on the base. Like *Acapulco Plywood, Layed Back* was enclosed in a Plexiglas case (figs. 3.19, 3.20). "The case expands the idea of preciousness and creates a hermetic bubble, which is part of the amusement," Kottler commented. "In an ordinary literary situation, there is a stream of words. Here the word is taken out of that visual context and isolated in its own environment. You become more aware of the placement and shape of the letters and their physicality, which sets up another layer of meaning. I was trying to create something that revealed itself in stages."[20]

For his next series Kottler created three-dimensional earthenware brushes that project vertically from horizontal plaques. In *Touch of Reality* (1974), for example, the panel beneath the trompe l'oeil ceramic brush, whose bristles are wallpapered with decals of Thomas Gainsborough's *The Blue Boy*, contains a three-dimensional cast of the same image made from a hobby-shop mold. The most complex demonstration of dimensional shifts in this group is a 1976 homage to the American bicentennial, *All-American Stroke* (figs 3.21, 3.22). As Kottler described it: "*All-American Stroke* is a sculpture that involves changes in scale between two-dimensional imagery and three-dimensional objects. It contrasts three different reproductions of the *Signing of the Declaration of Independence* by John Trumbull: the two-dollar bill, U.S. postage stamps, and a large ceramic decal. A three-dimensional, molded ceramic brush leaves a two-dimensional brushstroke across the ceramic decal. This stroke is composed of many small decals of the American flag. The stroke is a play on the Roy Lichtenstein 'pop stroke' painting series, which itself was a play on expressionistic brushwork. A negative shape of the same brushstroke is presented in decals on the inside of the top of the Plexiglas box."[21]

In retrospect, Kottler concluded, "this kind of work and a lot of what was being done in the Bay Area in the 1970s was really a footnote to a footnote of Surrealism. Except for Arneson's, it didn't really add much to the Surrealist tradition or to the history of sculpture. Even

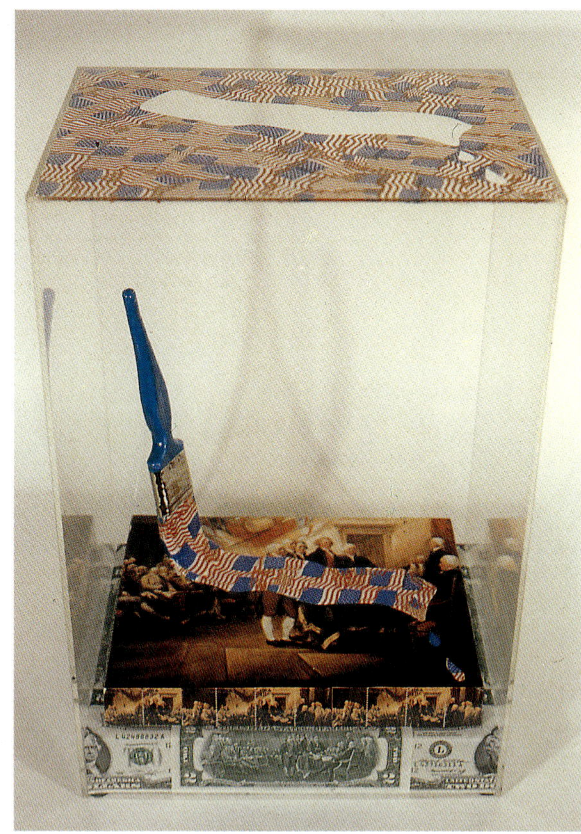

3.21 *All-American Stroke*, 1976. Mixed media, 16 x 11

though a lot of people were working in this direction, most of the work was jokey or kitschy or sentimental—collectively, it didn't raise the level of the field very much. What was most important about this period for me was that it brought me to something else."[22]

By the mid-1970s Kottler had developed a ceramics-world persona to complement his irreverent palace ware. For him, the artist's statement in exhibition catalogues was an occasion to provoke traditional ceramists. In 1978, for example, his work was included in "Eleven Updates: a profile of the Slocumb Gallery's interest in and enthusiasm for the craft renaissance," an exhibition mounted by the art gallery at East Tennessee State University in Johnson City, Tennessee. The catalogue Preface states, "For over a decade it has been evident that there was in progress a renaissance in the production of handcrafted works in clay, fiber, metals, wood and glass." In his artist's statement, however, Kottler declared:

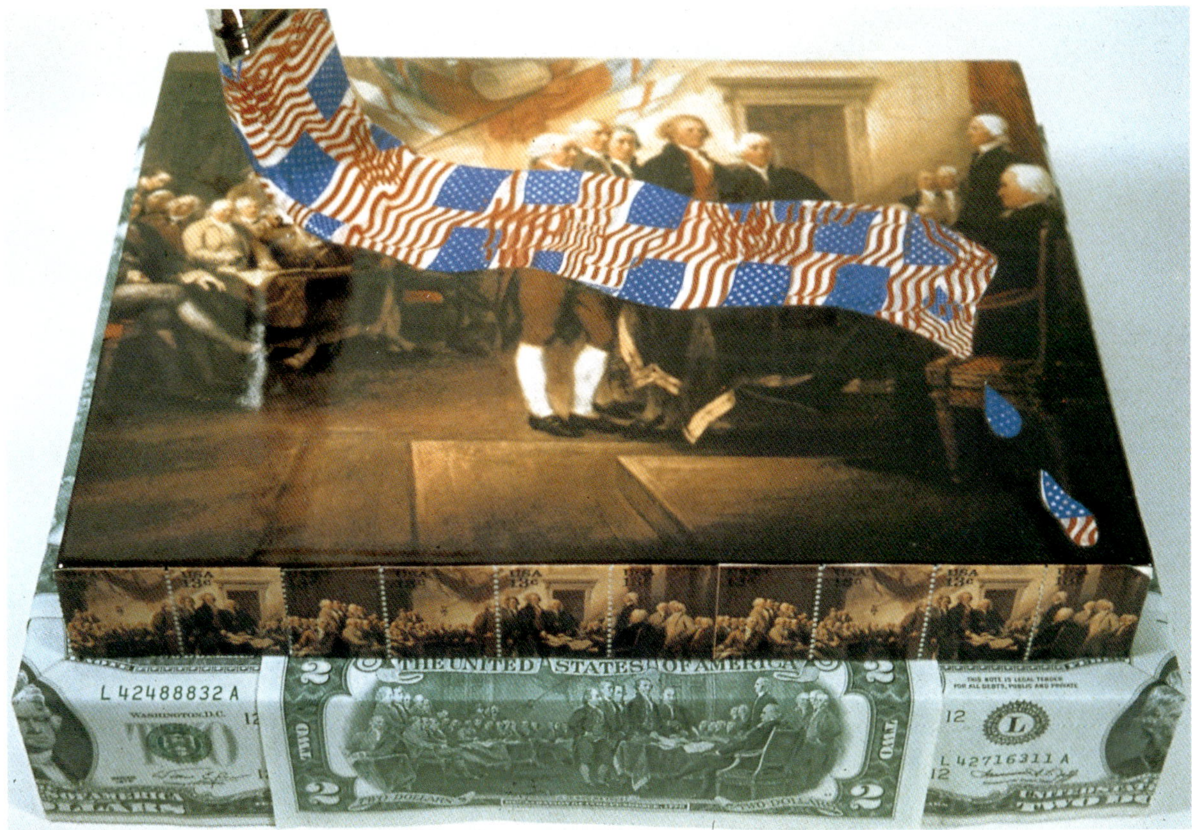

3.22 *All-American Stroke,* 1976. Detail

"There is no craft media revolution in the United States or anywhere else. Craft is craft and art is art; fortunately, the twain never meet."[23] For a 1977 catalogue he wrote, "I am lazy. I use images already available—casting is simpler and faster than modeling. I purchase molded pieces already cast, use prepared glazes and junked ceramic objects; in fact, I seldom touch clay. I use other people's molds, other people's ideas and other people make my ceramic decals. I just assemble the parts. The resulting work ranges from bad to interesting, with an occasional hot piece."[24]

This statement accompanied an illustration of *The Old Bag Next Door Is Nuts* (fig. 3.23), a 1976 ceramic assemblage that paired a Victorian house made from a hobby-shop mold with a cast of a paper bag containing cast walnuts, also reproduced from a commercial mold.[25] As Garth Clark points out, *The Old Bag* provoked a "long, ongoing correspondence between the left and

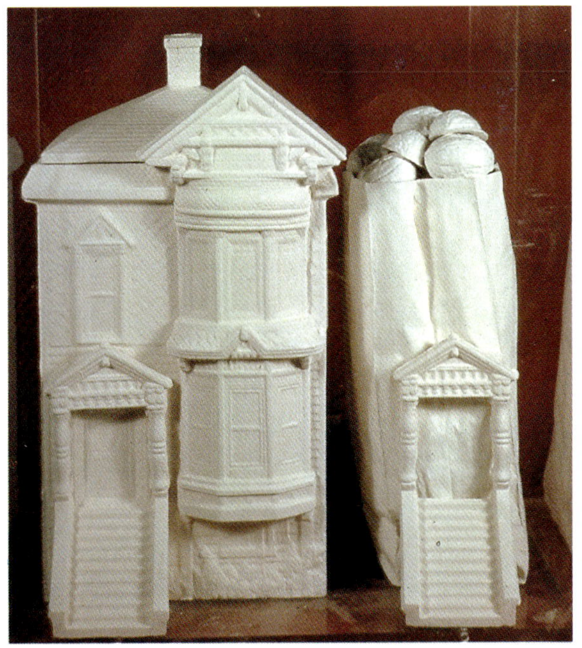

3.23 *The Old Bag Next Door Is Nuts,* 1976. Slipcast earthenware, 13 h

right wings of ceramic sculpture" when it was subsequently illustrated in *Ceramics Monthly*.[26] A letter from Ruth Poris, a ceramist from Farmington Hills, Michigan, launched the debate. "My sense of justice, honesty, integrity and aesthetic feeling have been affronted and I am completely outraged," she wrote. "Shown as one example of illusionistic realism [*The Old Bag Next Door Is Nuts*] is cynical and dishonest, stretching originality beyond my level of acceptance." Poris then cited the page and issue of the Duncan ceramics catalogue where the Victorian house molds Kottler used were illustrated. In a second letter, she explained that she did not object to the use of molds *per se*, "although my preference would be for the original model to be made by the artist. . . . I believe this controversy is a philosophical question of integrity, honesty and personal consideration of values and goals. The work in question was represented as 'earthenware with decals, wood and Plexiglas, 13 inches in height, by Howard Kottler,'—not as 'an assemblage with slip-cast Duncan molds, decals, wood and Plexiglas.' In all media, the use of another's work is called plagiarism, according to the dictionary." In her conclusion, Poris thanked other potters who had supported her position, adding that "working in clay, one cannot escape the timeless touch of thousands who came before us to use their imaginations and skills to pass down this very human art form for us to treasure and preserve."[27]

In their responses to Poris's letter, Kottler supporters pointed out that artists use many commercial products without crediting their inventors; furthermore, they argued, artists should be free to use commercial molds for their own artistic ends. Instead of diplomatically deferring to his allies, however, Kottler stuck to his black-sheep persona in a sarcastic letter to Poris.

> Indeed, Ruth Poris, I am a sinner. I have plagiarized from everyone. In my sculpture *The Old Bag Next Door Is Nuts,* the Victorian House mold (artist unknown), sold by Duncan Ceramics Products was cast at Lloyds Ceramics and Pottery of Seattle, Washington, the nuts were cast from another Duncan Ceramics Products mold (artist

unknown), the bag mold was made from a real paper bag (artist unknown) by one of my former students, V'Lou Oliveira, the ceramic decals were made by Tim Hall of Seattle, and the Plexiglas box was made by Continental Industries of Seattle. Even the title for the piece, I must confess, is not my own, but the brainstorm of two students, Michael Lucero and Alice Sundstrom. In fact, the only element that is mine was the concept for the sculpture and hopefully, Ms. Poris, you will permit me this one small glory.[28]

One legacy of this kind of rhetorical posturing was Kottler's portrayal in Clark's standard reference book, *American Ceramics* (1988), as an artist who "freely acknowledges the lack of depth or content in his work"; he is also described as a "supermannerist" who displays a "slick comedy of manners and a style that employs the visual sleight of hand of trompe l'oeil painting."[29] These observations might be consistent with Kottler's ironic rhetoric, but not with the evolution of his work: as the 1970s progressed, Kottler in fact became more and more concerned with the expressive content and conceptual status of his production. In 1978 he clipped, saved, and quoted to his students a *New Yorker* essay by critic Harold Rosenberg, who echoed some of his own views about art and craftsmanship. "Crafts, with their measurable skills," Rosenberg wrote, "cannot be reconciled with the interests and practices of art of our time. The skills of the modern artist are the opposite of those of the craftsman: instead of acquiring techniques for producing classes of objects, the artist today perfects the means suited to his particular work. His technique—and indeed, his self as an artist—tends to be his own creation."[30]

Like many avant-garde artists of the 1970s, Kottler came to regard ideas and concepts as the locus of artistic expression. In the physical execution of these concepts, efficiency was more desirable than were demonstrations of his own manual expertise; he was entirely comfortable, therefore, with ready-made images and materials and with skilled technical assistants. This neo-Duchampian outlook was familiar to artists in other

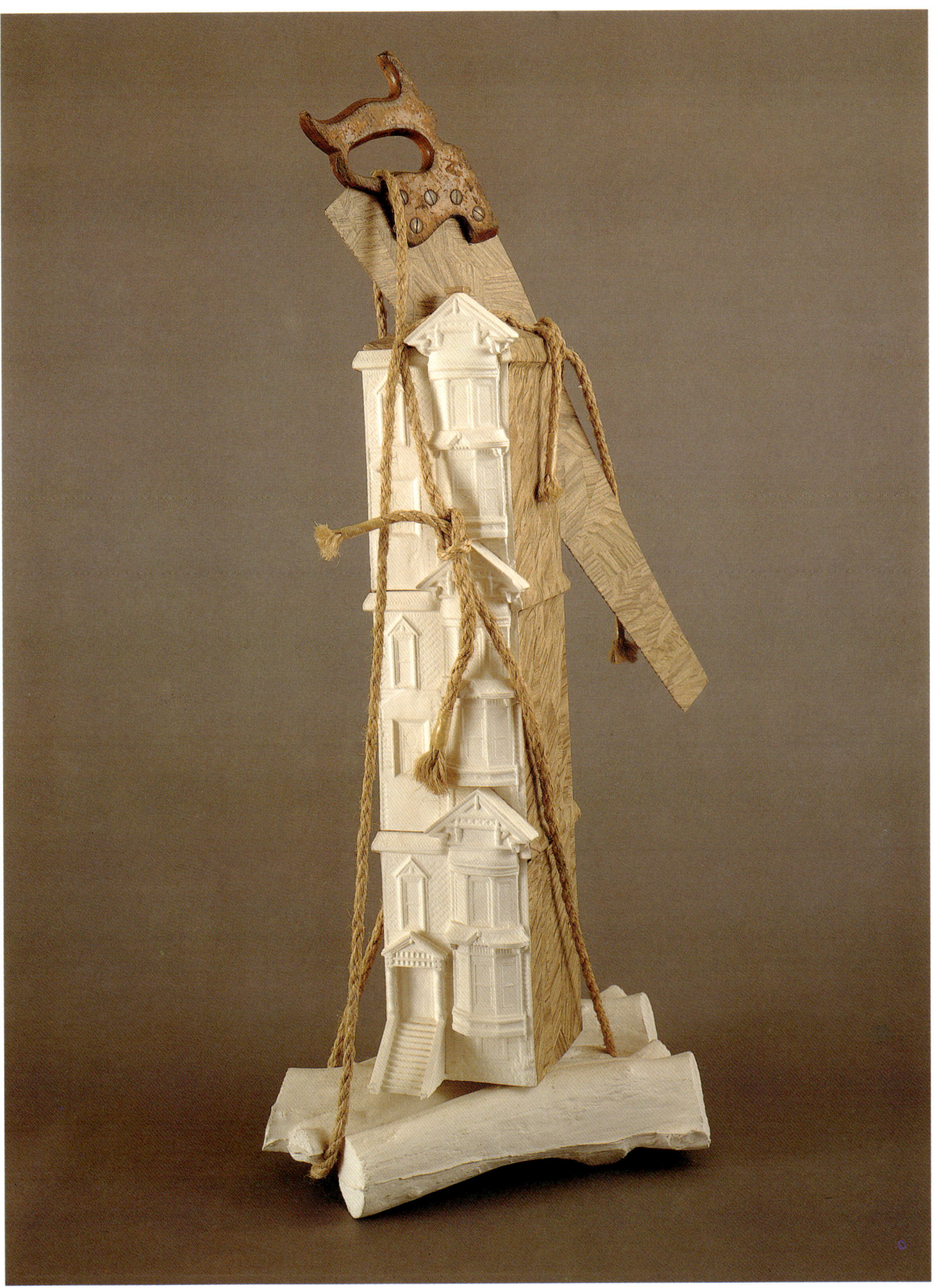

3.24 *Knotty Pine*, 1977. Mixed media, 40½ x 20

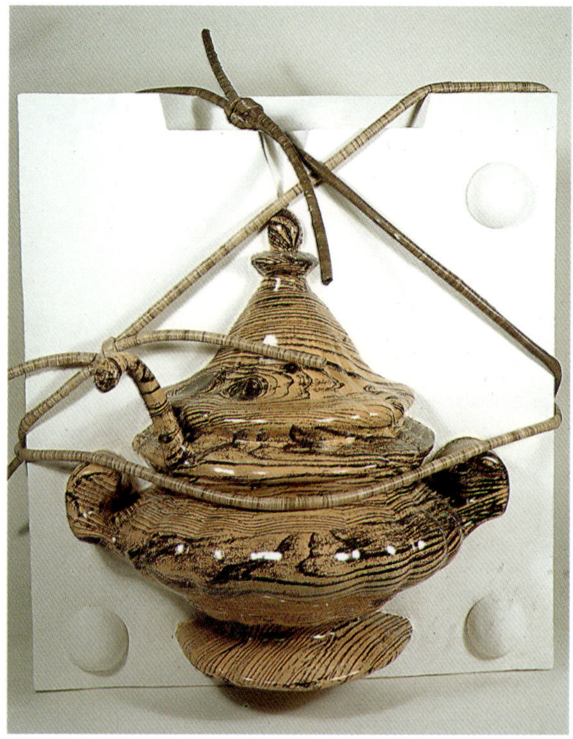

3.25 *Naughty Pine,* 1977. Mixed media, 15 x 15. Collection Henry Art Gallery, University of Washington

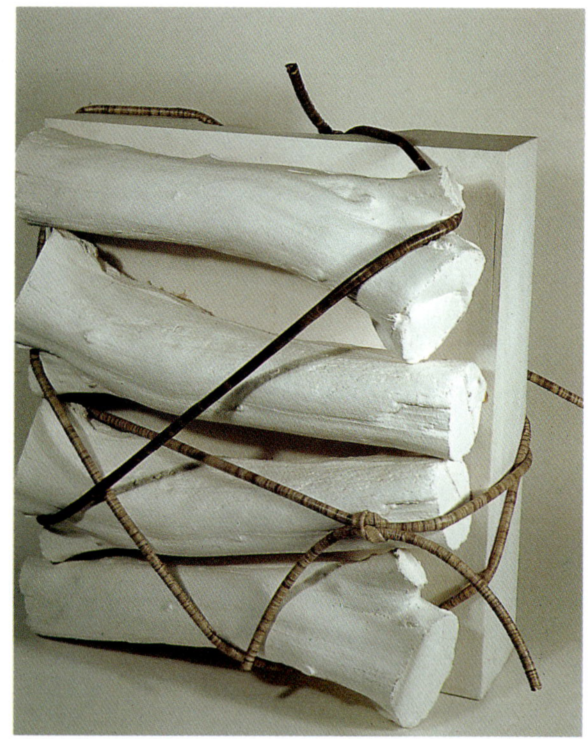

3.26 *Naughty Pine,* 1977. Rear view

fields, but in ceramics, where romantic views about the sanctity of hand labor are deeply entrenched, Kottler's reputation as a slick provocateur was blown out of proportion. By the end of the decade he had, in fact, begun to produce a number of truly evocative sculptural statements, particularly in the self-portrait series begun in 1977.[31] Some of the assemblages related to the *Old Bag Next Door Is Nuts*, in addition, approach the psychic depth charge of classic Surrealist poetry. In *Knotty Pine*, for example, a stack of Victorian houses cast from a commercial mold rests on a base of cast wooden logs; cutting through the top of the buildings is a real saw, wrapped and bound to the houses and logs with manufactured rope (fig. 3.24). The saw blade and three sides of the buildings are covered with wood-grain contact paper, but the casts of actual wooden logs are colorless ghosts of the original forms. Scale oscillates irrationally from logs to houses to saw, paralleling the unpredictable surface treatments. The rope and saw provide another layer of paradox: "You have something—in a domestic struc-

ture—being cut or sliced apart," Kottler pointed out, "yet at the same time it is being held together and bound in a kind of sadomasochistic way by a deep tie."[32]

Equally provocative is a related composition, *Naughty Pine*, which presents an elaborate Victorian soup tureen with a wood-grain decal surface trapped on one side by a slip-cast mold. Casts of four wooden logs are stacked against the back of the mold and the logs and tureen are bound together with plastic tubing covered with wood-grain contact paper (figs. 3.25, 3.26). As with the cup series, Kottler "wanted to emphasize that even functional forms represent a forum where ideas can come into play. Most of the people who make nonfunctional containers are just making decorative objects, a direction that doesn't really interest me—I'm interested in strangeness and revelation."[33]

According to Clark, Kottler's employment of molds and decals in the 1970s linked his production to "a highly crafted, trompe l'oeil style of still life/object making that I have entitled the 'Super-Object.' Most of this activity took place in San Francisco and the adjoining Bay Area. Seattle was the center of a similar movement in painted ceramic sculpture." Development of the Super-Object, he continues, "can be traced through the sixties in the work of Kottler, Melchert, Price, Nagle and others. The Super-Object in the seventies was identified with an elaborate, almost obsessive concern with craft, the use of trompe l'oeil as the primary stylistic device, and with simplistic references to assemblage and collage and to the art object in Dada and Surrealism. Form was approached as a kind of three-dimensional illustration, mostly through found objects that had been cast in clay."[34] Clark identifies Richard Shaw and Marilyn Levine as paradigmatic Super-Object makers of the 1970s, noting that their work was "slavishly imitated in almost every ceramics department by mid-decade." At the end of the 1970s, in Clark's assessment, the Super-Object movement had degenerated into "'Hollywood Magritte,' a debased and decorative use of Surrealism that completely lacked the passion, the wit and the visual literacy necessary to give the objects validity."[35]

Only one category of Kottler's ceramics in the 1960s, however, actually contributes to the Super-Object genre outlined by Clark—the ceramic-decal plate series begun in 1966 and continued until the early 1980s. In the 1970s his cast sculpture and cups could be classified as Super-Objects, yet Kottler's sculpture did not share the "elaborate, almost excessive concern with craft" associated with Levine and Shaw. Kottler approached trompe l'oeil as a vehicle for allusion rather than illusion—casts and decals were used not so much to effect a simulacrum as to set up a visual conundrum or as a form of art-historical commentary.[36] The layering of meanings and the coded suggestions in these assemblages also distances them from paradigmatic Super-Objects, even though Kottler's use of casts and decals paralleled the technical strategies developed by other artists associated with the movement.

Kottler is best known for his ceramic-decal plate series, which spanned the entire Super-Object era. These plates may have figured in the early history of the Super-Object, as Clark suggests, but they were not sculptural objects; they were antithetical, in addition, to the virtuoso demonstrations of hand-craftsmanship characteristic of the genre. In retrospect, the plates fit more easily into the discourse of language theory than into discussion of the early evolution of the Super-Object, even though Kottler was not familiar with this discourse and drew his inspiration from many of the same sources as did prominent Super-Object makers. To assess the relevance of a linguistic perspective, however, it is useful to review the evolution of the plate series.

Commercial decals began to play a significant role in Kottler's work in 1967, when they appeared in compositions such as *Hole Grabber*. In the plates, Kottler departed from the wallpaper-pattern effect used for other decal vessels in favor of a more adventuresome strategy: by strategically altering the manufactured images, he transformed banal reproductions into vehicles for social commentary and satire.

In a 1980 statement, Kottler reviewed his plate series:

> At first I did work using these factory ceramic decals on my sculpture, pots and plates. However, as I continued to use these decals for surface exploration, I began to concentrate my efforts in the use of the decals on plates. Most of the decals were purchased from wholesale houses or the manufacturer, but when I wanted an image that was not available commercially, I would make my own decal.
>
> At first, I made my own plates on the potter's wheel and used the commercial decals on these plates. However, I produced only a few of these plates because I was not satisfied with the combination of handmade plate and commercial ceramic decal. I wanted the precise, streamlined character that industry achieves with porcelain plates . . . which I was unable to achieve with any consistency in my thrown work. Furthermore, I also became interested in the idea of producing these plates in limited editions, and so it seemed foolish to throw the plates individually on the potter's wheel. I was

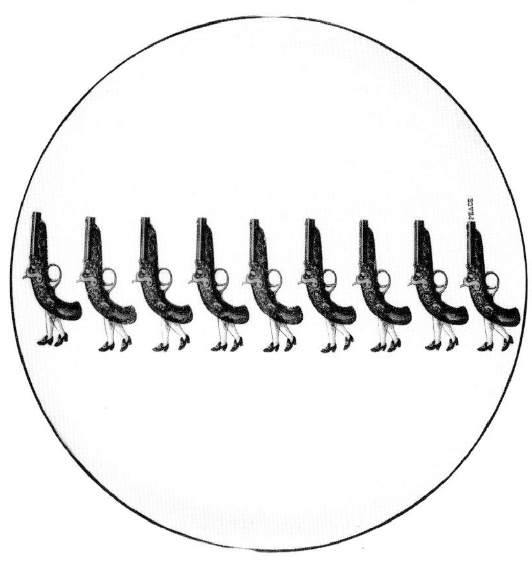

3.27 *Peace March,* 1967. Porcelain, decals, 10½ h

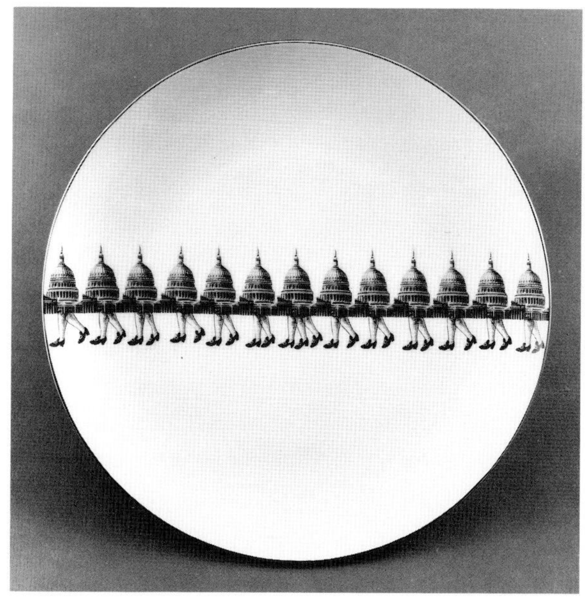

3.28 *Capitol Walk,* 1967. Porcelain, decals, 10½ h

primarily interested in the surface image with no concern for making a statement about the plate as a form or in developing a new plate shape. The logical answer was to use the porcelain glazed blanks from industry. These plates were inexpensive, simple in design, consistent in their machine perfection and of excellent quality porcelain. . . . The coupling of these two products [plates and decals] . . . showed the potential that industry had never developed—the use of images as a statement rather than simply as decoration. . . . Many contemporary craftsmen are overly concerned with the handmade qualities of craft. Machine perfection is just another aspect of ceramics and holds as much validity as the expressive character of thrown or hand-built work. Each of these opposite approaches to the use of clay reveals its own particularity. There is no one way to work with porcelain or any other clay body.

The statements he decided to make with the manufactured plates and ceramic decals, he continues, reflected the counterculture movement and its impact on American politics, religion, and society.

The 1960s was an unbelievable period in American life. No one can imagine the full extent of the social forces of change at work during this time without living it. On my trips to San Francisco, I experienced the full bloom of hippie life. The Vietnam war, with all its social unrest, had powerful ramifications throughout the U.S.A. in daily life and also in academia. Furthermore, there was a dramatic surge in the Bay Area into funk art, which manifested itself in ceramics through the use of bright colors, erotic images, narrative and the use of mixed media. It was a marvelous shocker. . . . It was a direction that worked perfectly for me, and gave me the freedom to let my craziness run amok. I became my own man and expressed my sarcastic wit through images and titles in my art work.[37]

Working on the plates, he adds, he changed the original commercial decals in three primary ways: cutting away sections of the decal; interchanging parts of the same image; and combining different images into collages. These techniques allowed him to combine Surrealist methods of image-disruption with social satire.

Among the first collage-decal plates were *Peace March* and *Capitol Walk*, both executed in 1967. For *Peace March*, he affixed the stockinged legs of a man in colonial attire to images of antique dueling pistols repeated in a band across the center of the plate. *Capitol Walk* has the same format except the legs are placed under decals representing the U.S. capitol building (figs. 3.27, 3.28). The serial format, visual punning and political content of these plates link them securely to their sixties historical context, but the images also humorously illustrate more recent theorizing about the dynamism of the signifying process. In these compositions the signifiers "pistol" and "capitol building" are represented as literally in motion, marching away from their conventional denotive references. In their new configurations, the visual signs for "gun" and "building" now read as the torso and head of a half-organic biped. The punning titles facilitate another multivalent shift: these verbal-visual composites can be viewed as comments upon broad public support for political change, the mindless conformity of peace demonstrators, or the absurdity of national governmental policies and processes.

In the six-plate "American Supperware" series (1969), one of his most widely exhibited political statements, Kottler deconstructed the American flag: on the *Hollow Dream* plate, the stars and stripes have been subtracted, leaving the flag's empty outline; stripes fly away in the wind in *Made in U.S.A.*, hang like a wet dishrag in *Drip Dry*, and unravel across the plate in *Charming Lyre*. Component parts of a flag image are inventoried in *Flag Kit*, and in *Exhausted Glory*, one stripe traces the path of a tiny race car stalled near the edge of the plate (figs. 3.29-3.34). Each plate in the set was later packaged in a white leather envelope with its title embroidered across the center and a small flag stitched to one edge.[38] Commenting on *Hollow Dream*, one reviewer concluded, "This beautifully packaged 'hollow American dream' (like political rhetoric) is a 'dream kit,' in which, upon opening, one finds an empty plate and an empty flag. Politics and plates, like any other consumer item, are packaged for consumption."[39]

In 1970 and early 1971 Kottler spent a sabbatical in

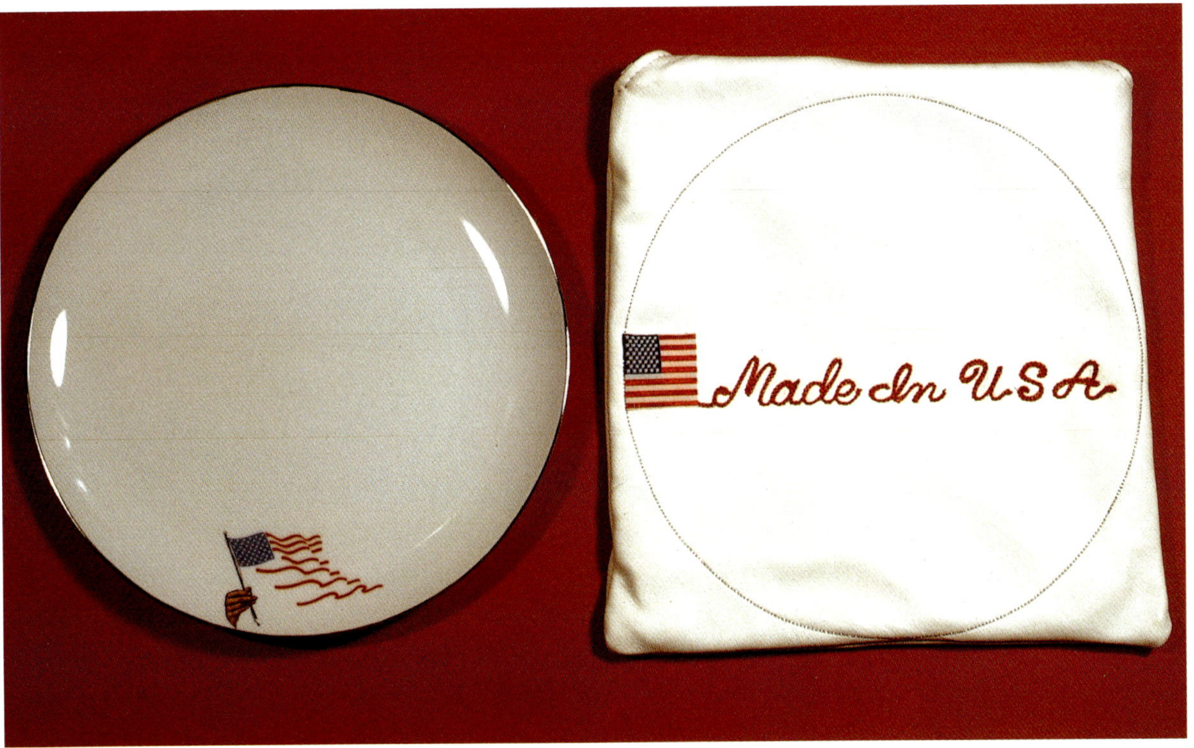

3.29 *Made in U.S.A.*, 1969. American Supperware series. Porcelain, 10½ h

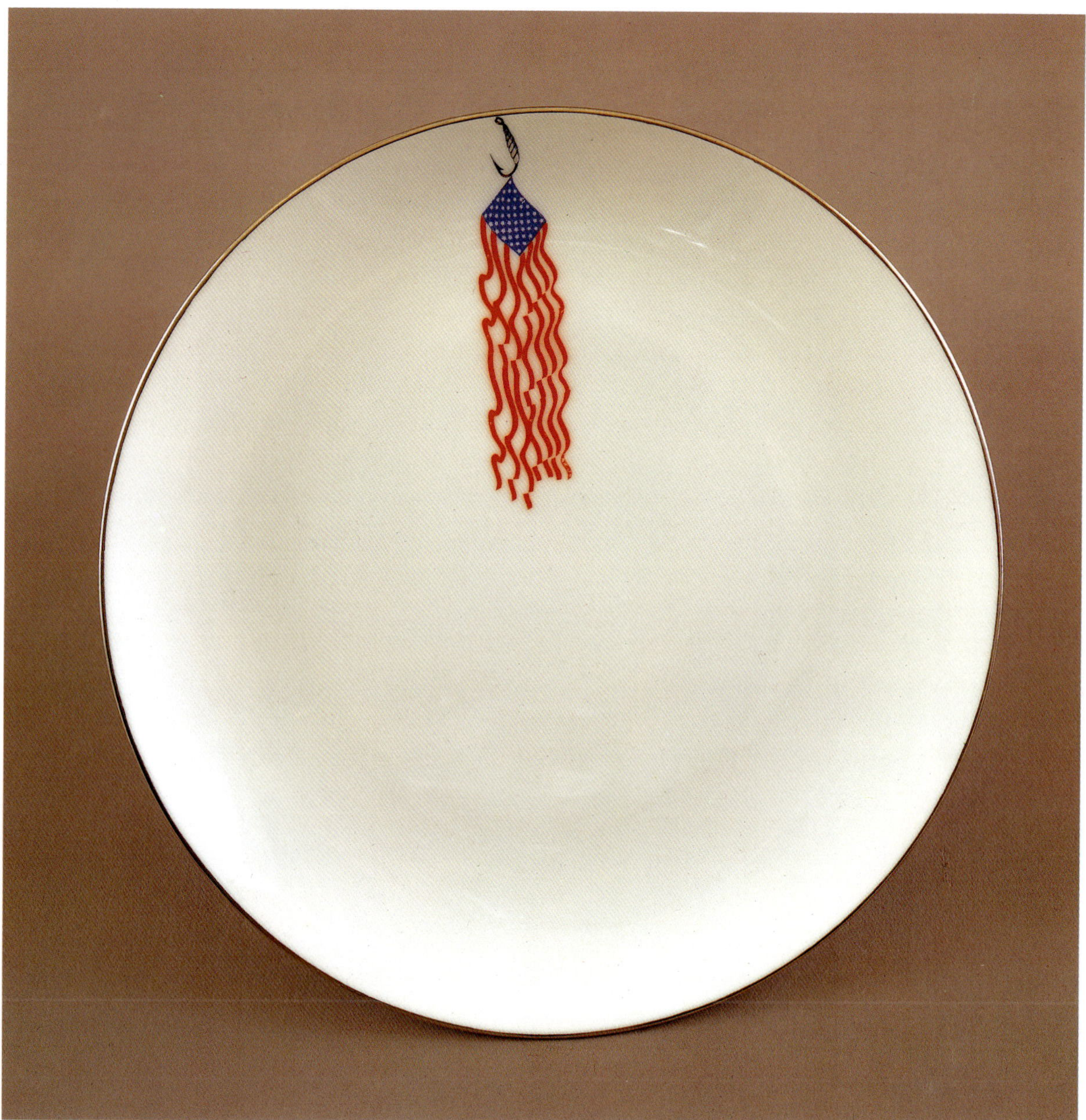

3.30 *Drip Dry,* 1969. American Supperware series. Porcelain, 10½ h

Western Europe, where he studied historical precedents for packaging plates. "Going around to museums, I started to look more and more at English tea sets in wonderful boxes made in the seventeenth and eighteenth centuries," he recalled. "I liked the idea of creating a surprise, the idea of opening a container to find another container and then the ceramics. It was another way of layering a viewer's experience."[40] According to Clark's text, the luxurious custom-made containers Kottler made for several of his decal plates represent a "supreme irony" because he "lavished more attention on the wrappings than the 'art objects' they contained."[41] In Kottler's view, however, "Clark really missed the boat," by focusing on the packaging instead of the plates. "Perhaps Clark focused on the wrappings in discussing this series because the wrappings seemed to have more craft value than the manufactured plates," he speculated. "Actually, the packaging was all farmed out: a friend who had a

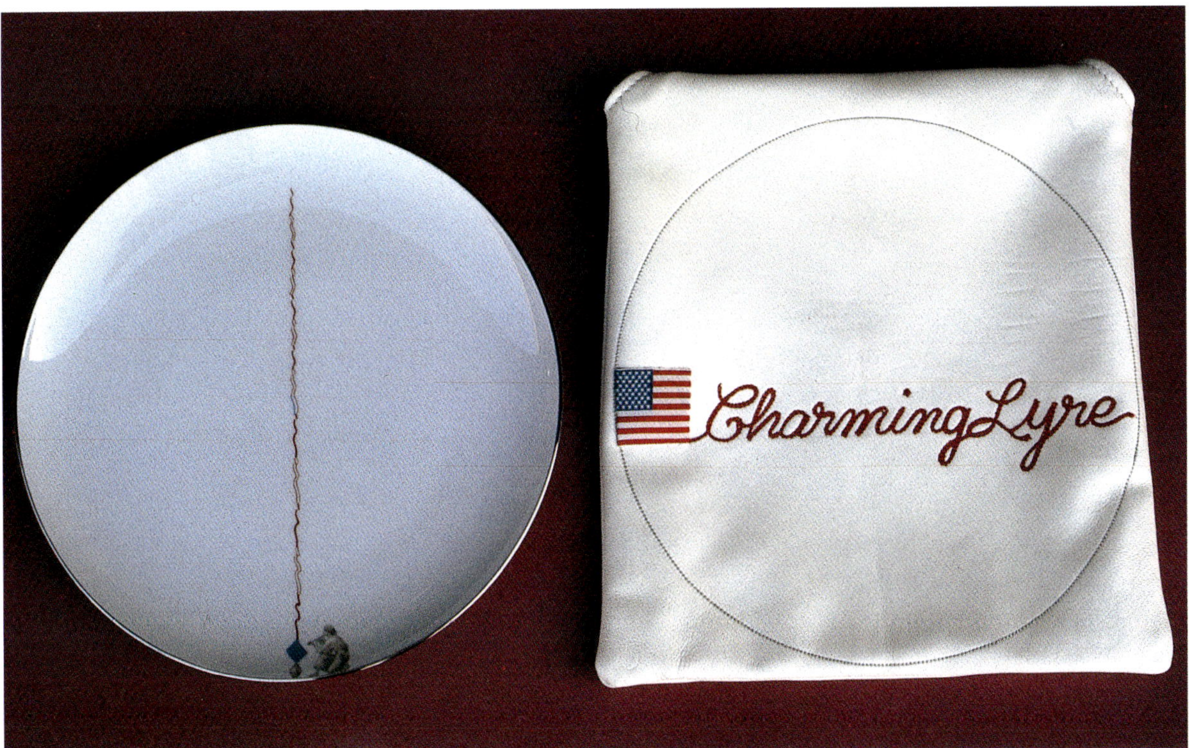

3.31 *Charming Lyre,* 1969. American Supperware series. Porcelain, 10½ h

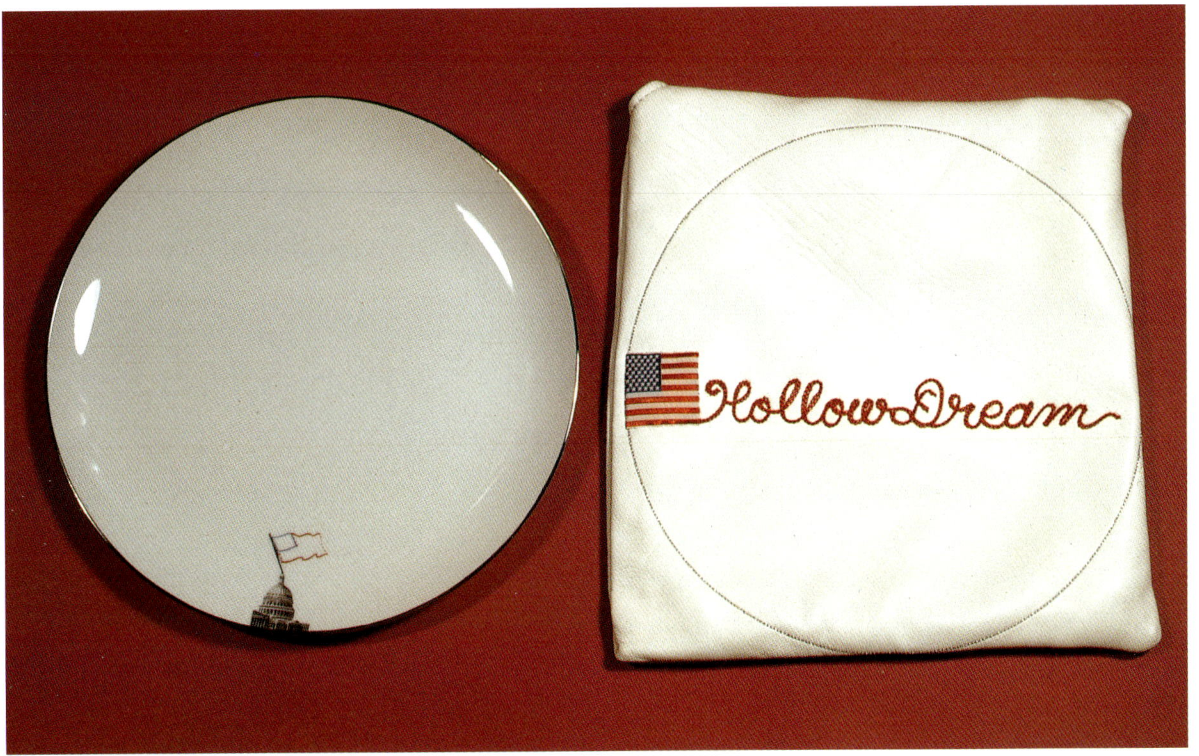

3.32 *Hollow Dream,* 1969. American Supperware series. Porcelain, 10½ h

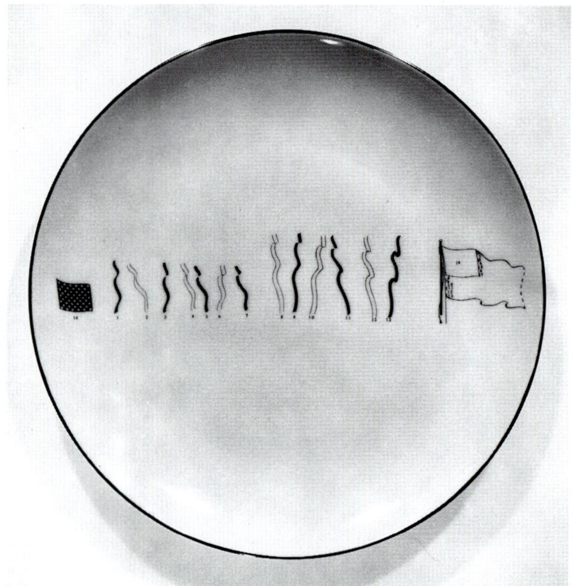

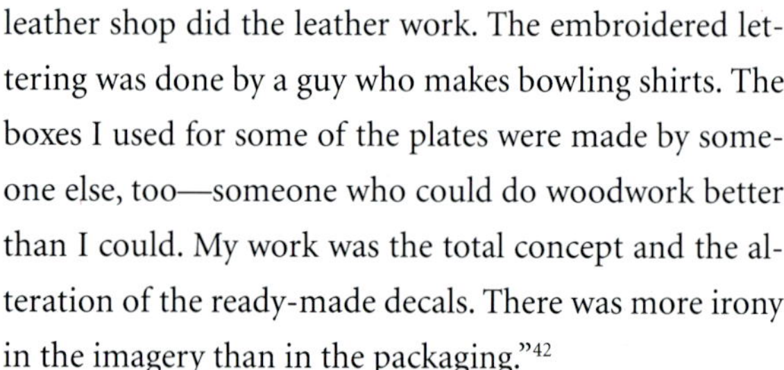

3.33. *Flag Kit,* 1969. American Supperware series. Porcelain, 10½ h

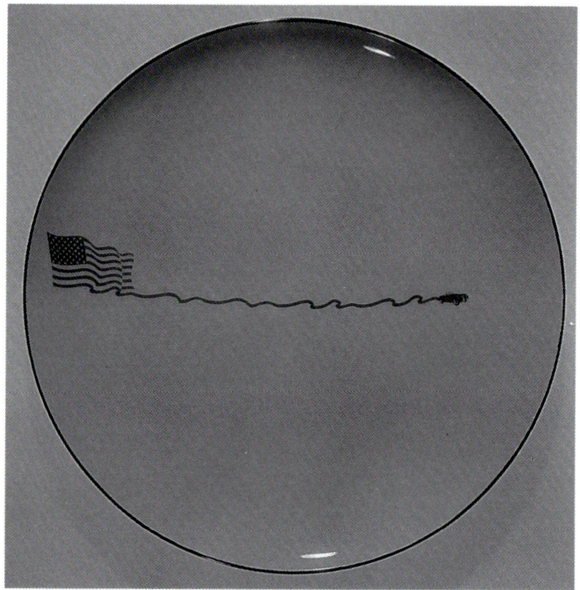

3.34. *Exhausted Glory,* 1969. American Supperware series. Porcelain, 10½ h

leather shop did the leather work. The embroidered lettering was done by a guy who makes bowling shirts. The boxes I used for some of the plates were made by someone else, too—someone who could do woodwork better than I could. My work was the total concept and the alteration of the ready-made decals. There was more irony in the imagery than in the packaging."[42]

Kottler eventually produced about 250 different decal plates. Reactions to the work, he found, were radically uneven. "The *Peace March* plate was popular and so was the 'American Supperware' series," he recalled. "They appealed to the hippie, antiwar crowd. But people weren't used to finding political commentary in ceramics—Michael Frimkess was the only other ceramist I knew at the time who was really involved in social commentary. In my case, I think people reacted to the humor, but they didn't really want to confront what the image was about. The images weren't deep, but they did raise some valid questions. How should we look at the American flag today? What kind of image is it for us?" Religious images, Kottler continued, "were an even bigger problem. I did a series using a commercial decal of Pope Paul. On one plate I made his skullcap into a yarmulke by adding a Jewish star. People were very offended. In another plate I

put a paisley decal over the pope's face (figs. 3.35-3.37). When the series was shown in Scotland it raised an incredible howl because people took it as a comment on Ian Paisley. Yet people were perfectly comfortable with the same decal on garish souvenir plates."[43]

Well-known works of art, Kottler found, had also been translated into commercial decals. "In the hobby

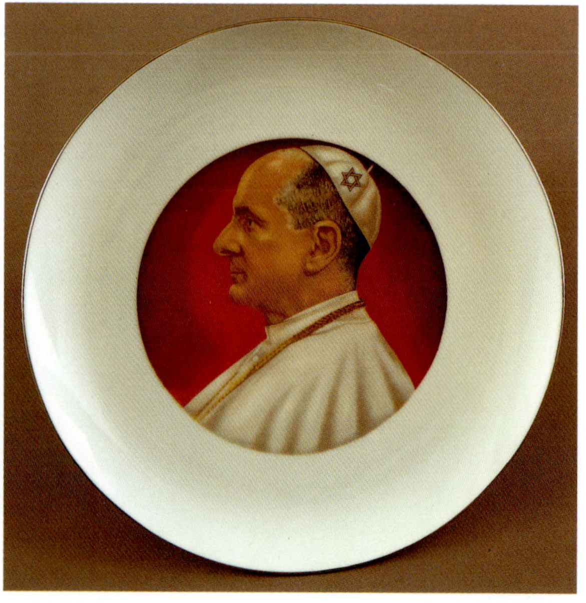

3.35 *Bar Mitzvah Boy,* 1969. Popeware series. Porcelain, 10½ h

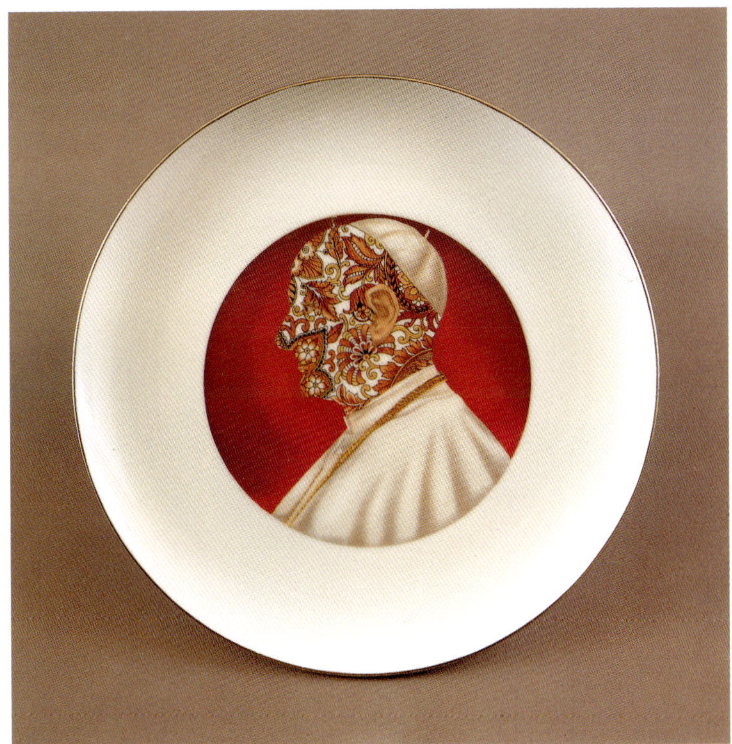

3.36 *Paisley Pope,* 1969. Popeware series. Porcelain, 10½ h

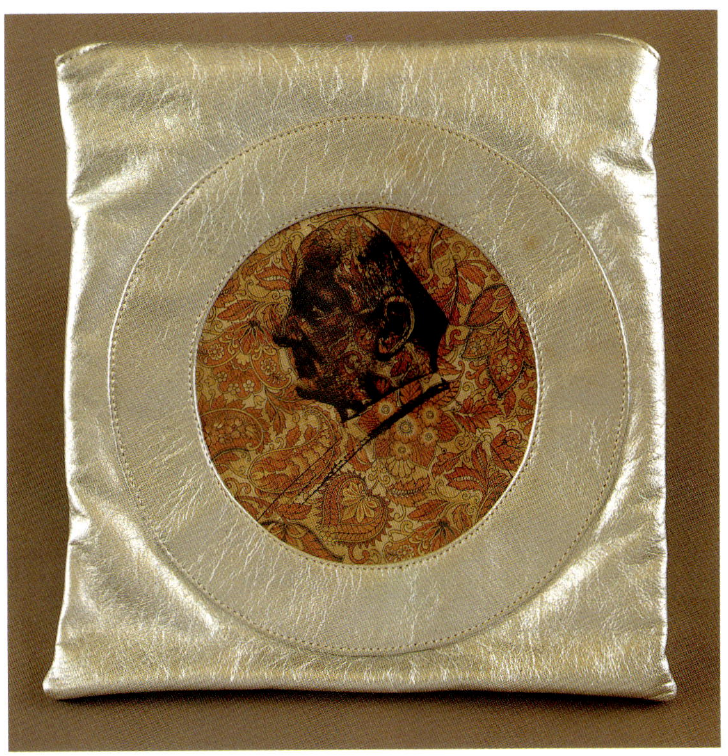

3.37 Leather envelope for *Paisley Pope*

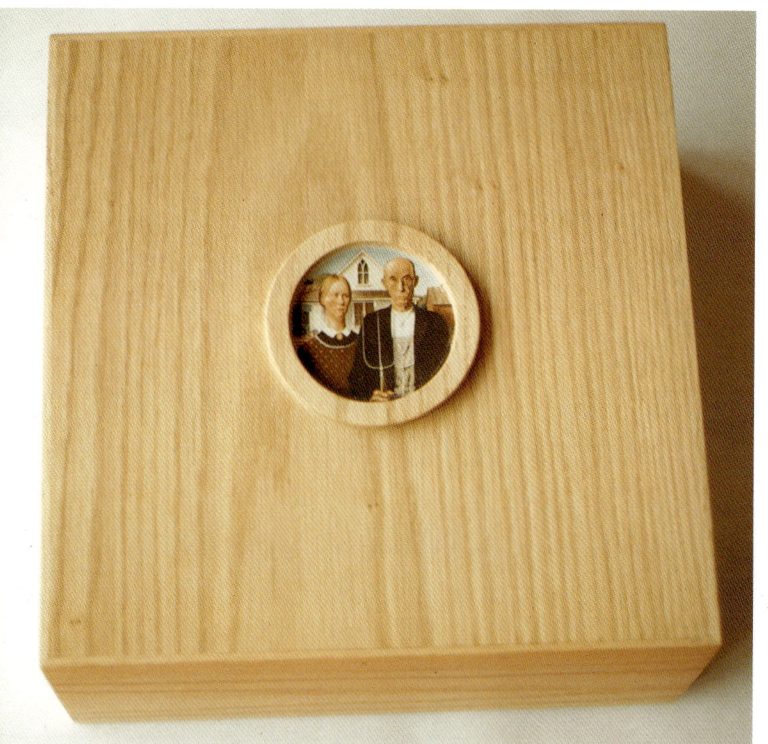

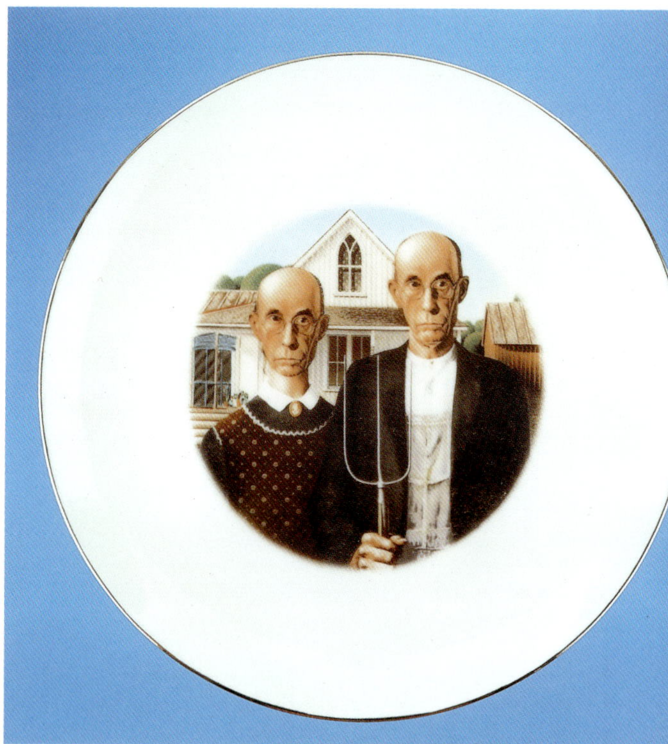

3.38 Box for American Gothicware, 1972. Walnut, 12 x 12

3.39 *Look Alikes,* 1972. American Gothicware series. Porcelain, 10½ h

shops, famous paintings are just another category of decals, like guns or flowers or U.S. presidents. I liked the way Andy Warhol re-presented media images, and I decided to try something similar with the decals of paintings. I wanted to see if small changes could forever alter the way we see these pictures."[44] Among the most frequently exhibited plates from this series were Kottler's variations on a decal of Grant Wood's painting, *American Gothic.* In 1972 he completed a four-plate set titled "American Gothicware": each plate was packaged in its own leather envelope and the set was enclosed in a woodgrain box (fig. 3.38). *Look Alikes,* a plate from this series in which the farmer's wife's head has been replaced with that of the farmer, was included in the 1978 "Art about Art" exhibition at the Whitney Museum of American Art (fig. 3.39). In a book based on the exhibition, the curators observe that "Grant Wood's *American Gothic . . .* has been extremely popular as a color reproduction since it was first painted. In this witty spoof of the strait-laced American farm family, the vertical lines of the house

seem to be echoed in the elongated, glum faces of the couple, and the Gothic window in the tines of the pitchfork. Wood's sister and a family friend, a dentist, posed for the painting. . . . When the picture was exhibited at the Art Institute [of Chicago], it won a prize, was bought for the collection, and created a storm of protest because of its satirical intent. Howard Kottler, an artist who has done a number of art parodies using ceramic decals on plates, has duplicated the dour dentist's face and nimbly satirized the satire."[45]

Other plates from the "American Gothicware" set include *The Silent White Majority,* an homage to former Vice-President Spiro Agnew's Vietnam War-era political rhetoric. In this composition, the farmer and his wife have white faces and no mouths; the same figures appear in whiteface *with* mouths in *American Minstrels.* For *Personal Possession,* Kottler created a form of imagery very much like the television "chromakey" effect by cutting away the bodies of the couple and replacing them with a decal of a rural landscape (figs. 3.40, 3.41). He also cre-

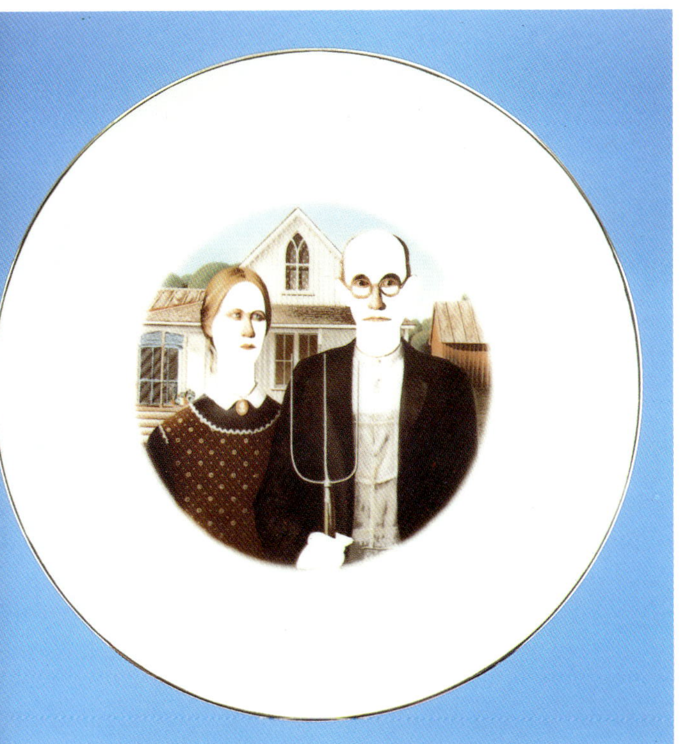

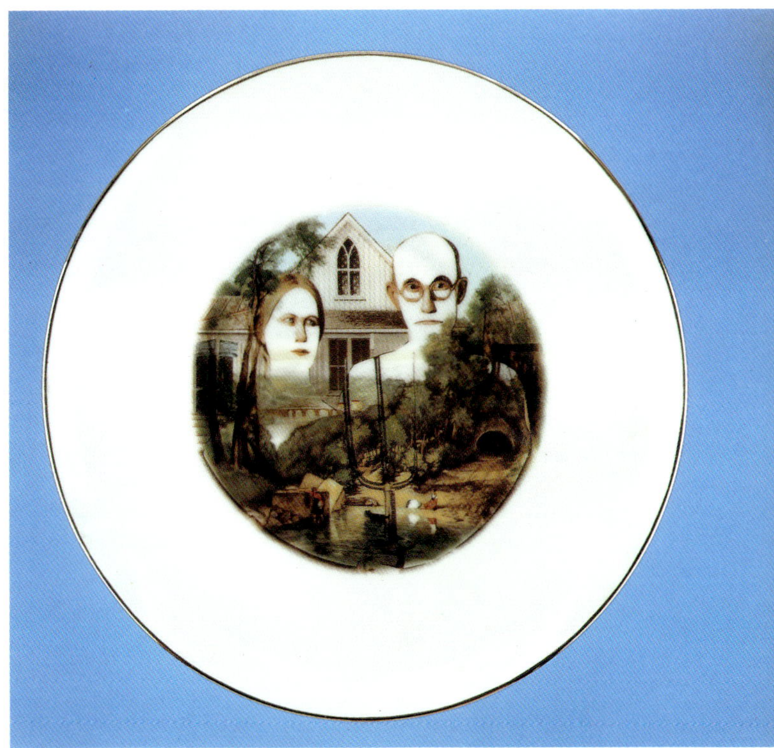

3.40 *American Minstrels,* 1972. American Gothicware series. Porcelain, 10½ h

3.41 *Personal Possession,* 1972. American Gothicware series. Porcelain, 10½ h

ated variations on the image not included in the "American Gothicware" set: *AC/DC* reverses the male and female heads, for example, and both figures have female heads in *Restless Sex.* Decals of Thomas Gainsborough's *Blue Boy* and *Pinkie,* and of Leonardo da Vinci's *Last Supper* and *Mona Lisa* were used in other extended series of plates dating from the late 1960s to the early 1970s. Kottler continued to produce decal plates throughout the seventies: *X-Rated,* which couples *Blue Boy* and *Pinkie* decals, for example, was executed in 1979.[46]

To create these compositions, Kottler imported techniques of photocollage into the field of contemporary ceramics. As the Berlin Dadaists demonstrated in the early 1920s, photocollage can serve as an effective mode of social commentary because the fragmented structure of collages conflates truth and absurdity, presenting both as equally real. Although the decals Kottler used were not actually photographs, they were derived from photographs and were understood to be veristic imitations of familiar icons, much as photographs are

understood to be two-dimensional records of the real world. By disrupting the imitative function of the decals, Kottler uncovered a new range of visual expression, just as the Dadaists did with their photocollages. In the "American Gothicware" series, for example, Kottler illustrated the pervasive uniformity of white middle America by slightly shifting the structure of a familiar visual sign. The resulting absurdities paradoxically reveal the truth, the most exalted goal of high art.

With the decal plates Kottler argued, in effect, that manufactured pottery and hobby-shop decals could be inserted into the category of high-art palace ware. Inspired by Warhol and Duchamp's assisted ready-mades, he attempted to shift the meaning of manufactured images with, in many cases, relatively minor alterations of the forms—alterations typically less severe than those of the decal manufacturers, who reduced the original scale and took great liberties with color. In re-presenting already-transmogrified decal reproductions on mass-produced porcelain blanks, Kottler tried to further

Duchamp's precedent by creating double-assisted ready-mades. This strategy, however, met with only limited success.

In his Ph.D. dissertation, Kottler had not only outlined the history and characteristics of palace ware but had also compared it to "folk pottery," a second major category of ceramics. Restating a conclusion first presented in his 1956 M.A. thesis, Kottler argued that folk potters—ceramists who make traditional functional pottery—are obsolete in modern industrial societies. Manufactured utilitarian ware "may seem cold and impersonal," he wrote, "but it is technically excellent and attests to the successful realization of the potentialities of clay when used in objects produced by the machine. Although mass-produced ceramic ware shares with folk pottery a concern with the production of quantities of utilitarian objects at low cost and an interest in solving problems in the most economical way, the coming of the machine age and the growth of the ceramics industry have literally precluded the folk potter [from] performing an active or significant role in society."[47] According to his own historical scheme, therefore, the decal plates represented an attempt to merge today's folk pottery, the manufactured dish, with palace ware, the artist-potter's personal statement. His ambition was to mass-produce the plates at low cost, utilizing the technology of folk ware to expand the output of an artist-potter.

"I began with a kind of ironic perspective that I thought art people would appreciate," Kottler explained. "Then I realized that the images were quite accessible and there was a potential for reaching a larger audience. I talked to some ceramics manufacturers but didn't get anywhere. They were interested in work with a straight decal, because they knew people would buy it. They weren't interested at all in a small alteration of the same decal that suggested an idea. They were right. There wasn't a broad audience willing to buy this work, even though it was inexpensive to begin with. The people who really related to the plates and enjoyed them were primarily art people. The galleries wanted documented, numbered editions for their collectors. Later I began to make signed limited editions, but that wasn't my first idea at

all. Another problem with the plates was that in ceramics you are supposed to attack the form and surface as a total entity. But in this case I wasn't interested in form—I used the same commercial blanks over and over again, like blank canvases. So the plates didn't meet certain standards of the ceramics world either."[48]

In retrospect, Kottler's effort to merge palace and folk pottery seems to have produced a neither/nor hybrid that remained suspended in critical limbo. The plates were exhibited all over the United States, but the Duchampian questions they raised about appropriation, art and technology, originality, and academic hierarchies received little serious attention.[49] Kottler's humor and reputation as a slick prankster might have distracted critics; his uneven production may have been a factor as well. Nevertheless, these prescient investigations of art-historical appropriation by a well-known ceramist, his explorations of photocollage techniques in altering the decals, and his rhetorical treatment of iconic images as cultural signs should have provoked, it would seem, a higher level of critical response.

But Kottler's interactions with his audiences after the mid-1960s were ambivalent and complex. He clearly enjoyed the role of provocateur, especially in confrontations with the antitechnology, truth-to-materials traditionalists who still play a significant role in contemporary ceramics. (Queried about the wages of his iconoclasm, Kottler replied, "I've always liked the line from a song Lena Horne sings—'If you can't take the punishment, honey, then don't commit the crime.'")[50]

But he was not simply a critic: his aspirations for the evolution of ceramics were ambitious, and he continued to believe that an artist-potter could and should participate in the vanguard art movements of his or her time. In one sense, he was a paradigmatic university ceramist, pursuing a singular direction without being inhibited by the marketplace: he was not unconcerned about the relatively low level of support he received from ceramics collectors, but he was able to go on without them. Even though his production was erratic in the 1970s, therefore, his work grew in maturity and sophistication to a degree that was not widely recognized.

FOUR

The Last Decade

In 1965 Kottler was offered a regular teaching position at the University of Washington, and by 1972 he was a full professor. For many years, however, he continued to regard his job as a temporary appointment. "I never really wanted to stay in Seattle," he said, "but in 1975, after being in Seattle for eleven years, I realized I was actually living here, and so I finally bought a house."[1] He enjoyed teaching and began identifying himself as "an educator as well as an artist. I found that I was a successful teacher because I tried to stimulate people without telling them what to do. I looked for a middle ground between being hard-nosed and stand-offish—standing off to let people do what they wanted to do, but at the same time being critically alert and providing a strong analysis of the direction being taken. I wanted students to develop a balance between intuition—'I'm doing it because I like it'—and critical reasoning. If that balance is present, the result is likely to be a strong individual personality. I would rather see bad stuff that's personal than good work that is really the result of teacher badgering."[2]

For both graduate students and undergraduates, Kottler stressed open-ended problem-solving over directed technical training. "I didn't really distinguish between grads and undergrads," he admitted. "I was interested in exploring and pulling out what was innate in each individual and in helping people recognize their own limitations—we all have limitations. Sometimes an undergrad would be brighter and more talented than the grads; then, two quarters later, the situation would reverse itself. My teaching was about zeroing in on particular people."[3]

Garth Clark ranks Kottler as "one of the most influential teachers in the ceramic sculpture movement." His students include a generation of innovative, successful artists, among them David Furman, Jacqueline Rice, Anne Currier, Irvin Tepper, Mark Burns, Clair Colquitt, Joyce Moty, Ann Perrigo, and Michael Lucero. Furman described his studies at the University of Washington in the 1970s:

> [Robert] Sperry broadened my horizons . . . he gave me insight into myself so I didn't take myself so seriously. Howard, on the other hand, took me . . . very seriously. He was always joking and song-and-dancing it, and coming out of his closet and being crazy, and it was tough to discern when he was talking to you and when he was horsing around. But, he was *always* talking to you, and it was up to you, the student, to listen, to read beneath the lines. He was always constructive and positive, and, if you weren't listening, you'd miss it,

because of the way he presented himself. Metaphorically, he kicked me in the ass and said, 'It's time you start thinking about why you're doing what you're doing, and stop relying on things that you've been floating on without questioning.' He provided me that instrument to re-examine and re-evaluate what I was doing. He was a good teacher.[4]

First encounters with Kottler, however, were often trying, as Irvin Tepper relates:

I was a prospective grad when I first met Kottler. I liked his work and heard that he had a strange personality, but I didn't know how the strangeness manifested itself. I happened to catch him in one of his moods when he would play cruel jokes on people. We began to talk and he said he couldn't understand me—he accused me of speaking Japanese instead of English. It wasn't a pleasant meeting. Later on, when I was a teaching assistant, I'd watch nervous new students come in and knock on the door to his office. He would answer the knock and before the student had a chance to

say a word, he'd say, "Did you have an appointment to see the doctor?" But this kind of strangeness was ultimately a positive thing. He disarmed you.[5]

Kottler worked with a team of educators at the University of Washington who were also well-known ceramists, including Fred Bauer, Robert Sperry, and Patti Warashina. Sperry, Kottler, and Warashina became long-time colleagues, and the three artists forged a fruitful and reasonably harmonious rapport. "The good thing was that Bob and Patty teach differently than I do," he said. "I let students make more mistakes—the work in Patty's beginning class seemed to me almost too well done. I talked more about form and Bob has great expertise with surfaces. We didn't get in each other's way. But when we got together for major grad crits, our critical input often came together. I always thought that was surprising.[6]

In the 1970s Kottler also lectured and taught at ceramics workshops across the country.[7] After these professional gatherings, many participants remembered his eccentric behavior better than his work. In a report on a 1978 ceramics symposium in Vail, Colorado (fig. 4.1), one of the participants summarized his impressions:

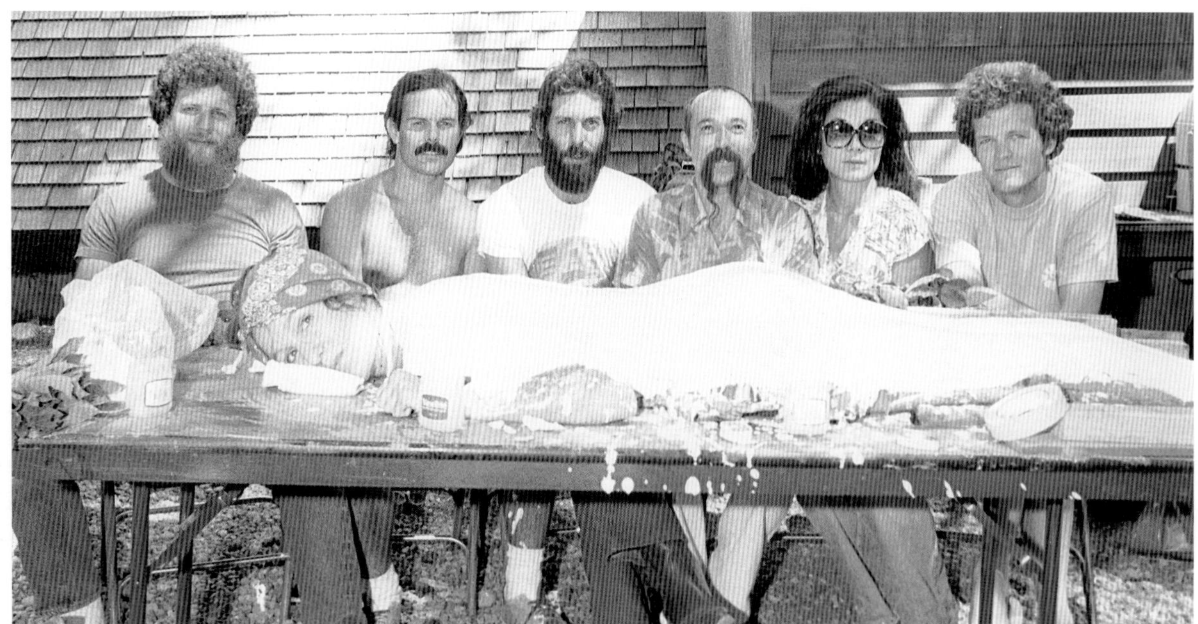

4.1 Howard Kottler (third from right) at the Summervail Art Workshop, Colorado Mountain College, Vail, Colorado

I've left Howard Kottler for last . . . but in this case it's a place of honor. Howard Kottler is one of the craziest sons-of-bitches I've ever had the pleasure to meet. Like many poets I know, Howard is liable to say anything for the sake of seeing what reaction it might bring. And he doesn't care much where or when he says it—or sings it. He wore a peach-colored shirt with a gaudily screened "Kottler" across the back. Whenever the group was together, in workshop or restaurant or tavern, it was not unusual for Howard to launch into a schmaltzy rendition of "Together, wherever we go-o," in a voice that was definitely "Kottler." He was a joy, and a source of lunacy that never allowed the people or the symposium in general to fall into self-importance.[8]

Richard Notkin, one of Kottler's colleagues at the Colorado workshop, recalled that "you couldn't be faint-hearted and go into a restaurant with Kottler. You never knew *what* he would say to people, or what he would do. I remember once when he was embarrassing all of us by giving a nice but bimboish waitress a hard time. Finally I signaled her to come over behind his back where he couldn't see. I whispered to her 'Don't mind Dad—they've just let him out of the home for a while.' After that, we survived the evening."[9]

Kottler took a sabbatical from teaching during the 1980 school year and rented a studio in Manhattan, where he spent several months visiting galleries and familiarizing himself with new work by European and younger American artists. "While I was in New York I also decided to go back to making small pots because I knew they would be easier to ship," he said. "I usually started out with a linear drawing. Then I wanted to see the relationships between the forms, so I made small maquettes to play around with the proportions. I made maybe fifty or seventy-five models in New York, but it was very damp that summer and things dried slowly. I completed only about ten pots, but I worked out a lot of ideas."[10]

These new vessels reinterpreted the stylish geom-

etry of the Deco-inspired pots of 1969-70. As he elaborated the series in the early 1980s, Kottler also incorporated formal references to Memphis, the Milan-based design group. Memphis colors, according to one reviewer, were "unlike anything seen in furniture before—hard, shrill, childlike and funny. The same was true of its fanciful new shapes, with their odd angles, saw-toothed edges and flat discs, combined in startling ways. . . . Using this new vocabulary, the designers announced that . . . furniture no longer had to be strictly functional; it could provoke, challenge, entertain and, above all, communicate."[11] Friends in Milan, Kottler recalled, "sent me the first book published on Memphis. I knew Peter Shire's work too, and I liked it very much, especially the pristine edges, the contemporary materials and the boldness of the colors. My direction, though, was considerably different. The Memphis School isn't really erotically oriented, and I wanted to use forms that have some erotic connections. But the colors in these new pots were certainly influenced by Memphis."[12]

Hard-edged balls, shafts, and triangles are the basic compositional units Kottler configured in the new vessels such as *Toro* and *Rockets*.[13] In *Toro* and *Romaine*, executed in 1982, the shiny balls and shafts are bracketed with voluptuous biomorphic extrusions colored softly with underglaze (figs. 4.2-4.4). These unmediated juxtapositions of crystalline shafts and organic flanges are reminiscent of mid-1960s multimedia compositions with fur, such as *Guilt Feeler*. In *Guilt Feeler* the hard/soft, organic/inorganic dichotomies are literal and blatant; in the 1980s vessels, by contrast, the mode of address is one of implication and inference. Vases such as *Romaine* and *Blue Balls* (fig. 4.5) are also reminiscent of the winged raku bottles Kottler executed in 1966 and 1967. In fact, many of Kottler's pots from different periods, ranging from the Egyptian paste *Madame Chiquita Pot*, to the bright-colored *Hustler's Delight*, to the Deco-inspired *Fountain Fun Pot* and *Romaine* share the same basic composition: the body of each pot is a smooth oval or rectangle framed by curvilinear flanges that reach into or up to a hole in the top. Each has a strong front/back orientation, minimal interior volume, and color-coded formal zones, and each

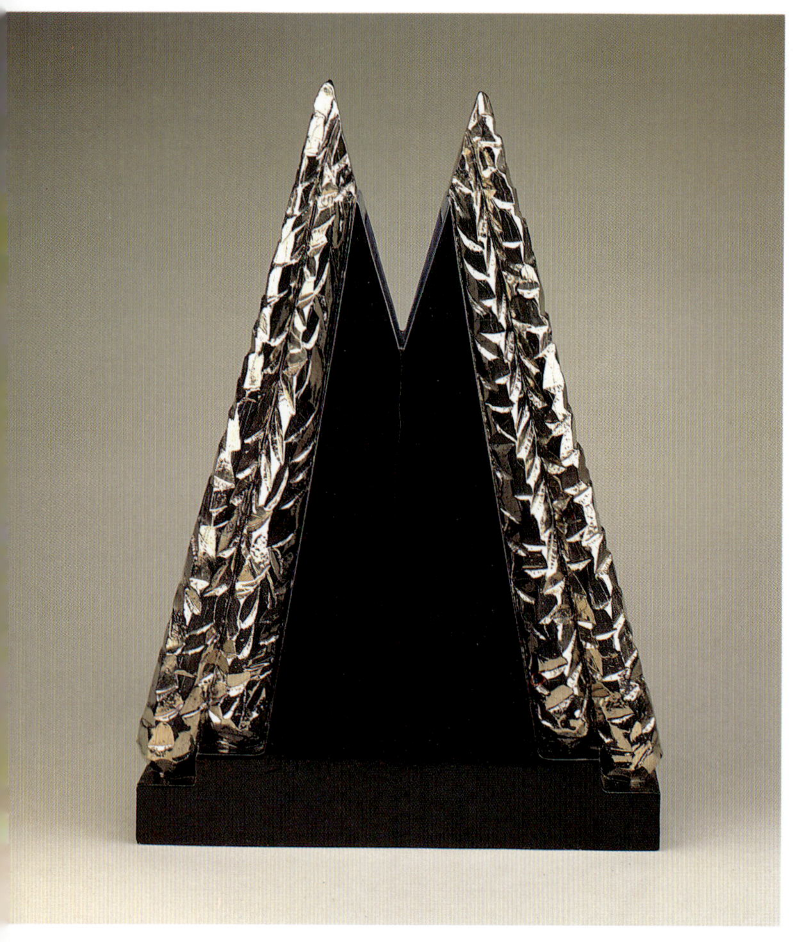

4.2 *Rockets*, 1982-83. Earthenware, 24 x 16½

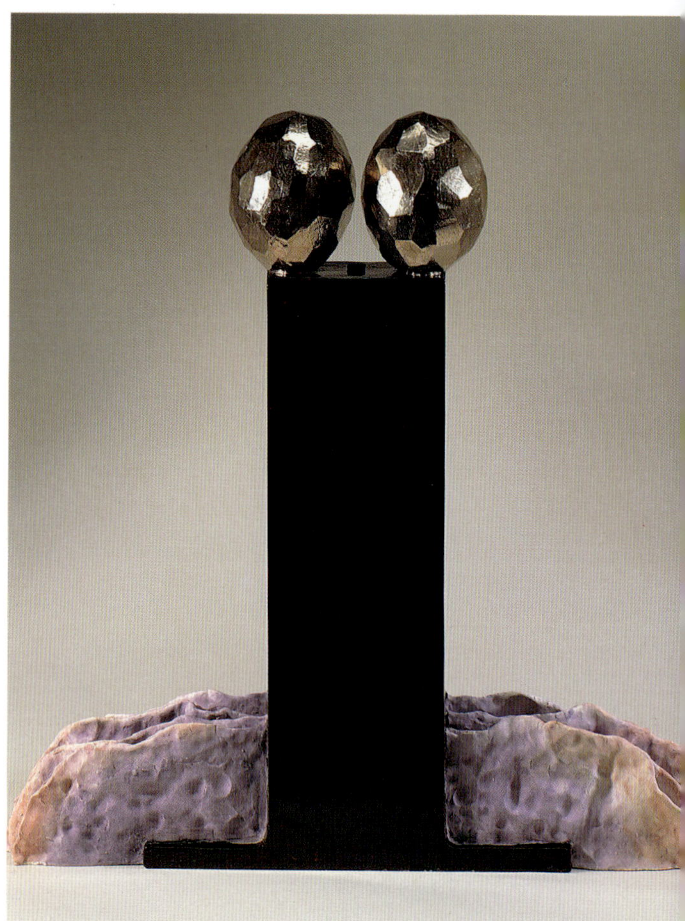

4.3 *Toro*, 1982. Earthenware, 22½ h

is conceived as an additive construction rather than a holistic unit. Some of the 1980s pots depart from this pattern in the contrasting surface textures of the body and the frame which play up the element of counterpoint.

In many compositions, the bodies and the frames were also executed separately. In 1984 Kottler hired Dan Neish as his technical assistant, and the two artists developed an intuitive and efficient rapport. "It was easy to draw up diagrams for the shafts—or for any hard-edged forms—so Danny would build the shafts," Kottler explained. "I would make the wings if they involved a more expressionistic handling of the clay, which I had to work out on my own. But there were many pieces Danny built entirely; he is an excellent craftsman and could translate my ideas into clay as well as I could. It freed me up to develop more ideas."[14]

In the mid-1980s Kottler extended his compositional formula to include bottle-and-stopper pots with unframed geometric bodies crowned by faceted balls (figs. 4.6, 4.7). In the Memphis-colored *Lemon Lips Pot*, the ball is literally a stopper with a projection that extends downward into the interior of the pot. "You have to pick up this big ball to see that it has a cone point that goes into the opening," Kottler explained. "There's a kind of sexual relationship between the forms which is hidden and which you must reveal. The experience of uncovering and surprise has been important to a lot of my work, although eroticism wasn't always involved. But I think that a utilitarian object can have a psychological dimension too, as well as a strong design."[15]

The decal plates and cup series of the early 1970s demonstrated that Kottler could also use utilitarian ob-

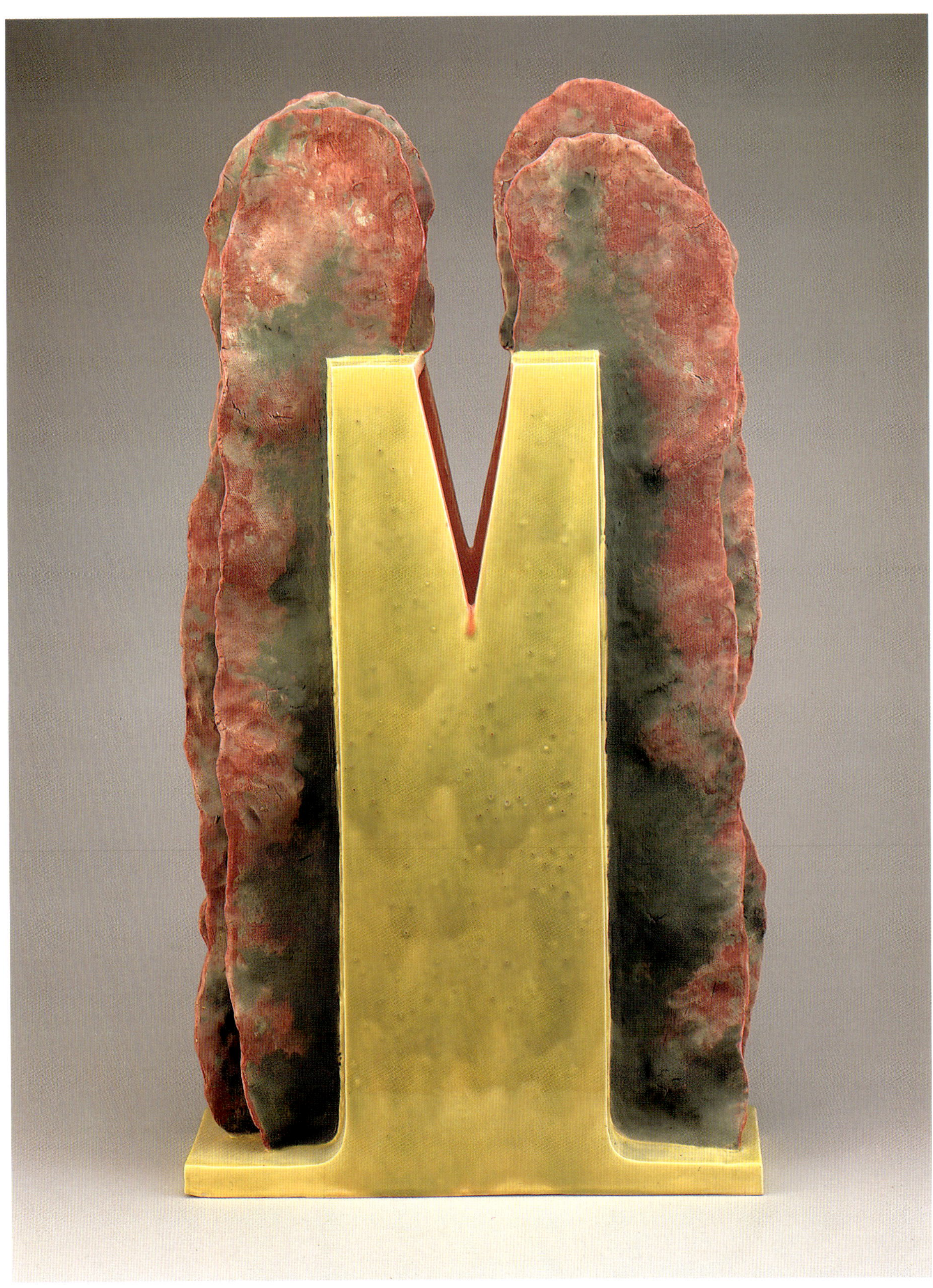

4.4 *Romaine*, 1982. Earthenware, 23½ x 12

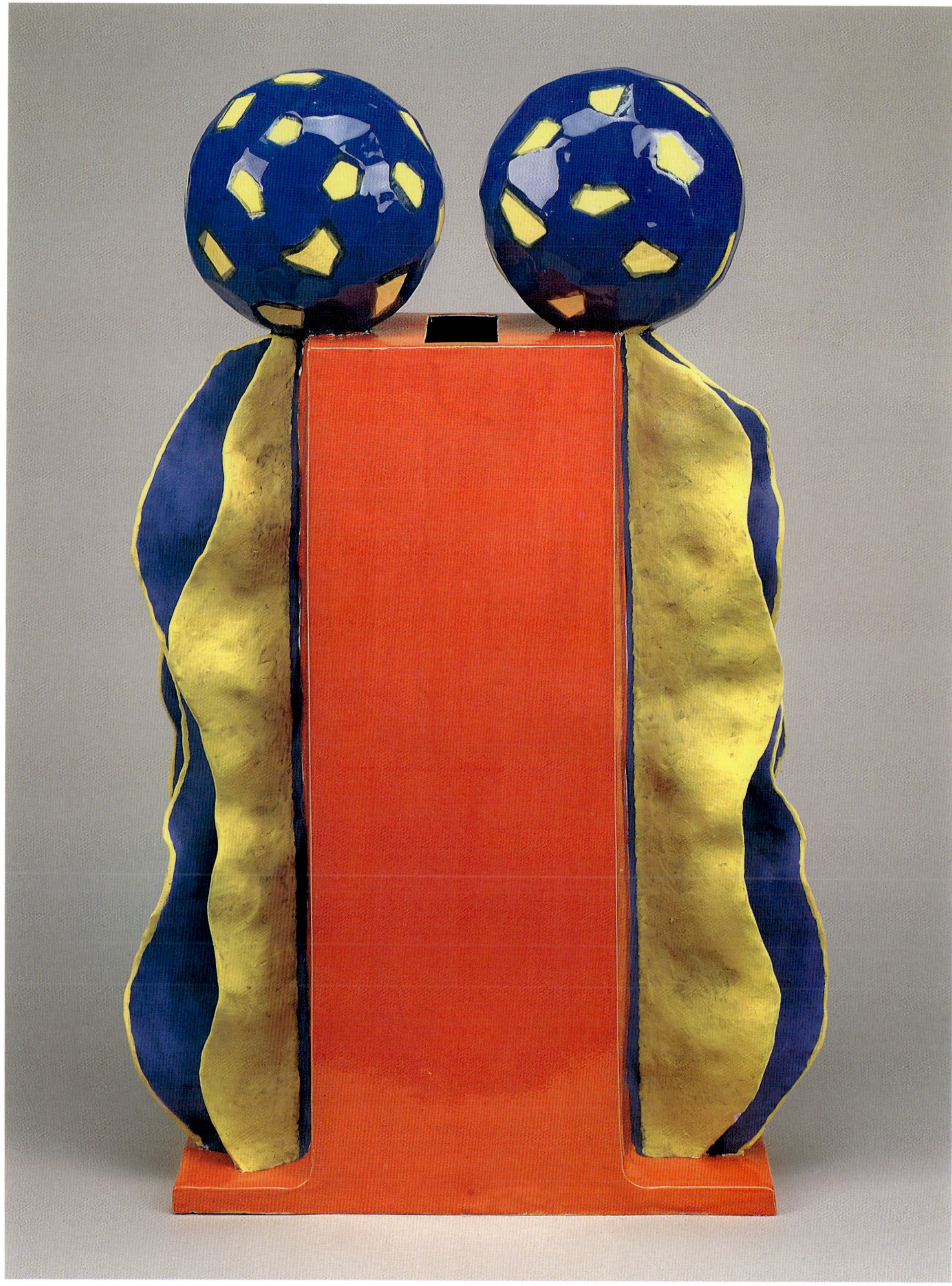

4.5 *Blue Balls*, 1982-86. Earthenware, 23 x 15½. Collection Los Angeles County Museum of Art. Gift of Howard Kottler Testamentary Trust

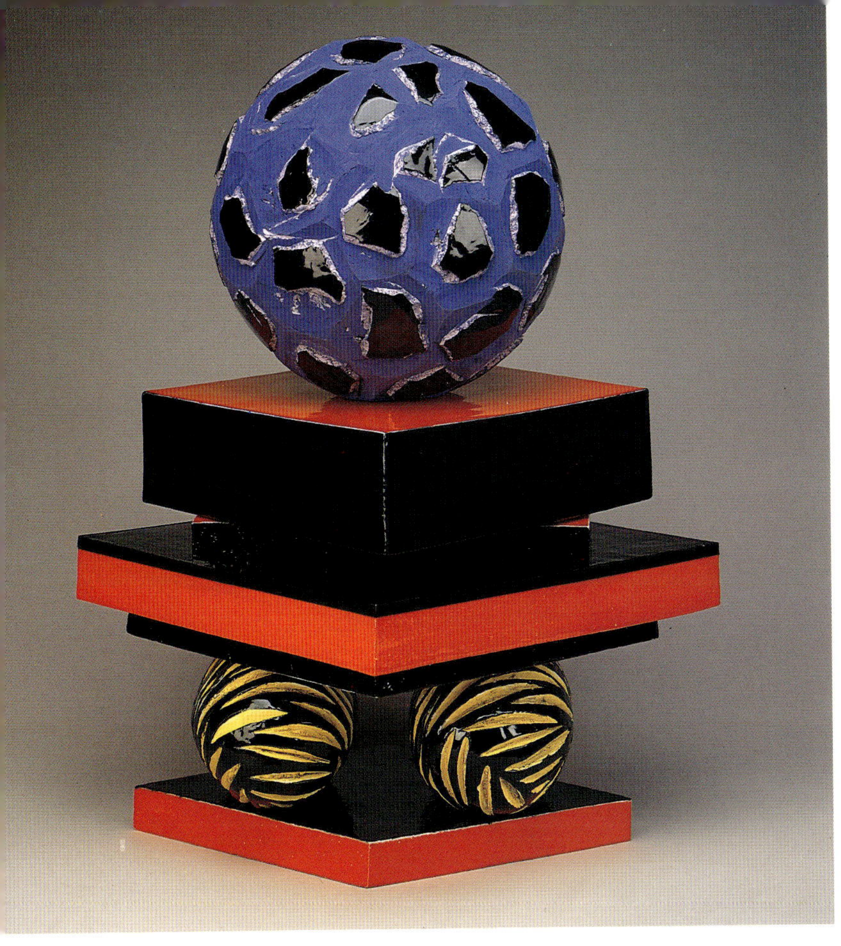

4.6 *Super Ball*, 1986. Earthenware, 25 x 20

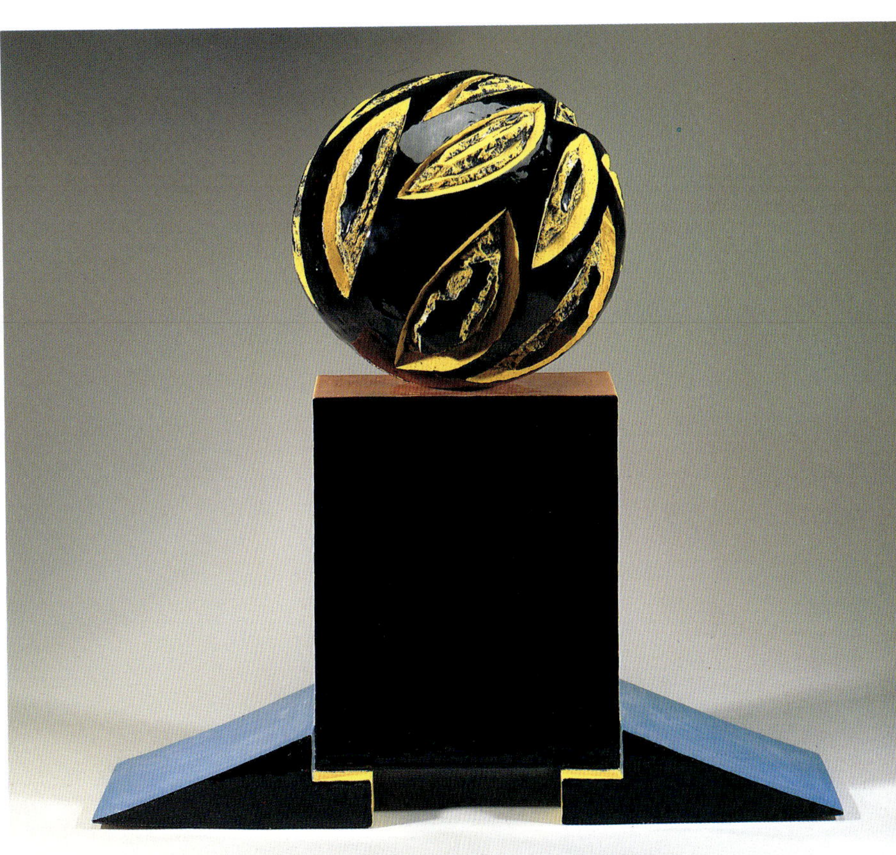

4.7 *Lemon Lips Pot*, 1985-86. Earthenware, 25 x 20

jects as vehicles for social and art-historical commentary. In 1985 he ruminated again upon art-historical hierarchies with another small series of coded vessels. From one perspective, these new vases were standard variations on an established historical precedent, but they also represented a further attempt to conflate modern folk pottery—manufactured ceramic vessels—and fine-art palace ware.

After purchasing his house in Seattle in 1975, Kottler began collecting Japanese-manufactured Art Deco pottery, especially Noritake porcelain. His 1985 container series was based on a crisp, streamlined vase from his collection manufactured in the 1920s by the Royal Trico Company (fig. 4.8). "I had Danny make five

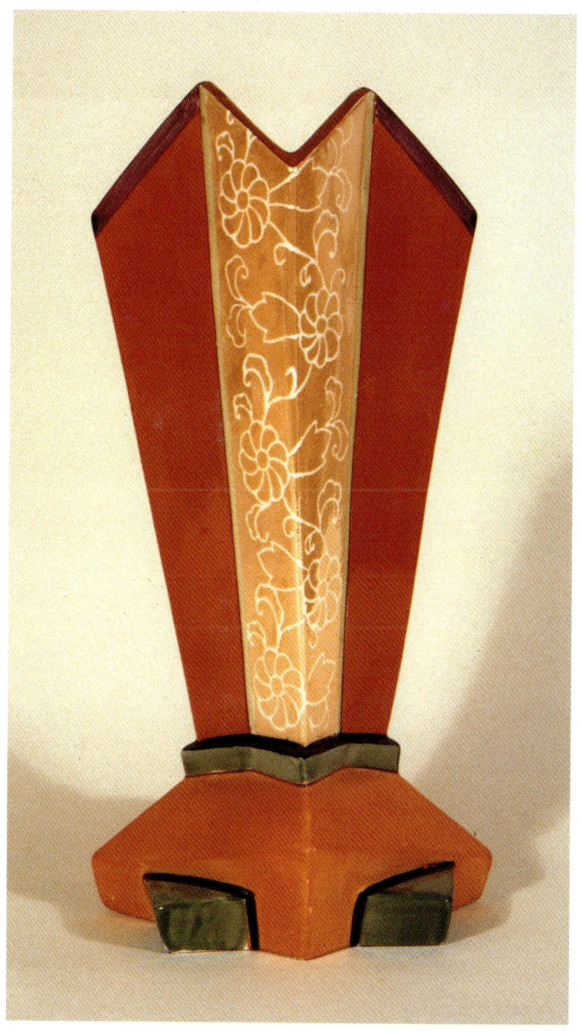

4.8 Royal trico vase, 1920s. 9 h

variations on this Trico vase, changing the distribution of parts and colors," Kottler said. "I was still interested in appropriating manufactured art and making my own changes—in this case I was trying to reconceive the piece in a bolder way (figs. 4.9, 4.10). I think *Skyscraper Pot*, which stands thirty-one inches high, was my favorite of the group. It's a mannered homage to great Deco buildings, coupled with a Memphis-style foot. *Twist Pot*, I think, was also successful. It has a stopper in the form of a green bud on top, with a long shaft below—it's a pot with a dildo inside."[16]

References to Art Deco had first appeared in Kottler's work in the late 1960s, but they resurfaced in new guises after he became an authoritative collector of Noritake (figs. 4.11-4.13). In 1982 his Noritake collection was circulated in a Smithsonian Institution traveling exhibition, accompanied by a substantial catalogue. According to the catalogue's introduction, Kottler "began to build his collection of Noritake ware, focusing on the two decades (1921-1941) prior to the closing of the New York offices of the Morimura Brothers (the Japanese conglomerate which up till 1941 included the Noritake Company). By 1976 Kottler had amassed a major part of the collection, which now consists of some 500 objects and stands as a rare and extensive document." The objects in Kottler's collection are "unusual artifacts, hybrids manufactured in the Orient for the American market. The Art Deco objects are especially unusual; they are the result of an ingenious plan involving international designers living in New York to create designs for ceramics to be produced in Nagoya and exported back to the U.S." The influence of Bernard Leach, the introduction continues, had inhibited serious consideration of Noritake Art Deco ware; Kottler's lecture about Noritake ware, presented at the 1981 International Ceramics Symposium in New York, not only undermined this prejudice, according to the show's curators, but also stimulated new scholarship and research.[17]

In his own catalogue statement, Kottler reviewed his activities as a collector, beginning with cut fingernails and cake icing. As a college student, he collected beaded bags and soapstone vases before moving on to Art

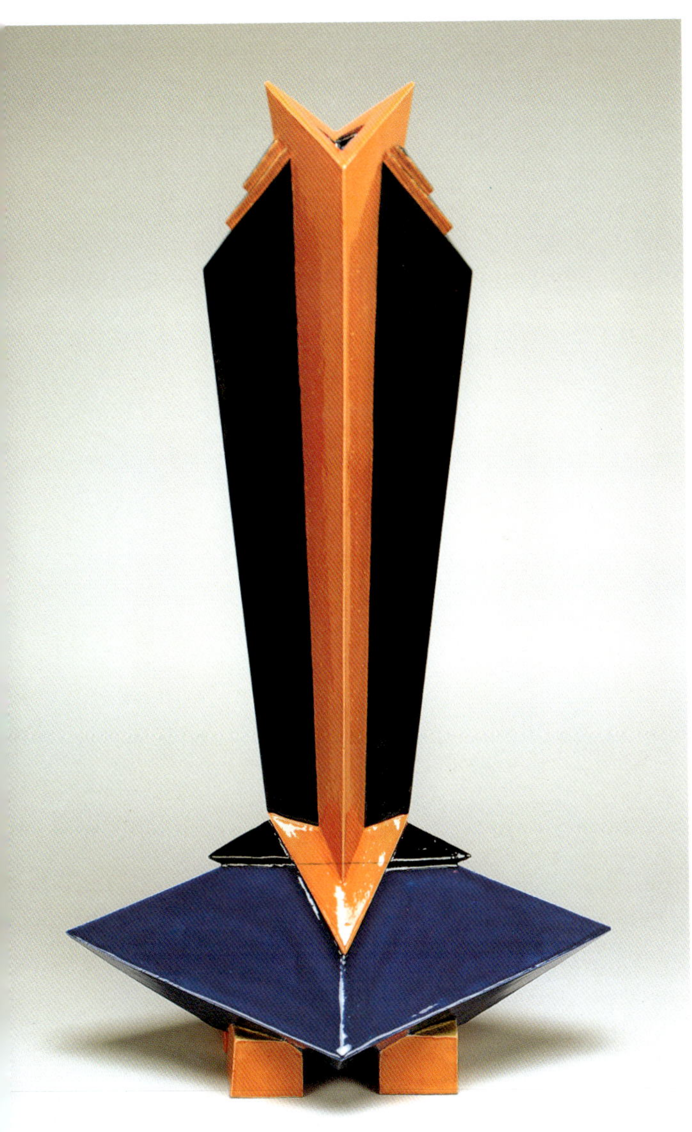

4.9 *Skyscraper Pot,* 1986. Earthenware, 31 x 18

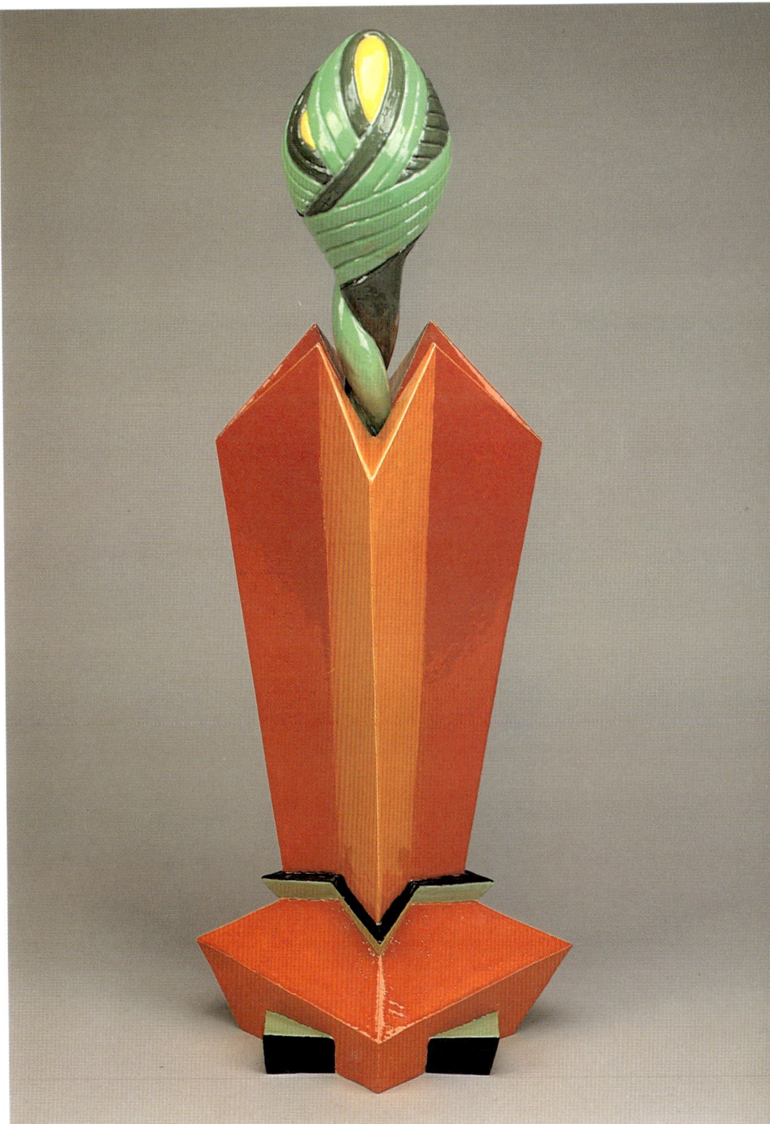

4.10 *Twist Pot,* 1986. Earthenware, 29 x 11

Nouveau jewelry. In Seattle in 1970, he began to notice Noritake pieces during his weekly haunts of antique shops and flea markets. "I knew I was on the right track when nearly every antique dealer looked down his nose at the mere mention of Noritake. My antique-hunting soon revealed that Noritake porcelains were readily available at reasonable prices and, best of all, the ware had a variety of motifs. It was definitely untapped and unspoiled virgin territory. Bongo! Here was the perfect combination and the perfect collectible." These Deco porcelains, he points out, were a vivid visual record of the

1920s lifestyle. "This is particularly true of the figurative pieces which reflect the joyous love for living associated with the Roaring Twenties and its rage for parties and costume balls. . . . The Noritake porcelains came close to expressing the very essence of the Art Deco style so exuberantly manifest in New York's Chrysler building and Rockefeller Center. These structures incorporate decorative details ranging from abstract to figurative, embodying floral and animal themes that are expressed in the same visual vocabulary as those used in Noritake porcelains."[18]

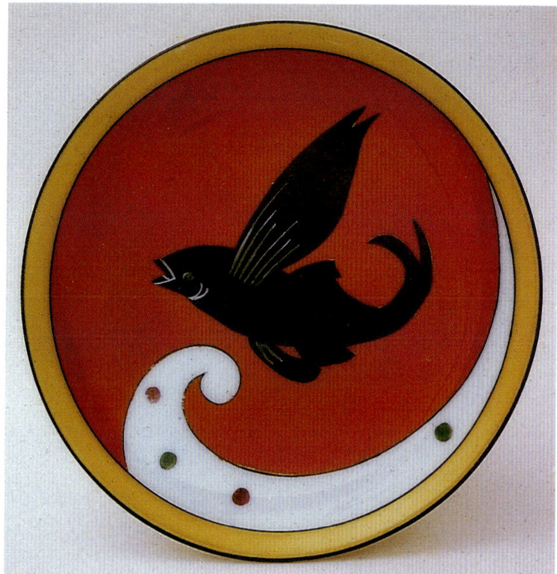

4.11 Noritake Deco plate, Kottler collection

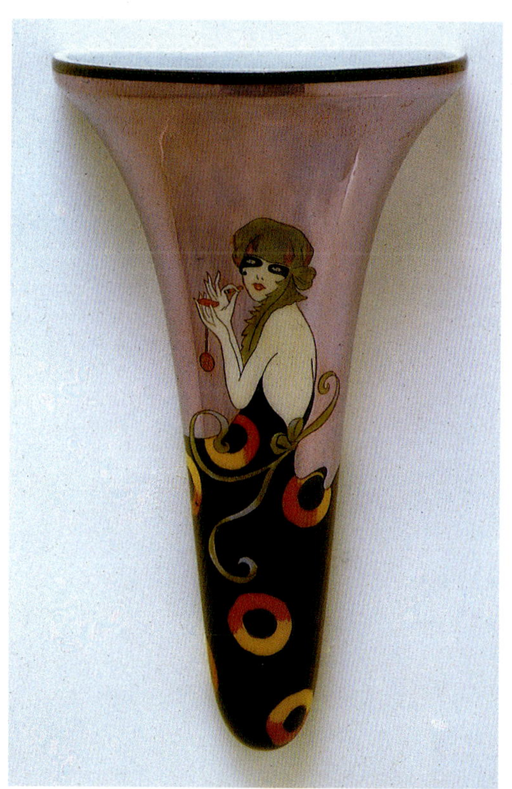

4.13 Noritake Deco wall pocket, Kottler collection

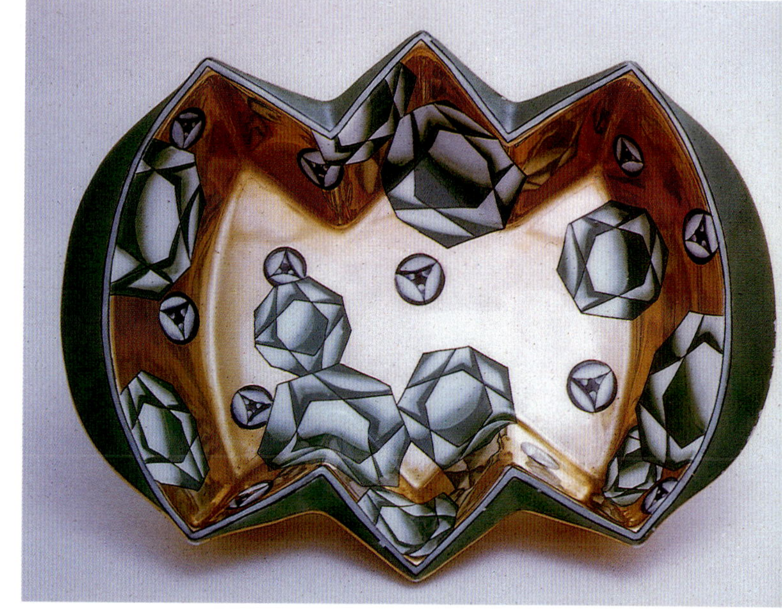

4.12 Noritake Deco plate, Kottler collection

Noritake Art Deco porcelain and Memphis design, two major influences on Kottler's work in the early 1980s, have evident formal commonalities consistent with his taste: hard-edged, clearly articulated forms, broad color planes, shiny accents, and a vivid palette. Each of these commercial design systems, however, also reflects its own time and cultural ambiance—the coy decadence and whimsy of the 1920s in the populist Noritake ware and the knowing, mannered postmodernism in the case of elitist Memphis design. Joining references to both design systems in the 1985 Royal Trico series, Kottler created an uneasy hybrid of wisdom and naïveté that barely holds up. His renewed enthusiasm for the vessel format in the first half of the 1980s, however, manifested itself primarily in slick, elegant ball-and-shaft forms that are formally more indebted to postmodern architecture and design than to Art Deco (fig. 4.14). But the shifts of meaning involved in recontextualizing Deco design in manufactured Noritake ware—the mobility of visual signs circulating from high art to low—was an equally important stimulus for many of his last artistic explorations. Because this stimulus was theoretical as well as stylistic, gauging the full impact of Noritake on the development of his work requires further review of his 1980s production.

In his last decade Kottler was among the few major ceramics artists in the United States actively involved with both vessel-making and sculpture, and his assessments of his own position were not always consistent. On the one hand, he maintained that "what I'm trying to do is to give crafts a good name by continuing to make pots that are definitely functional, but whose form and surface involve an eighties' approach to the vessel. In my case, an eighties' approach means loading the work with multiple meanings and references that communicate ideas or erotic suggestions. I try to approach functionalism as a challenge, not a burden. The obstacle I've faced with this work is the big market for mindless decorative objects like most of the work in the 'Eloquent Object' show [a widely reviewed 1987 traveling exhibition that included ceramics, jewelry, glass, metalwork, and textiles]. That exhibition should have been called the 'elegant object' show because it didn't have much to do with eloquence—only a few of the pieces had anything to say at all. These lush objects really need to be put down because they don't deal with new ideas or have content that reflects our time," he continued. "Yet this kind of work is getting the most attention from ceramics curators and critics. What's happened is that the artists with ideas have moved into sculpture, and there are few key figures working in the craft-utilitarian area to move it on to new dimensions."[19]

On the other hand, while he lamented this defection Kottler also admitted that "people who work with utilitarian forms have been held back because they haven't found a way to introduce an intensive layer of comment into the work. They are not second-class citizens, but I don't think there's been anyone who has been able to shore up the crafts to give them the kind of power we can find in objects designated as painting and sculpture. Even the artists, including myself, who make ceramic sculpture are not probing the limits of what sculpture is all about. In the 1980s there weren't any major changes either in the approaches to ceramic sculpture or in functional ware—there was a kind of plateau. Ceramics has never had a leadership role and still doesn't deal very much with the broader ideas that are pulling the twentieth century to its end. But that doesn't mean it can't happen—the most important thing is to keep pushing."[20]

The most adventuresome work Kottler executed in the 1980s, his ceramic sculpture and self-portraits, represents a bold attempt to forge intersections between ceramics and a postmodernist sensibility recognized and appreciated in the "fine arts." His earlier conclusion that concepts are the locus of artistic expression, his appreciation of Duchampian irony, his investigations of simulated materials and art-historical appropriation, and his study of the high-art/low-art shifts in the production and reception of Noritake Art Deco porcelains provided a framework for these new excursions. Another pivotal development was his decision in the late 1970s to investigate the inner and outer appearances of the Self as a new province of subject matter.

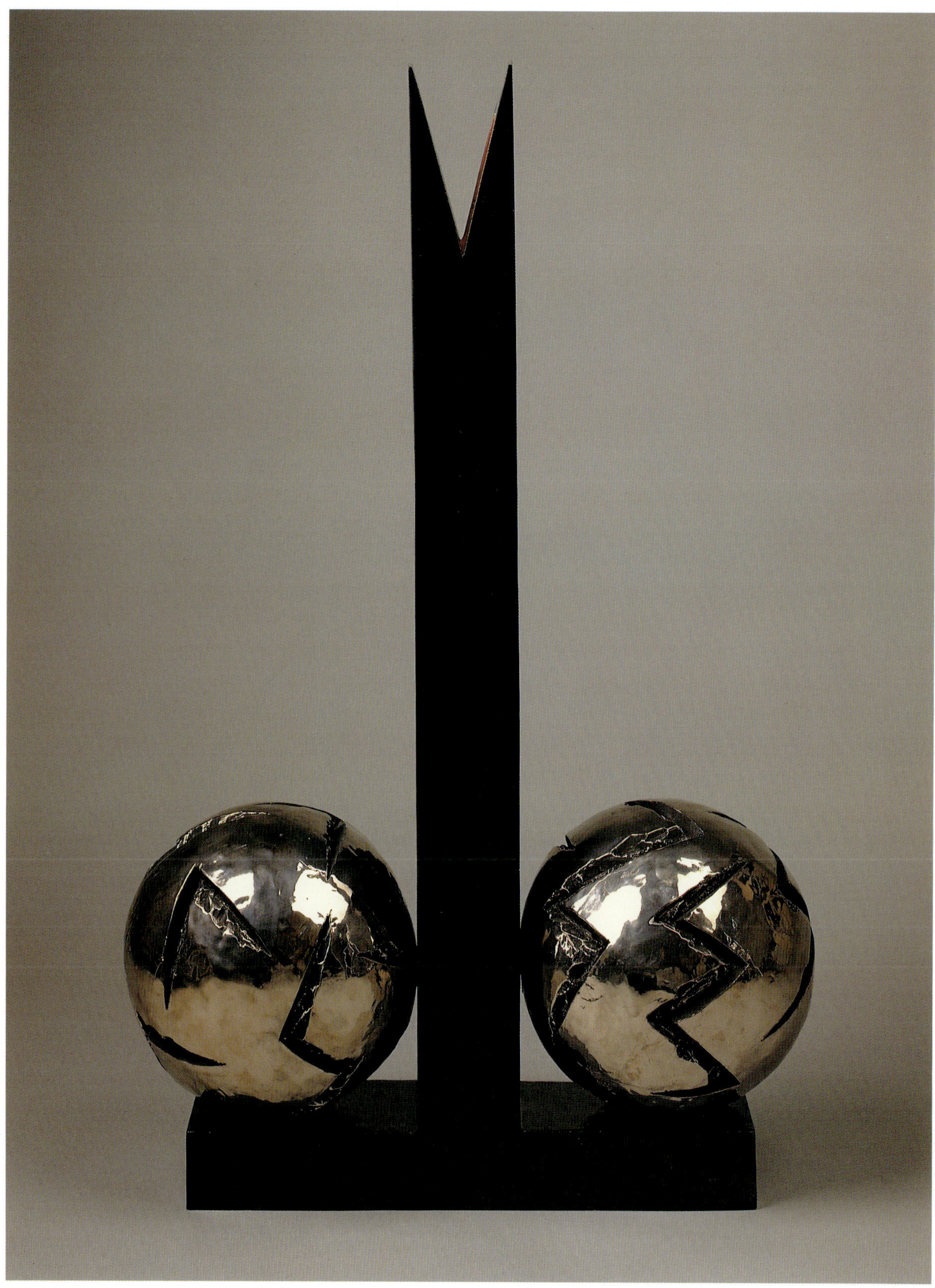

4.14 *Devil Tongue Pot*, 1987. Earthenware

Kottler began a series of self-portraits in 1977 based on his silhouette in profile. These two-dimensional images, which revived a high-school hobby (snipping paper silhouette portraits) provided a personal/impersonal sign for "head." "I really thought of the head first of all in generic formal terms," Kottler said (figs. 4.15). "I could have used anyone's portrait." On the other hand, he admitted, "I do like my own silhouette, which is pretty idiosyncratic. I won't deny that narcissism entered in. But when I began the portraits I wasn't trying to say anything about my inner secrets."[21]

His first silhouette compositions, however, are very much about his public persona. First of all, the profile, which outlines his puffy mustache and pointed goatee, is unmistakable. On occasion, he waxed and sculpted his mustache and beard as an homage to George Ohr, although his silhouette portraits were based on a profile with his beard and mustache in a conventional position (figs. 4.16-4.17). Many of his early self-portraits also commented upon his professional preoccupations. In

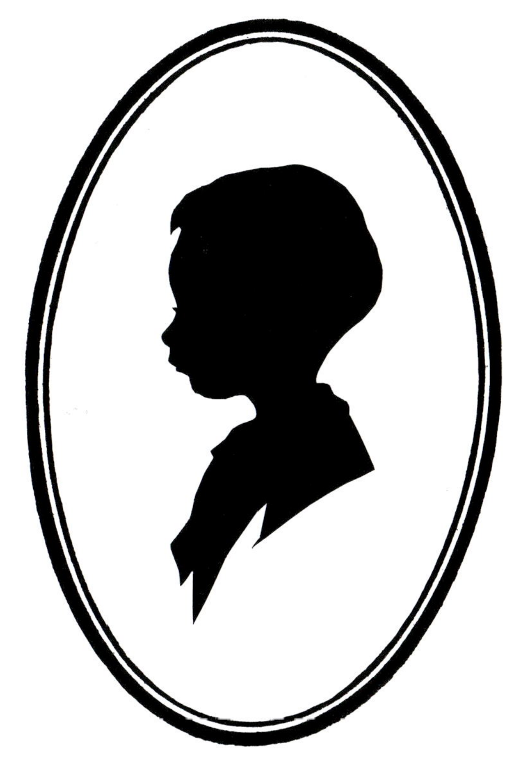

4.15 Silhouette of Howard Kottler, age six (1936)

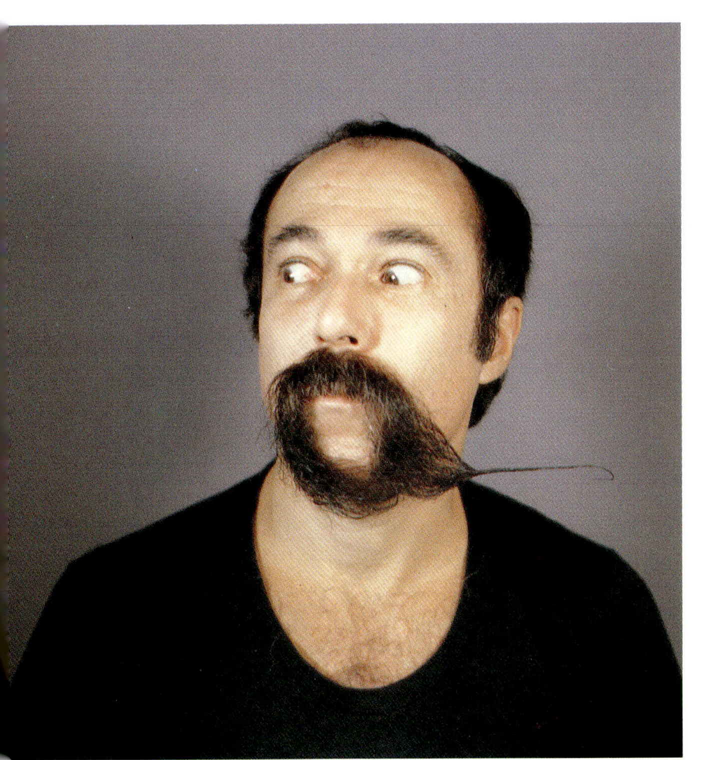

4.16 Howard Kottler, 1979, imitating photographs of George Ohr

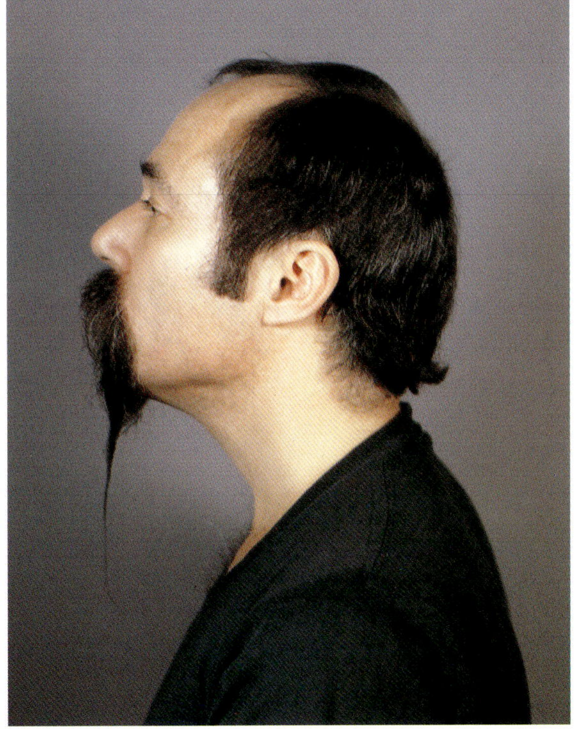

4.17 Howard Kottler, 1979, in profile

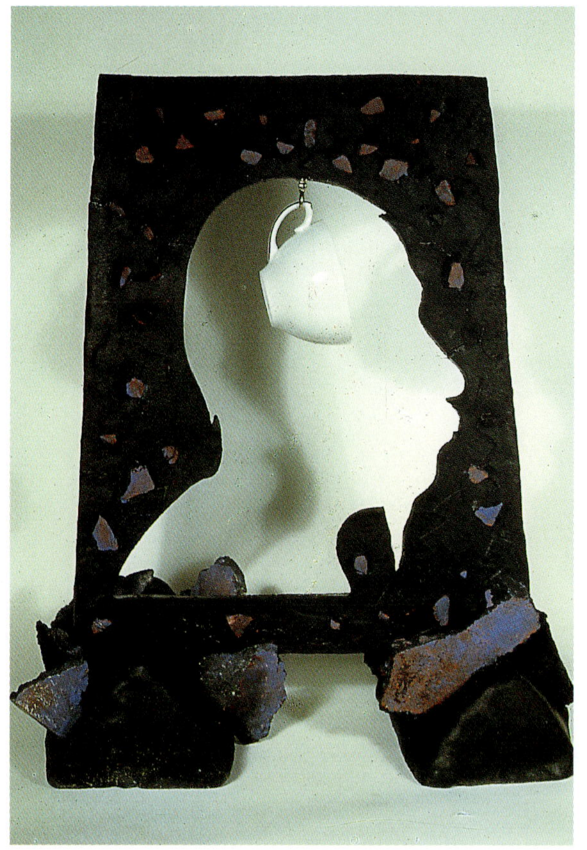

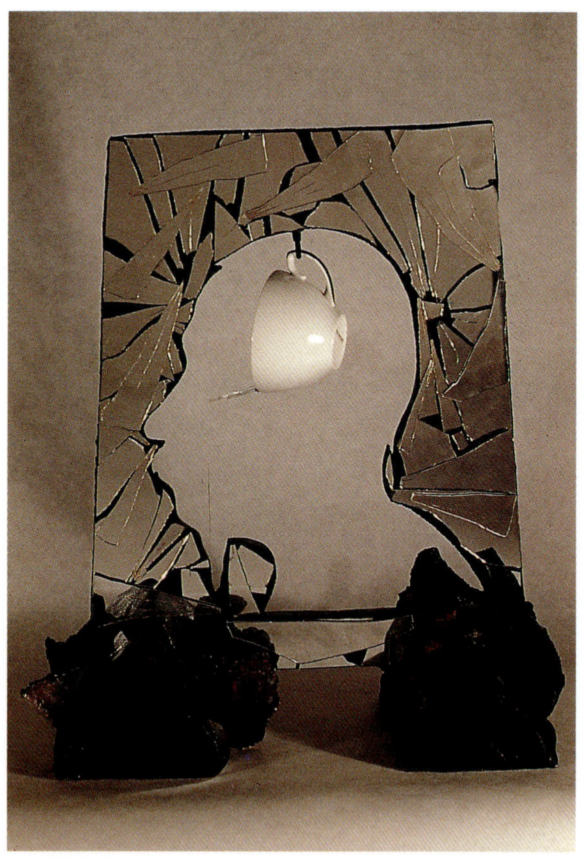

4.18 *Kottler by Kottler,* 1977. 19 h. Collection Everson
Museum of Art, Syracuse, N.Y. Gift of Howard Kottler
Testamentary Trust

4.19 *Kottler by Kottler,* 1977. Rear view

the 1977 compositions *Cracked Up* and *Kottler by Kottler,*
for example, the silhouette's brain has been invaded by a
manufactured cup; in *Bits and Pieces of Reality,* the flat
profile is surrounded by a potpourri of apparently unre-
lated ceramic decals, including fruits, vegetables, and
Gainsborough's *Blue Boy.* The Arcimboldo-style face is
piled high with illogically scaled hobby-shop casts of figures, vegetables, and architecture, playing the literal
three-dimensionality of the piled profile against the de-
picted dimensionality in the flat decals. In *Heads West
Young Man,* the profile of the artist's forehead, nose, and
mouth echo the Pacific Coast of the United States, while
the goatee serves as an analogue for Baja California. On
the reverse side of this flat panel are small casts of, among
other objects, a wagon wheel, trunks, and figures of nineteenth-century pioneers (figs. 4.18-4.24).

Bits and Pieces of Reality* is a plaque designed to be

hung on the wall, but most of the self-portraits are free-
standing, two-sided panel sculptures. *Cracked Up* is supported in the rear by a stack of trompe l'oeil books;
Kottler by Kottler rests on cast logs placed at right angles
to the face panel, and the triangular wedge of wagons and
pioneers hold up *Heads West.* "I had recognized at a certain point that my pieces tend to have flat planes and a
strong front and back," Kottler observed. "But this
worked out well for me because I liked the idea of incorporating different images and materials on the front and
back of the same piece. I wanted to build in an experience
of change—this is especially important in my later
work."[22]

The obverse and reverse sides of these portraits often present separate, but thematically related, physical
statements. The two sides typically represent two aspects
or dimensions of the same idea: in part because the com-

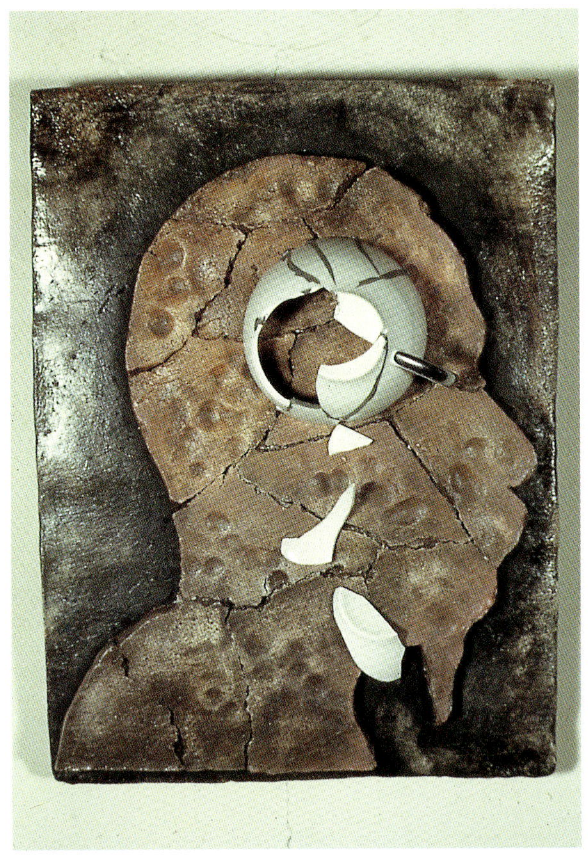

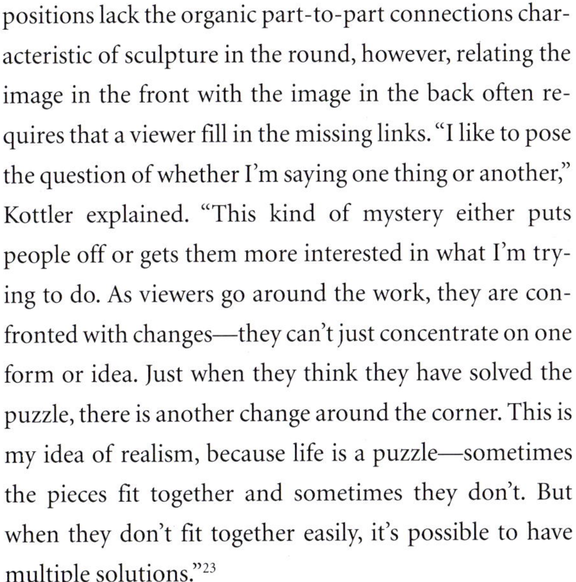

4.20 *Cracked Up*, 1977-78, 14 x 12. Collection Everson Museum of Art, Syracuse, N.Y. Gift of Howard Kottler Testamentary Trust

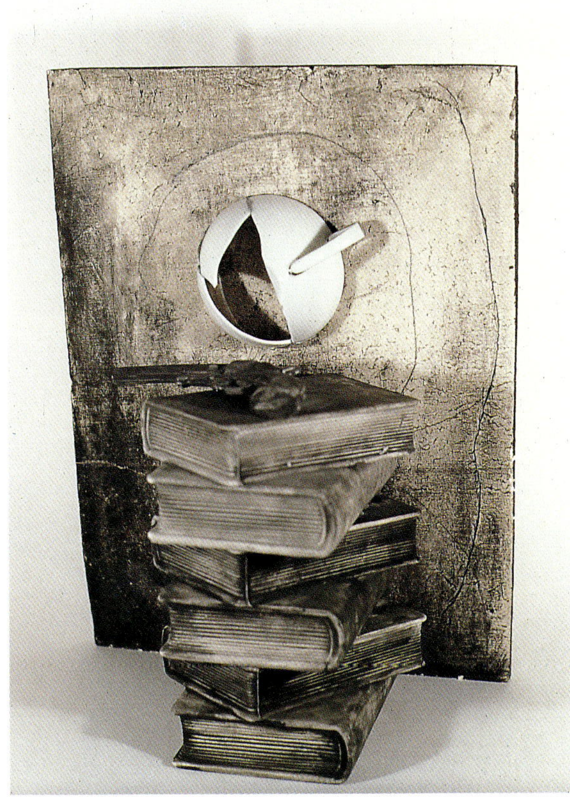

4.21 *Cracked Up*, 1977-78. Back view.

positions lack the organic part-to-part connections characteristic of sculpture in the round, however, relating the image in the front with the image in the back often requires that a viewer fill in the missing links. "I like to pose the question of whether I'm saying one thing or another," Kottler explained. "This kind of mystery either puts people off or gets them more interested in what I'm trying to do. As viewers go around the work, they are confronted with changes—they can't just concentrate on one form or idea. Just when they think they have solved the puzzle, there is another change around the corner. This is my idea of realism, because life is a puzzle—sometimes the pieces fit together and sometimes they don't. But when they don't fit together easily, it's possible to have multiple solutions."[23]

In 1978 Kottler began pairing his profiles to create a Rubens-Vase effect, as did Andy Warhol in his portrait of

Liza Minnelli. In *Portrait of a Vase* (1979), the front surface of the face-vase panel is covered with small pebbles; two fake rocks hold the portrait upright from the rear (figs. 4.25, 4.26). The sculpture comments again on Kottler's professional role as a paradoxical vessel-maker working with geological materials, but the image also represents a two-faced person—or, in this case, four-faced, if one counts both the front and back sides. The multiple facets of an individual personality, a theme introduced in these portraits of the late 1970s, develops into another point of departure for his final body of work.

Portrait of a Vase was included in a widely reviewed traveling exhibition mounted by the Seattle Art Museum in 1987, "Clay Revisions: Plate, Cup and Vase." Critical assessment of *Portrait of a Vase* ranged from A to F. For William Hunt, editor of *Ceramics Monthly*, almost all the

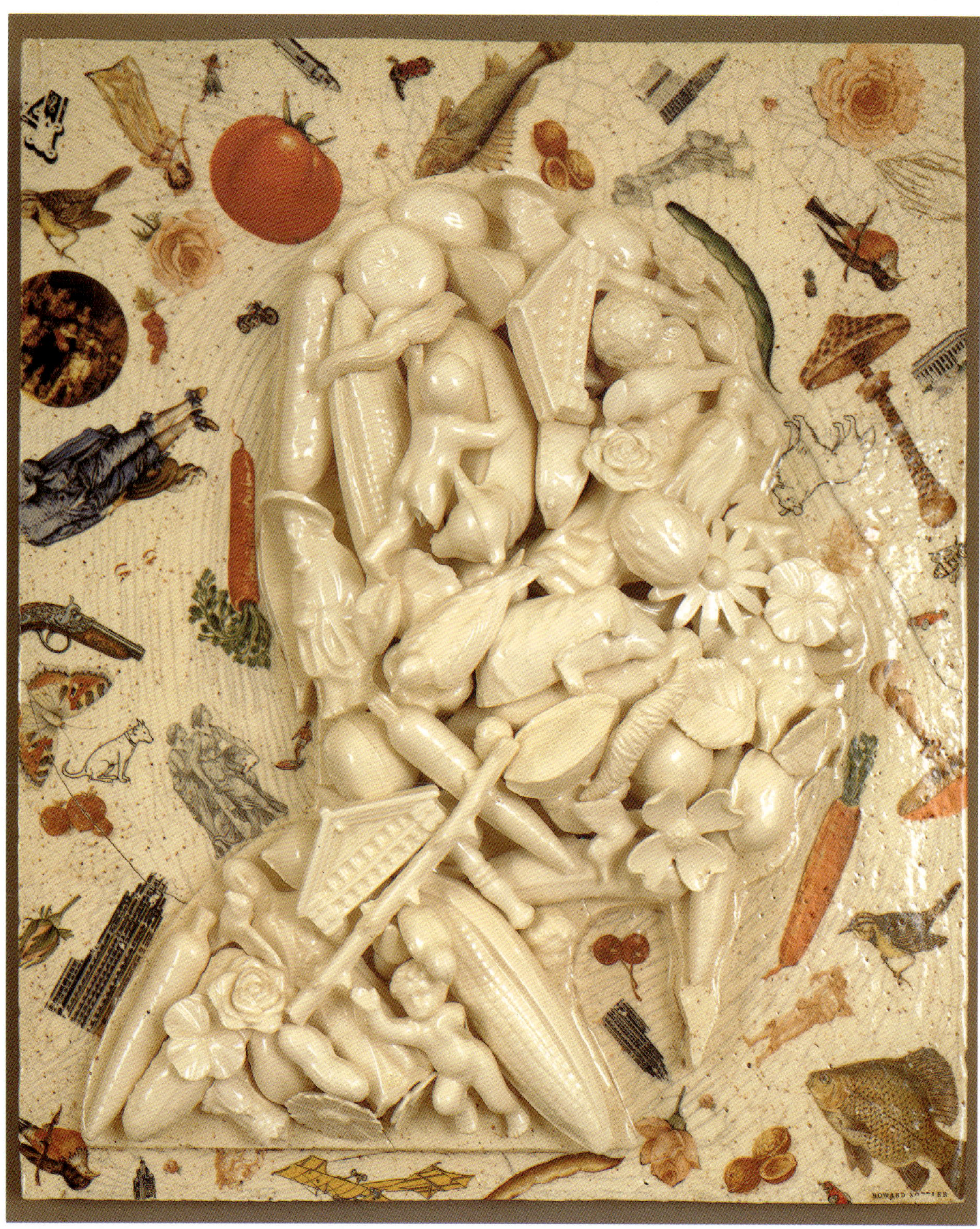

4.22 *Bits and Pieces of Reality,* 1978. 16 x 13

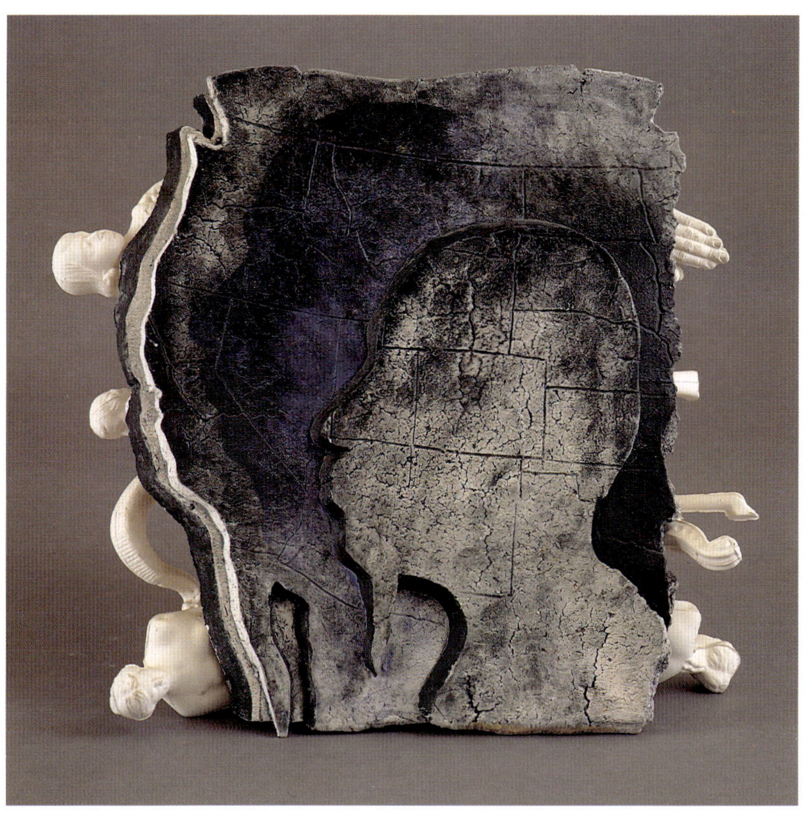

4.23 *Heads West Young Man*, 1979.
16 x 18

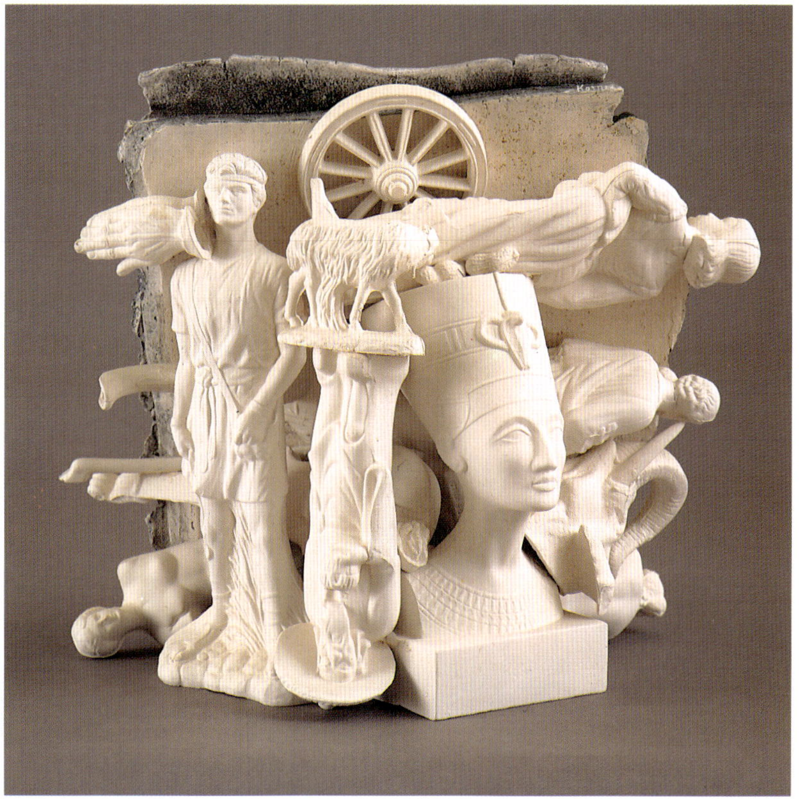

4.24 *Heads West Young Man*. Rear view

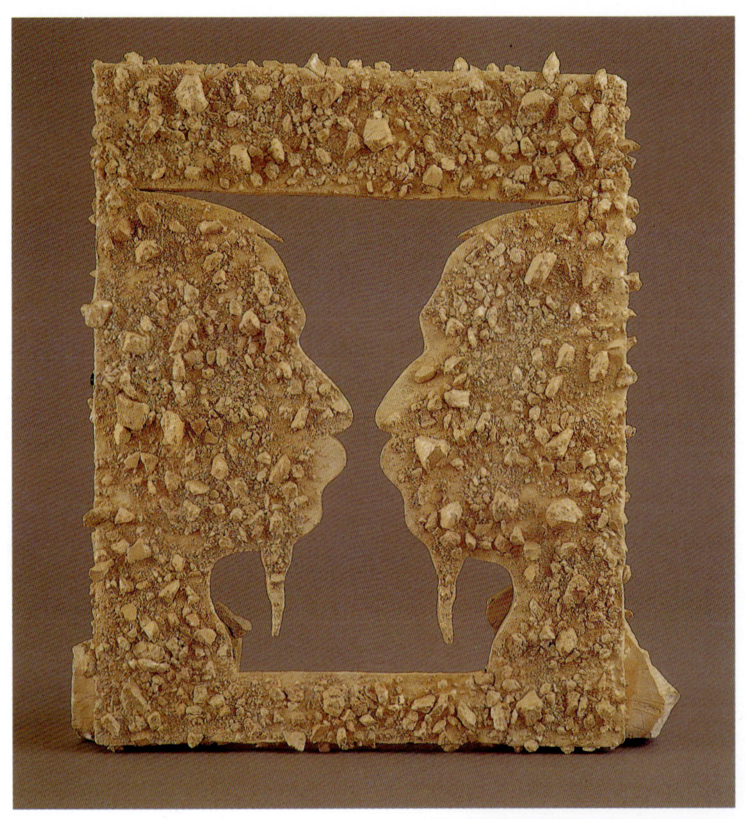

4.25 *Portrait of a Vase*, 1979. Whiteware,
19 x 18

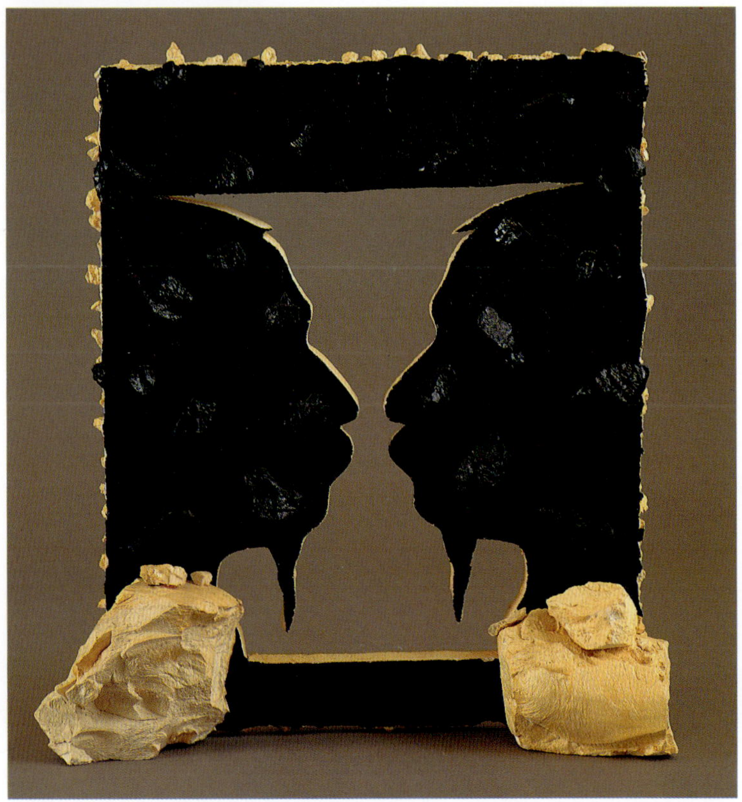

4.26 *Portrait of a Vase*, 1979. Rear view

artists in the "Clay Revisions" show deserved a critical C- because their work "begs for new thinking and new directions." The only exceptions, in his view, were Donna Polseno, Robert Sperry, and Kottler. "I give Kottler an A- because I'm hoping that denying him an A+ will make him work harder and smarter. . . . In the years to come when the current prices of most of the other pieces in the show have been forgotten in order to avoid embarrassing their collectors . . . Howard Kottler's work will continue to irritate, provoke and communicate to future generations." Kottler's superior achievement, he concludes, demonstrates by contrast "the nearly total lack of real meaning present in the contemporary ceramics movement."[24]

Portrait of a Vase also appeared on the cover of the *New Art Examiner* in 1988, where the composition was singled out to illustrate the "vacuous, insipid, and cliché-ridden ceramic art that has portrayed itself as the cutting edge of contemporary ceramics." On their surfaces, most of the objects in "Clay Revisions" reflect major stylistic trends in the fine arts, observed *New Art Examiner* ceramics editor Rob Barnard. "The application of [this] tired, trite and derivative imagery over ambiguous shapes," he writes, "results in objects whose form is in constant battle with its surface imagery." A few artists nevertheless managed to achieve a "conceptual and visual integrity, balancing material, technique and personal vision." At the other extreme, in Barnard's view, "is Howard Kottler. In *Portrait of a Vase*, for example, Kottler abuts two profiles of himself to form a void that resembles a vase. This kind of jejune visual proposition might be rejected out of hand if Kottler was not a skilled ceramicist using clay to make a pun on the vase inside the safety of the ceramics world."[25] Barnard's fundamental complaint is that artists in the show have lost interest in functionalism and respect for the "inherent romance and tactile nature" of clay. Why do so many of these artists "cling to clay, the vessel, and the ceramics field itself, long after they have rejected its history and language?" he inquires. Narrow-minded modernism that dismisses functionalism as a major criterion for judging the significance of a vessel is the ultimate culprit, he argues,

wrapping up his review with a paean to Japanese tea bowls.

Kottler's concept of the artist-potter thus encountered a neo-conservative "let-crafts-be-crafts" backlash in the 1980s. Swept up in the broad dissatisfaction with modernist art-for-art's-sake criticism that began to wash over the U.S. art world in the late 1960s, the let-crafts-be-crafts partisans developed a romantic nostalgia for the physicality and tactility of functional craft objects, which were seen as antidotes to the cerebralism engendered by computers and electronic communication. According to *New Art Examiner* publisher Derek Guthrie, in modern culture "the reconnection between aesthetic experience and the body is essential to survival. The aesthetics of function are essentially tactile. Useful craft objects relate to the body. . . . They adorn it and serve it. The intimacy of tactility is essential to human happiness. As many studies have shown, the absence of a mother's or parenting touch in baby's early years can lead to retardation, anxiety, anomie and ultimately psychosis. And craft objects are and always have been a culturally nurturing substitute for a mother's touch and warmth."[26]

Guthrie made these observations in his negative review of the "Eloquent Object" show, which featured work by artists who "explore form apart from function." Kottler's negative opinion of the same exhibition was also pegged to its focus on formal values; his complaint, however, was that form was being celebrated at the expense of content, not function. Kottler's concept of the artist-potter in the 1980s, therefore, wedged itself between two critical factions: the let-crafts-be-crafts contingent, many of whom revered what Kottler regarded as obsolete folk pottery, and late modern formalists, who favored refined luxury objects. Kottler's vases of the early 1980s were both functional and formally elegant; they might have drawn the attention, it would seem, of either critical camp. Why they did not is an intriguing question. One possible explanation is that the intellectualized stylistic commentary and phallic sexuality that were important to him in conceiving the vessels did not patch into the critical discourse of either group. The content of his self-portraits and sculptures of the 1980s, in addition, was even more at odds with a nostalgia for handicrafts or modernist formalism.

Ceramics criticism was not simply divided into two camps during Kottler's last decade, however, and he did receive significant critical support. But these instances were comparatively rare: Clark reports that Kottler "withdrew from the exhibition circuit from 1981 to 1987," although, in fact, his work was included in twenty-three invitational shows all over the United States between 1981 and 1986. The favorable attention he did receive, furthermore, was often pegged to older work: Hunt's 1988 review of *Portrait of a Vase*, urging him to work "harder and smarter," was a commentary about a sculpture executed ten years earlier. Kottler's conception of the artist-potter was largely a product of sixties optimism about the collapse of the ceramics academy and of traditional critical categories: he continued to be optimistic, reacting to the relative lack of serious critical and collector response to his art by creating progressively more difficult work.

Face to Face (1978), for example, is a complex fifty-six-inch-high assemblage incorporating a nightstand, a clay vase, a hobby-shop cast of King Tutankhamen's head, and plastic flowers, all covered with wood-grain contact paper (fig. 4.27). The vase is a Rubens Vase in positive form created by matching cut-away profiles of Kottler, who described the composition as paying "homage to the twentieth-century re-presentations of Tut" in the 1978 blockbuster King Tut exhibition.[27] Kottler's ironic response to Tut-as-commodity was to substitute a two-dimensional image of a vessel—his own double profile—for the king's torso, and to blanket the entire form with simulated surface materials. Tut's torso is a structure literally formed by representations of an observer; these images of a contemporary viewer in turn support the manufactured reproduction of the King's head. The doubly fake flowers—plastic wrapped in contact paper—convey the concept of homage, reflecting one of Kottler's personal idiosyncrasies. "I don't like real flowers," he admitted, "because they are a responsibility—you have to take care of them. So when I buy flowers, I buy artificial ones like French glass flowers or the great

Plexiglas flowers from the 1930s. You get exactly what you want and they stay that way. Besides, just like a lot of people, I really *enjoy* artificiality—the obviously fake."[28]

In 1980 Kottler created two related multimedia compositions of exceptional autobiographical candor. *Dinner for Me* includes a wooden triangular table and chair fabricated by a woodworker, and a table setting of commercial ceramic ware. The chair and table were coated with black paint; over the table was a "tablecloth" made from simulated wood-grain contact paper. Incised in the back of the chair was a Rubens-Vase portrait of Kottler, who was an accomplished cook and connoisseur of restaurants; his double portrait also appeared on the dinner plate. "In this piece I tried to present multiple shadows cast from the objects, and the shadows were all done in different fake woodgrains," he explained. "The piece was supposed to be lighted to cast actual shadows as well, so in some cases there were double shadows. The knife covered with contact paper, for example, had a shadow done in contact paper, but it also had a real shadow" (figs. 4.28, 4.29). The triangular form of the table was chosen in part, he said, "to thumb my nose at Judy Chicago's *Dinner Party*, which had a triangular table. What bothered me about the *Dinner Party* is that it was a real throwback to old romantic ideas about craft."[29]

The sharp triangular forms, Kottler added, were also chosen as a comment on "a personal relationship I was having at the time which was being brought into sharper focus. I wanted the relationship to be more pointed. I also wrote a narrative text for this piece and printed it on clear Dymotape, which picks up the different backgrounds—the different references to illusion and reality—in the surface materials. I let the tape hang down from the table onto the floor. It was unraveling, just as the relationship was unraveling."[30]

The narrative on the tape read:

> I feel sad and alone, but hopeful. I liked what you said before leaving—I wouldn't have missed it for the world. I want to continue as friends. I think we have been just that, friends, for a long time now. We respect each other, but seem unable to relate.

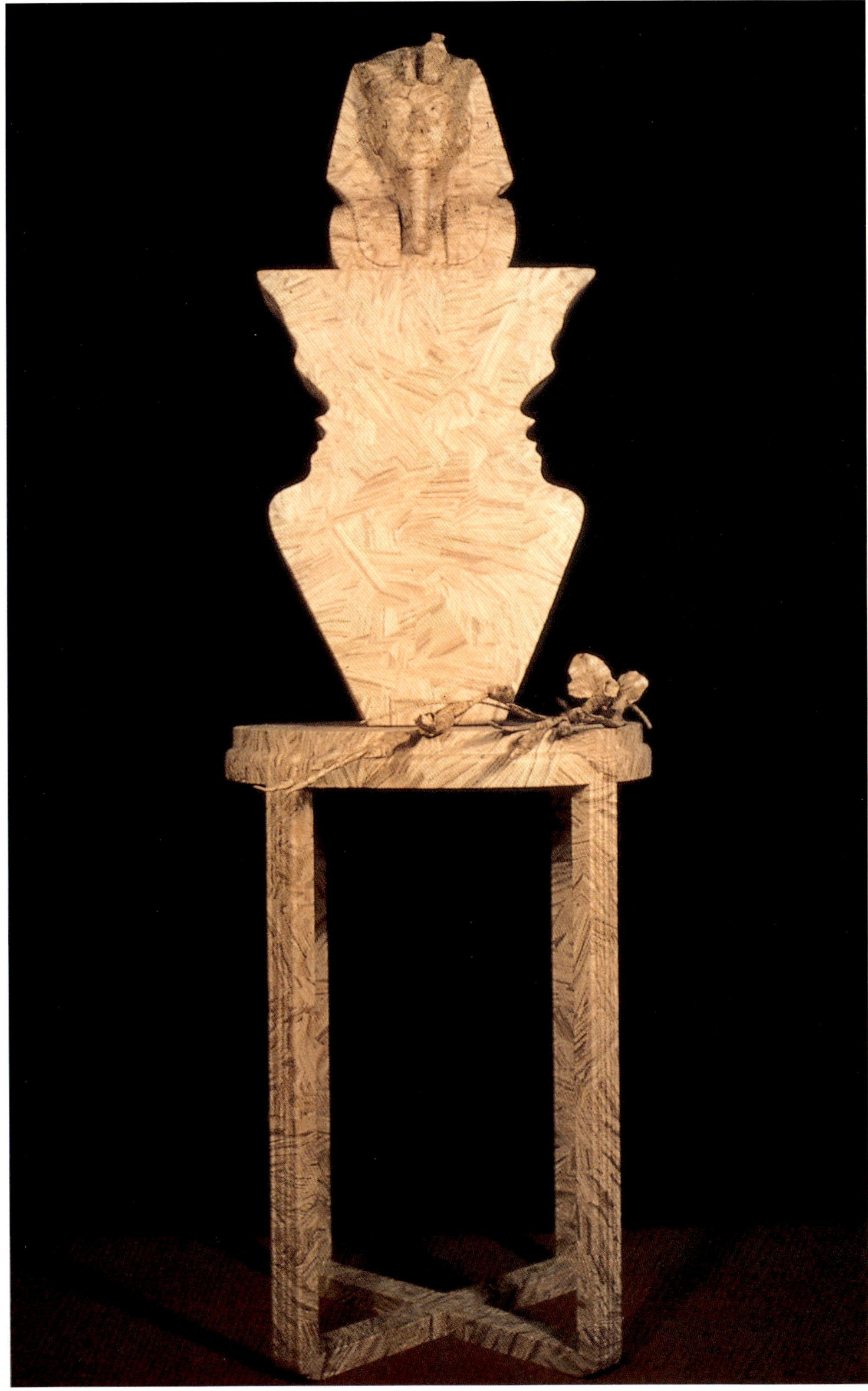

4.27 *Face to Face,* 1978. Mixed media, 56 h. Collection American Craft Museum, New York. Gift of Howard Kottler Testamentary Trust

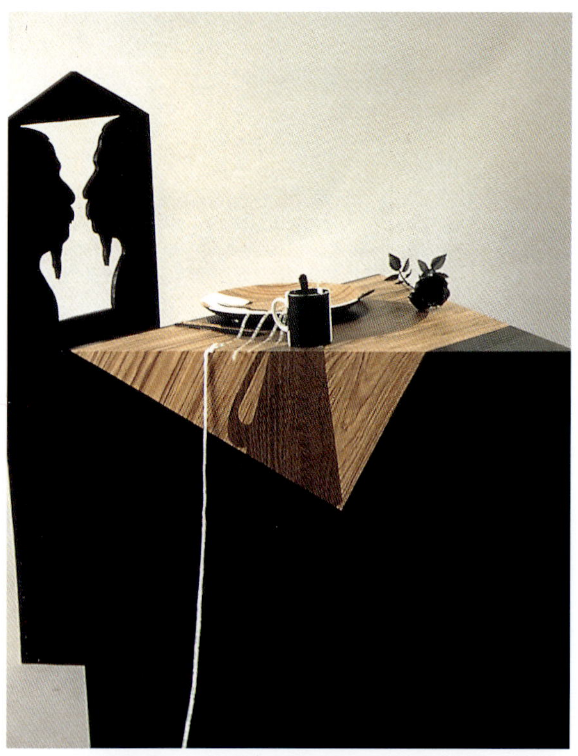

4.28 *Dinner for Me,* 1980. Mixed media, 48 x 36. Collection American Craft Museum, New York. Gift of Howard Kottler Testamentary Trust

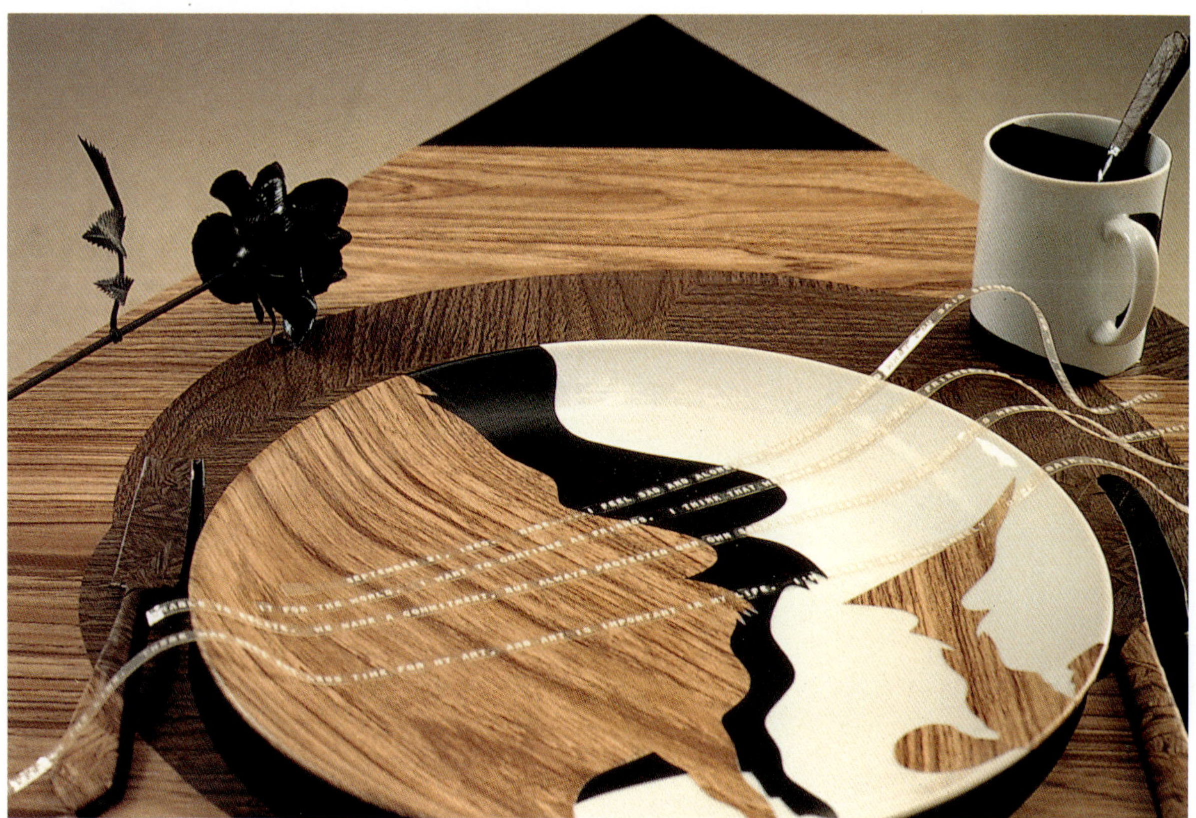

4.29 *Dinner for Me,* 1980. Detail of dinner plate

We made a commitment, but always protected our own selfish interests. In the end this made for a growing distance. We avoided conflict, but destroyed closeness by never putting ourselves on the line. There was more but less time for my art, and art is important in my life. I'm alone but not lonely. Once again, it's dinner for me.

A second version of this assemblage, in which nearly all the forms were black, was entitled *Alone at Last*. The following message was presented on the Dymotape:

> We can't get together again because we have never been together. We walk, we eat, we fuck, but we are not together. We are alone together and we are tearing each other apart. Holding on is torture. We must make the final break. I must solve my art myself. I can share a few things with you. I want to share everything with someone. It's hell.
> Love, Howard.

"Looking back on this work I realize it was an audacious thing to do," Kottler concluded. "The two tables were exhibited at the Henry Gallery when I was still with the person involved, and he saw them for the first time in the gallery. It wasn't a very subtle way to present a situation to someone. I'd just recently come back from my sabbatical in New York, and I was impressed with the pluralistic direction art seemed to be taking. This encouraged me to try to present things—and myself—more as they really were. I was trying to put more of myself on the line and I sometimes hurt other people. But even when I was offensive I was trying to get a better focus on myself and grapple with my own problems. The work became a kind of catharsis. But I also thought other people might see their own personal situations reflected in mine—that was really the point of including the narratives."[31]

In *Putting on the Dog* (1984), Kottler broached an even more intimate subject: sexual fantasies not widely acknowledged by heterosexual culture. In this sculpture the triangular table and chair are merged into a hieratic five-foot-high altar or shrine which is covered with faux-marble contact paper. The triangular base is empty at the back; this "doghouse" space contains a dog dish, a razor blade, and a photograph of a dog wearing a hat. Above the altar, under a Rubens-Vase portrait of Kottler, is a photograph of a row of dogs standing on two legs. Below, a dog figurine chained to the sculpture stares intently at a dogbone/phallus. Sections of text on Dymotape or small panels are attached to the altar in various locations. To read the text in the interior triangle at the rear, readers are obliged to descend on hands and knees, assuming a dog's vantage point (figs. 4.31-4.33). The text was excerpted from "Dog Dik," a 1981 essay by Jack Fritcher, which first appeared in a San Francisco gay newspaper.[32] The selections were both salacious and silly. One read:

> A dog who was quite appealing
> Yelled to the dog next door
> If you let me see your bone
> I'll take you to my home
> The dog suspected what he was in for.

Another example:

> Tonight it's ultimate obedience training. K9 patrol. Wild barking of delight, pacing, watching the bone, eager. Only the commanding look from the hairy dogmaster's eye. Only the whim of the dogmaster. Only minutes now.

Themes introduced in *Putting on the Dog*—the animal side of human nature, the pleasures of sadomasochism, relationships of master and pet, and dogs as a measure of man—provided the groundwork for a shift in Kottler's approach to the self-portrait. Although his profile still frequently appeared, in the mid-1980s his portraits began to allude less to his professional persona and more to his private preoccupations. The 1980 three-table series was an anomaly: he never again presented his personal life in his work in such simplistic or straightforward terms. Questions about what he was saying and not saying in his portraits became simultaneously more intricate and more open-ended as the decade progressed.

Kottler's collection of Japanese manufactured pottery included novelty animal figurines dating from the 1920s as well as plates, vases, and cosmetic boxes elaborately decorated with Art Deco–inspired designs. Many of these animal figurines were dogs with stylized geometric anatomy ultimately derived from cubism, which had been modified and reinterpreted by Deco designers hired by Japanese manufacturers. Studying the figurines, Kottler realized that cubist construction utilized flat, hard-edged planes to express volume, a formal strategy compatible with his long-standing preference for planar forms. After reviewing illustrations of early cubist paint-

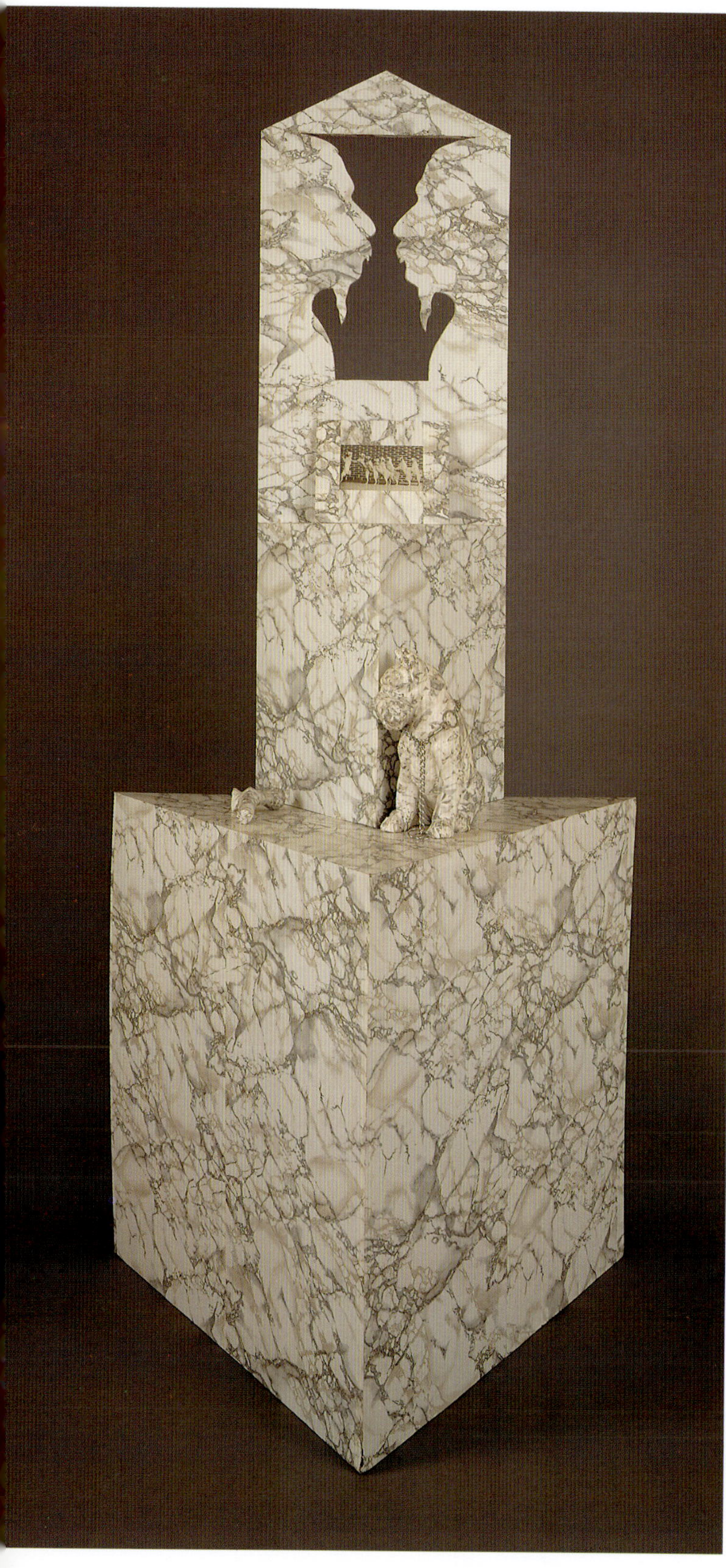

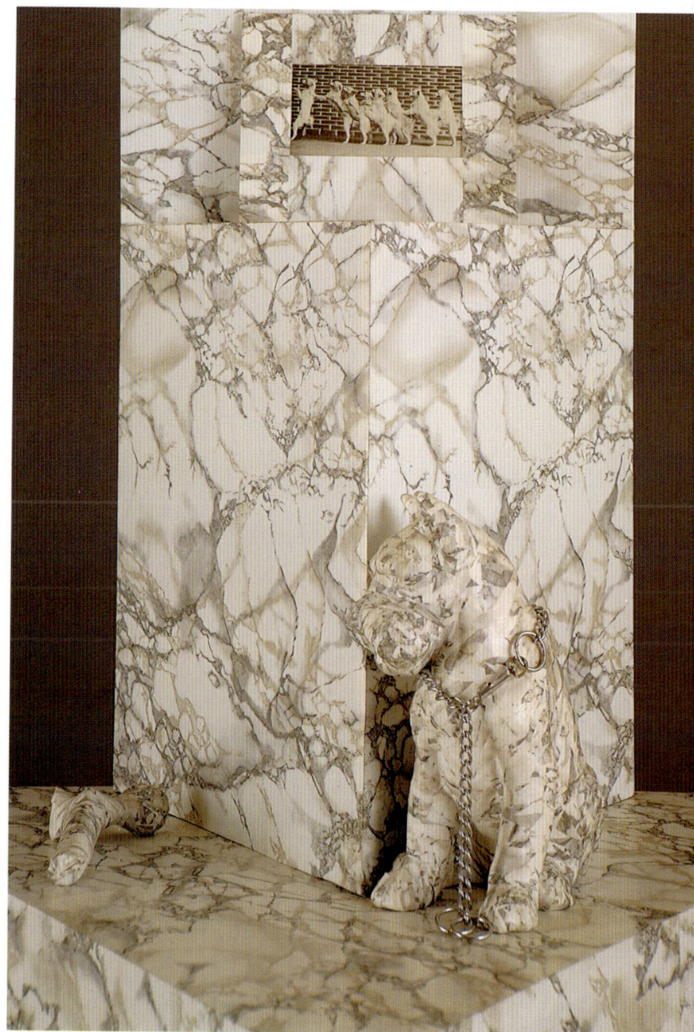

4.30 *Putting on the Dog*, 1984. Mixed media, 79 h

4.31 *Putting on the Dog*, 1984. Detail, front view

ings by Georges Braque and Pablo Picasso, he began to elaborate the faceting technique introduced in bottle-and-stopper compositions such as *Lemon Lips Pot* (see fig. 4.7). Cubist-style planes soon begin to appear in his self-portraits, where they function not only as a means for articulating planar space but also as a metaphor for the many sides of an individual personality and as a new form of art-historical commentary. In these portraits, the high art of cubism, recycled downward as low-art Noritake porcelain, rises to the top again as palace ware—but in an art form not fully accepted as "fine art."

Face Vase (1985) bridges Kottler's sculpture of the early 1980s and the forays into cubism that inform the

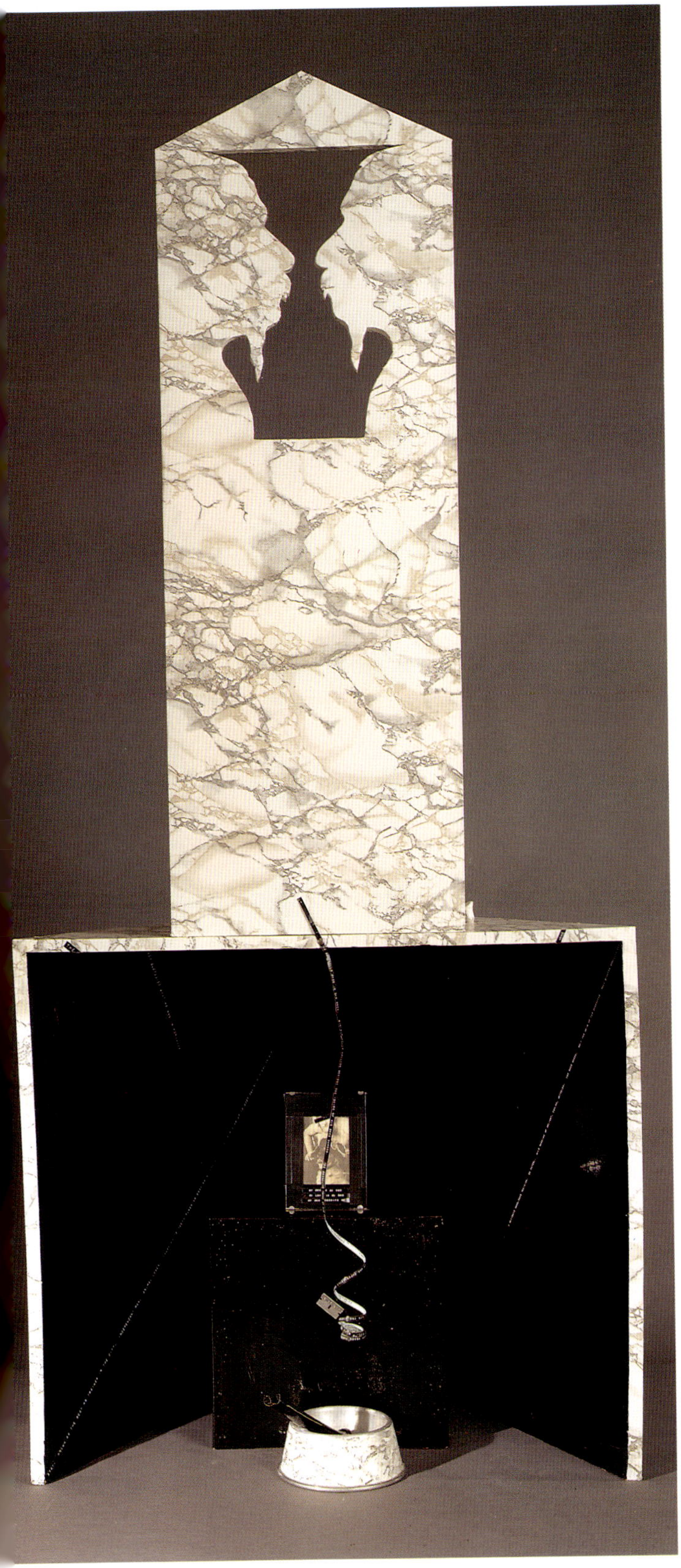

4.32 *Putting on the Dog*, 1984. Rear view

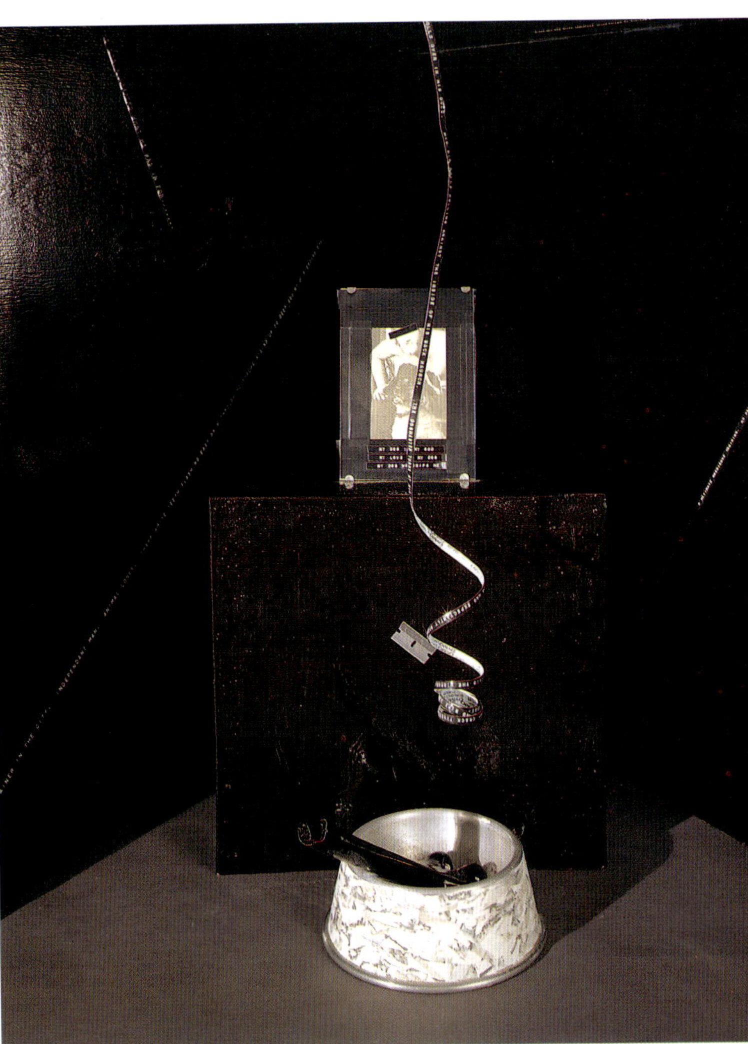

4.33 *Putting on the Dog*, 1984. Detail, rear view

remainder of his work. *Face Vase* is eighty-four inches tall and is composed of seven sections that interlock to form a triangular base mounted with a portrait head, which is flat on one side and filled out with cubist faceting on the other. Screwball forms—a ball attached to a long screw—penetrate the head, which is composed of removable sections. Inside are more balls and screws, some of which function as keys that hold the form together. On the front of the triangular base are double profiles of the artist in black—flat negative forms facing one another on a three-dimensional plinth covered with simulated gold leaf. Like the portrait head, the plinth is flat on the back side, except for a recessed niche containing a removable Rubens Vase. The inscription on the back of the vase reads:

> The face I face is a vase. The vase is my face. My face is the face vase I face. My face head is in my vase head I hold. My head is in my hand that holds my face that is in my face vase. My face knows my hand but not my head. The face I know is the face I like is the face I don't like. The face I know I know. Not knowing and knowing about me. When I think I know the face I know I know I don't know. Facing the face I don't know I face the known unknown face to face. The unknown known is reality. I fix on this unknown known reality I know. I know about it only about it. I fix my fix. And make it. Make it. Make it. Make it. Make it. Make it. Make it. Make it. Make it. Make it. Make it. Make it. Make it. Make it. Make it. Make it. Make it. Make it. Make it.

One section of the base also includes a text—word-plays about being outside and inside—printed over two interior double profiles (figs. 4.34-4.37). The inclusion of writing not only reflects Kottler's long-standing desire to incorporate titles directly into his work but also his recognition that many of his peers in painting, sculpture, and photography had begun to incorporate narrative texts in their work.

Between 1985 and 1987 Kottler executed several multicomponent sculptures incorporating words and interior landscapes. The secret interiors were introduced to provide spaces for hidden narratives and to enable an experience of revelation. In his earlier work, Kottler employed boxes and packaging to induce surprise; he also attempted to incorporate multilayered forms and signs that would extend the process of revelation in time. In his late portraits he adapted these layered presentations to address the evolution of intimacy in personal relationships.

"I don't use the idea of concealment in my work to hide myself," he said. "What I'm interested in is the process by which observers learn to see things about people that are not immediately apparent. We might assert ourselves with our dress or in communication with language, but we seldom present ourselves immediately. Our mode of living is a slow revelation of what we are about." Part of the fascination with sexual encounters, he continued, is that "during sexual scenes people are vulnerable and will often totally reveal themselves for the first time. They keep their innermost desires and feelings to themselves and stand waiting for an occasion to release them. The sexual act, properly orchestrated, gives both people an opportunity for release. It doesn't happen in ordinary conversation, when people almost never reveal their inner thoughts." Meaningful personal relationships, he concluded, "always involve extended time. Time makes it possible for two people to understand each other despite their preconceived ideas or regardless of lifestyle differences. That's important to me, and I wanted to deal with these concerns in my work."[33]

In 1988 several of Kottler's self-portraits were included in "Shattered Self: Northwest Figurative Ceramics," an exhibition mounted by writer and curator Matthew Kangas. One of the few critics who seriously explored the content of Kottler's late work, Kangas argued that his self-portraits could be interpreted "in psychoanalytical terms, chiefly as an effort to reconstitute a shattered or damaged sense of self through the act of artmaking and literally through the act of reassembling body parts into symbolic structures." According to Kangas, Kottler was a true exhibitionist who embraced

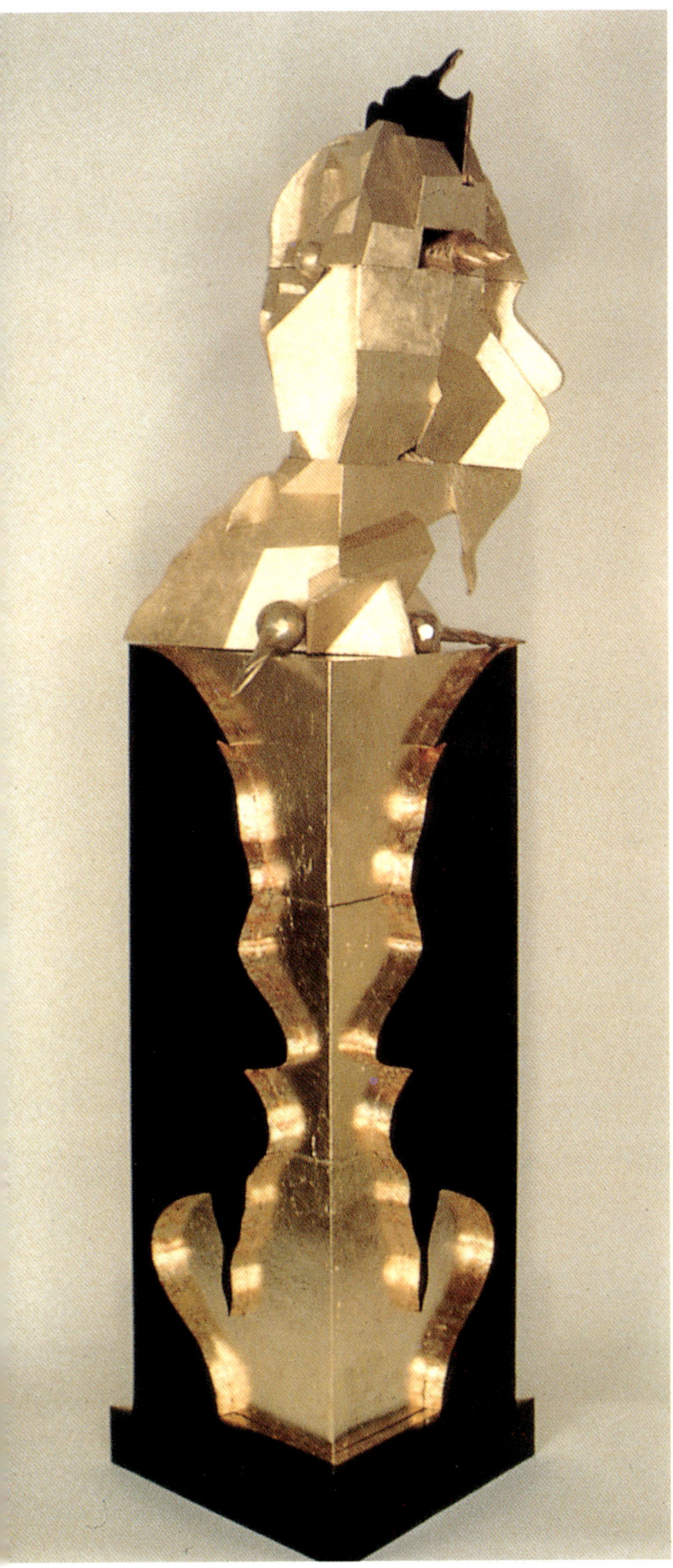

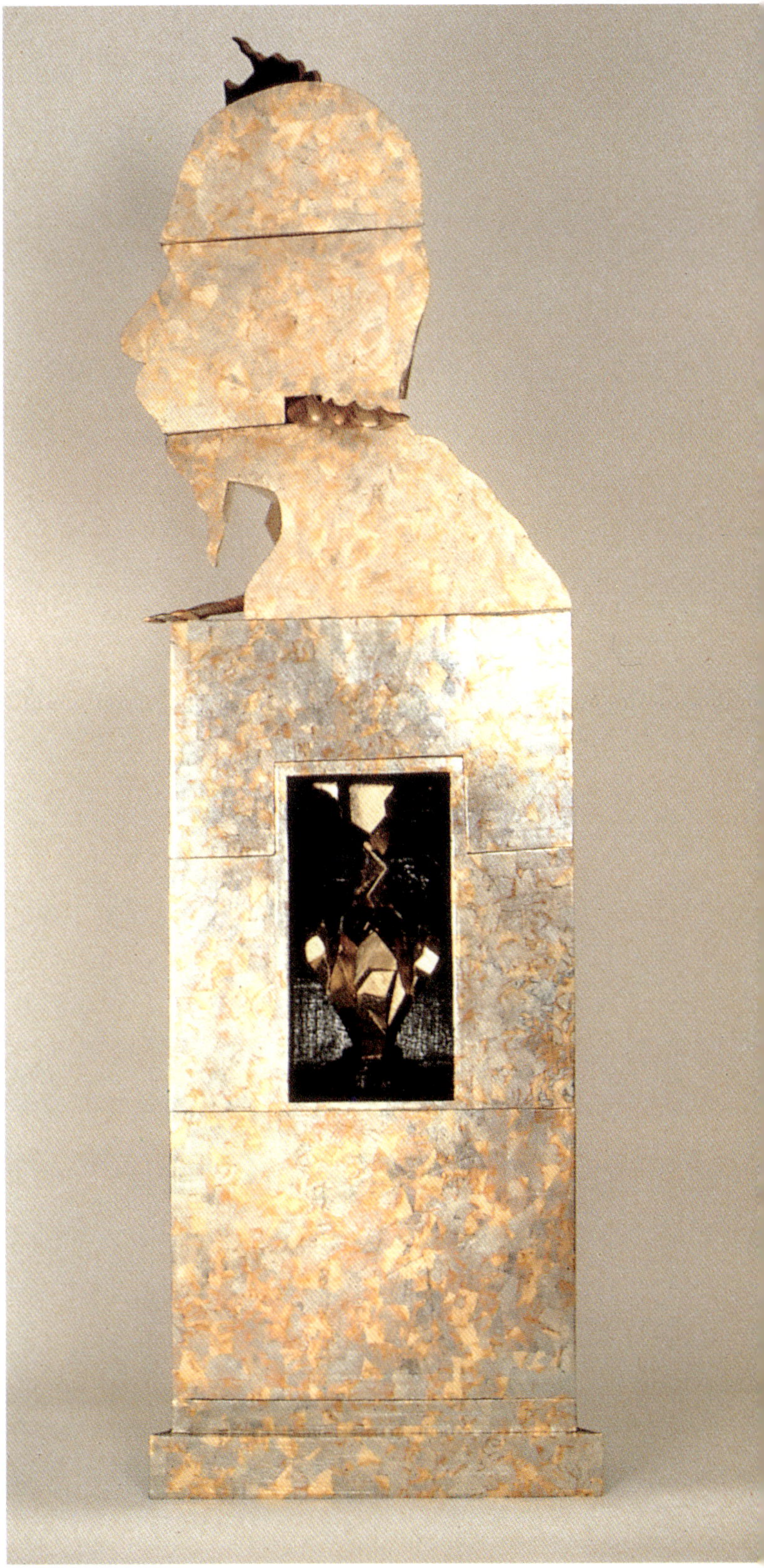

(Left) 4.34 *Face Vase*, 1985. Front view. Earthenware, 83 x 26. Collection American Craft Museum, New York. Gift of Howard Kottler Testamentary Trust; (Right) 4.35 *Face Vase*, 1985. Rear view

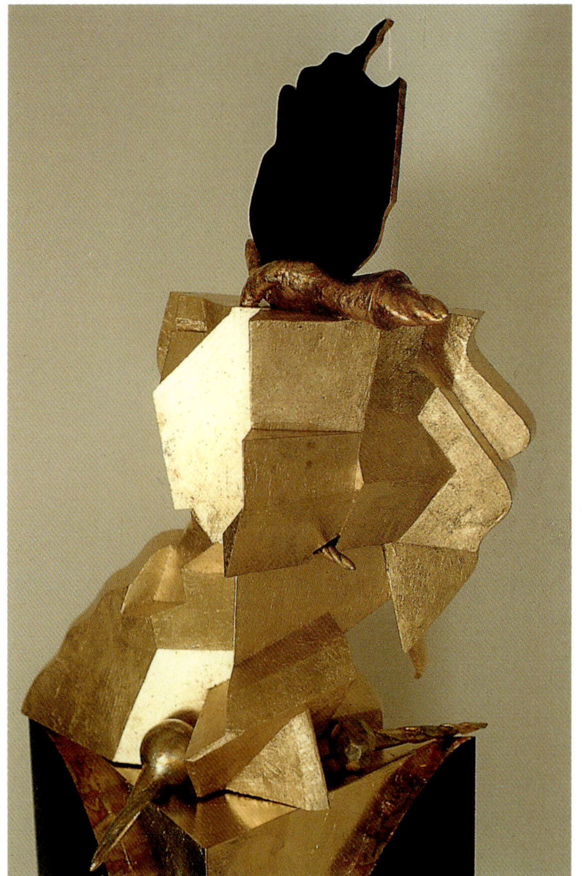

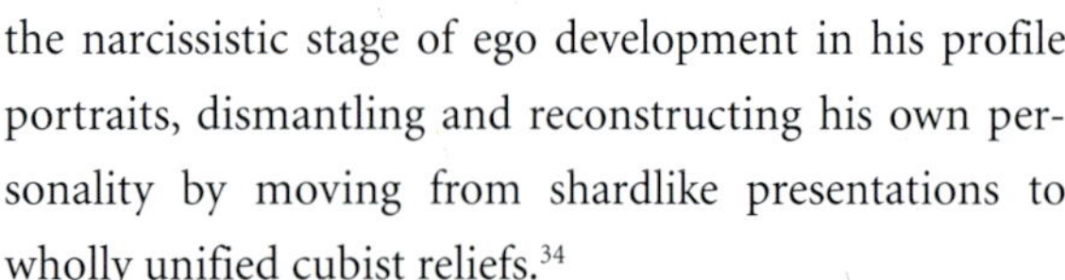

4.36 *Face Vase,* 1985. Detail, interior of head

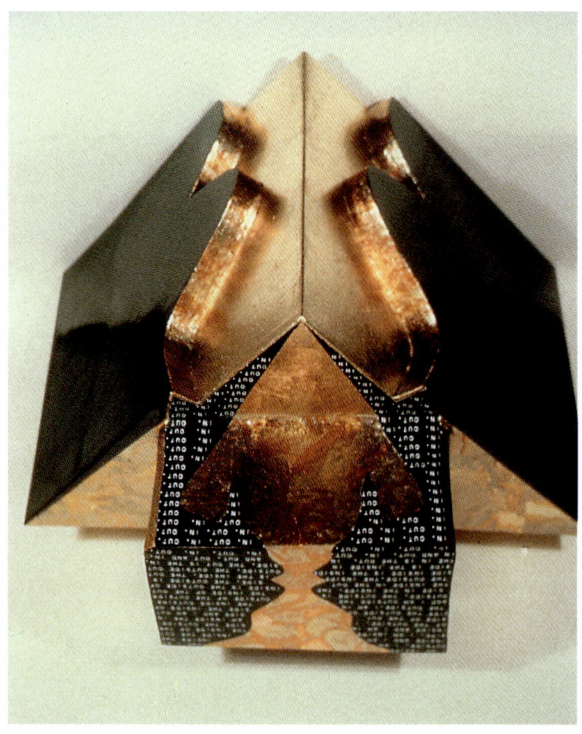

4.37 *Face Vase,* 1985. Detail, interior of base

the narcissistic stage of ego development in his profile portraits, dismantling and reconstructing his own personality by moving from shardlike presentations to wholly unified cubist reliefs.[34]

Kottler appreciated Kangas' thoughtful analysis but disputed his "shattered self" thesis. "For me, faceted forms represent the multiple personalities we all have and move back and forth between, depending on the situation," he said. "I don't think there is any kind of essential core of the self that can be shattered—there is no 'me,' but [there are] many 'me's' depending on the relationship and the situation. All the 'me's' are authentic—reality is always changing. . . . I did use gold and silver lusters to visually shatter or dematerialize the forms," he added, "but I think the conclusion that these techniques symbolize a shattering of the self is just not supported by the work."[35]

Comparing Kottler's self-portraits with those of Robert Arneson, however, it is clear that Kangas was responding to an elusiveness and lack of closure which distinguishes Kottler's oblique approach to images of the self. The relationship between his own self-portraits and Arneson's was a significant issue for Kottler, as he indicated in *Hallowed Gesture* (1987), an homage to Arneson's 1971 self-portrait, *A Hollow Jesture* (figs. 4.38-4.40).[36] In Arneson's veristic portrait, the physical strain and tension required to stick out one's tongue is vividly rendered, underlining the artist's own humorous response to art-world pretense. Kottler, by contrast, presents himself in an expressionistically distorted profile, built up on one side with large, faceted fire-engine-red cubes of clay. The back side, the "dark side," is black and completely flat. Projecting from the open mouth is a triangular projection pointed like a saber, an allusion to the sarcastic "devil tongue" with which he skewered his friends and also traditional ceramists. ("My sarcasm throws people off guard, so they sometimes reveal things about themselves they wouldn't divulge ordinarily," Kottler said. "And I have to be on my toes with a snappy reply."[37]) Kottler's tongue is an erotic organ, too, as well as a slightly absurd anatomical protuberance.

Kottler's homage to Arneson also comments upon the similarities and differences between his and Arneson's historical profiles. In their work and teaching, both artists were known for speaking out against the prescriptions of academic ceramics, and each used the self-portrait as an extended venue for art-historical commentary. Compared with Arneson's direct, frontal assault, however, Kottler's visual discourse is more indirect and his humor more ironic and cerebral. Both images are highly theatrical, but Kottler's is more elusive and paradoxical, befitting his involvement with gay culture as well as his unsettled standing in the field of contemporary ceramics. The two portraits contrast on other levels as well. Arneson's *A Hollow Jesture* is a fully realized physical surrogate. This holistic clone is also a clown, mugging for the back row; the gesture is an accessible, unambiguous, and confident display of body language. According to critic Donald Kuspit, Arneson's self-portraits indicate that he is "playing with a firm sense of self rather than playacting as a self." Searching for "a public style with carrying power," he says, Arneson created figures that "can be experienced as autonomous subjects."[38]

In *Hallowed Gesture* and many other self-portraits, Kottler represents himself with profile silhouettes, shadows, and faceted reflections. These two-dimensional forms apparently refer to a three-dimensional, noumenal being who is "out there" in a world never directly represented in his sculptures. When Arneson began including text in his portraits, he inscribed messages on a base that functioned like a kiosk, an open public forum. In Kottler's portraits, by contrast, the narrative is often concealed within the interior of the form, and is revealed slowly and cautiously. One writer characterizes gay life in America as "a capacity to hide in the mass of life and show passions behind a scrim or in the shade,"[39] a

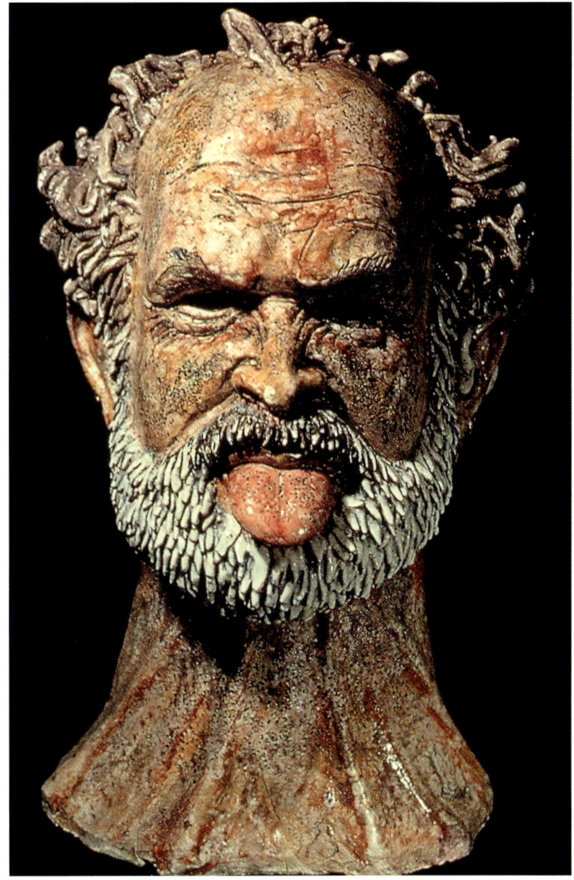

4.38 Robert Arneson, *A Hollow Jesture*, 1971. Earthenware, 20¼ h

lifestyle description that parallels Kottler's approach to this genre of his work.

Kottler also reverses inner and outer modes of appearance by referring to himself almost exclusively with flat or abstract images of the head, that is, with allusions to the mental or conceptual dimensions of being. References to the physical form of the body below the neck are usually concealed inside his sculpture, where they must be revealed by a symbolic "undressing." In the few sculptures that openly display body parts other than the head, the anatomy is dematerialized, parodied, or dislocated. In *Trilogy*, for example, the head from *Hallowed Gesture*, an eye, and a hand are each recessed into one side of a black triangular block. The refracted anatomical forms are covered with shiny gold lusters, reflecting both each other and the ambient light. As a result, the images shift elusively between negative and positive space, their

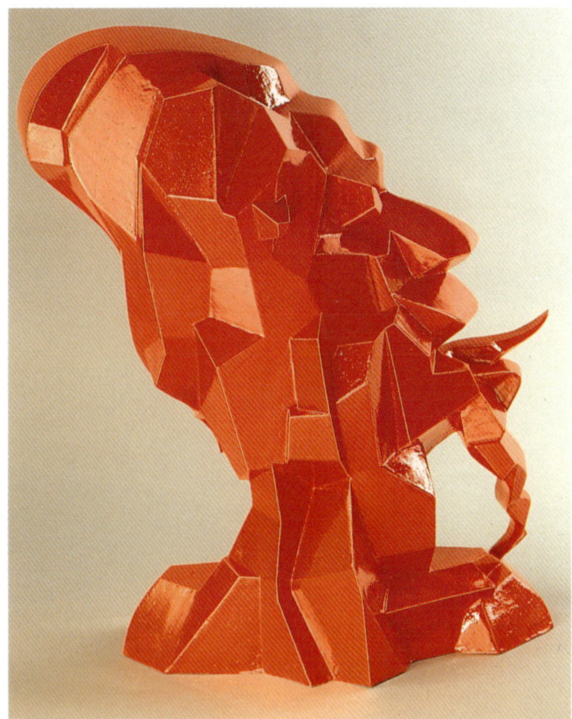

4.39 *Hallowed Jesture,* 1987. Earthenware, 28 h

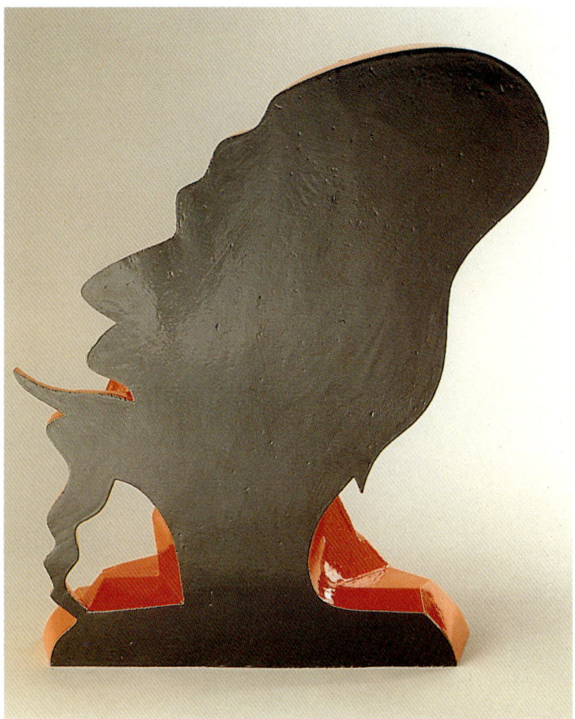

4.40 *Hallowed Jesture,* 1987. Rear view

physicality dissolved in optical illusion. The faceted eye in *Trilogy* stands in for the entire face in *Kottler Posing As a Cubist*; the poseur's torso, in turn, parodies the ball-and-shaft vases of the early 1980s (figs. 4.41, 4.42). *Bent* (1986) combines a volumetric, cubist portrait head with a flat two-faced portrait silhouette. A three-dimensional hand emerges from the top of the cubist cranium, loosely gripping the plastic tubing that binds the two heads together (figs. 4.43, 4.44). The dislocated hand projecting from the brain reads as a mental image, suggesting a preoccupation that unifies the two faces.

This preoccupation informs many of Kottler's late sculptures, and represents one of the clear lines of demarcation between his work and the production of his peers. *Bent* is about bondage and the psychodynamics of submission and control, especially within the context, as the title suggests, of a gay relationship. The dynamic tension Kottler represents in this figure calls to mind Jean Genet's play, *The Maids.* "I feel that a person being dominated knows exactly what he wants to have happen to him," Kottler observed. "In many cases the slave has more

of a sense of self-identity than the master. In every relationship, one person is bound to dominate the other, and yet who is really in control? There is always a flow of energy back and forth, and I tried to indicate that with the tubing that loops between the two." In *Bent,* he continued, "I wanted to show two kinds of personalities in the same piece. Each head has a dark side covered in dark formica, and a light side done in wood-grain contact paper. The tubing is covered with contact paper too. The title has a sexual reference, but it also refers to bent wood—you could do this piece in wood, but the contact paper was simpler."[40] In a 1986 statement, Kottler explained that his recent work was "about materials and not about materials. All the work uses clay as the primary building material, but the medium is not always the message. It is about material seen and materials unseen. It is about materials that are real, and materials that are fake. Our culture is obsessed with a desire for the real thing, but we often settle for what is fake—both with things as well as in relationships with others."[41]

Dominance and submission are also thematic in

Devil Walk (1986), a two-sided self-portrait, ninety inches high, flat on one side and elaborated on the other with a totem pole of faces made from cubist planes. This red-devil man is walking a bright blue double-faced dog's head. The dog's eyes and snout also appear on the devil's multifaceted façade (figs. 4.45, 4.46), and the dog's head, based on one of the Japanese novelty figurines in Kottler's collection, can be pulled apart in sections to reveal the artist's silhouette. A spiraling yellow leash encircles the devil's head and neck, suggesting uncertainty about who controls whom.

Devil Walk elaborates several themes introduced two years earlier in *Putting on the Dog*—the animal facets of the human personality, relationships between master and pet, and dogs as human surrogates. These topics were also explored in several remarkable sculptures ex-

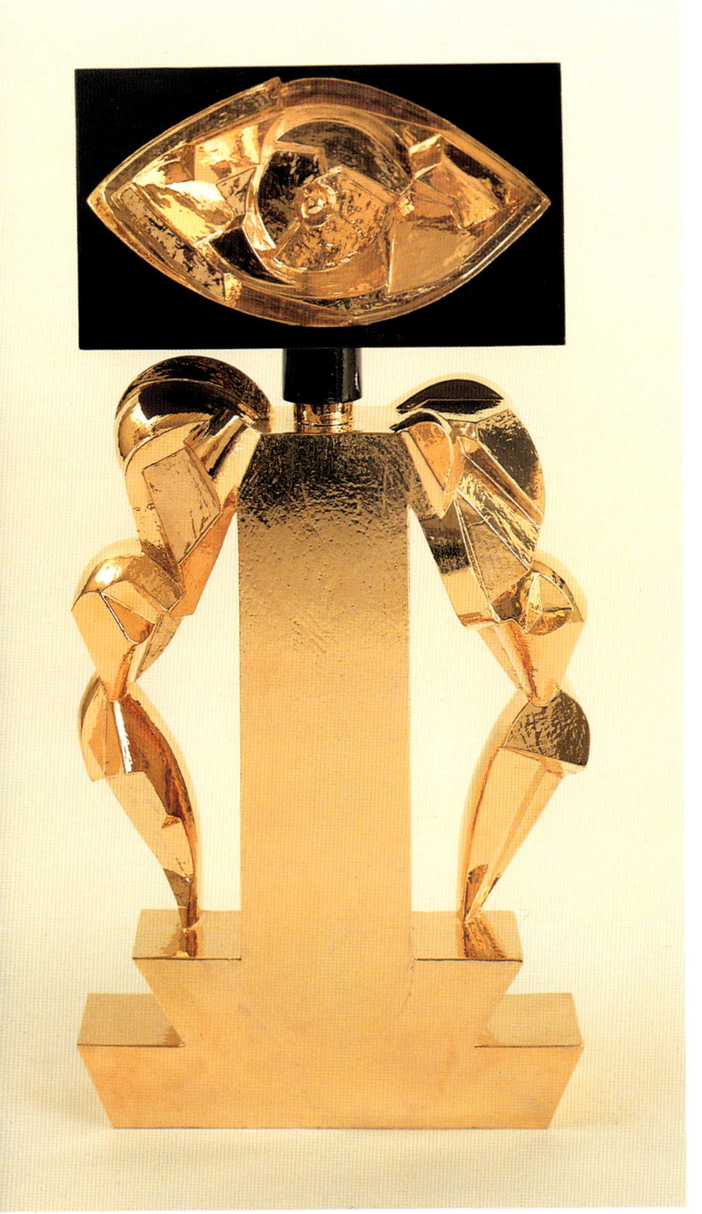

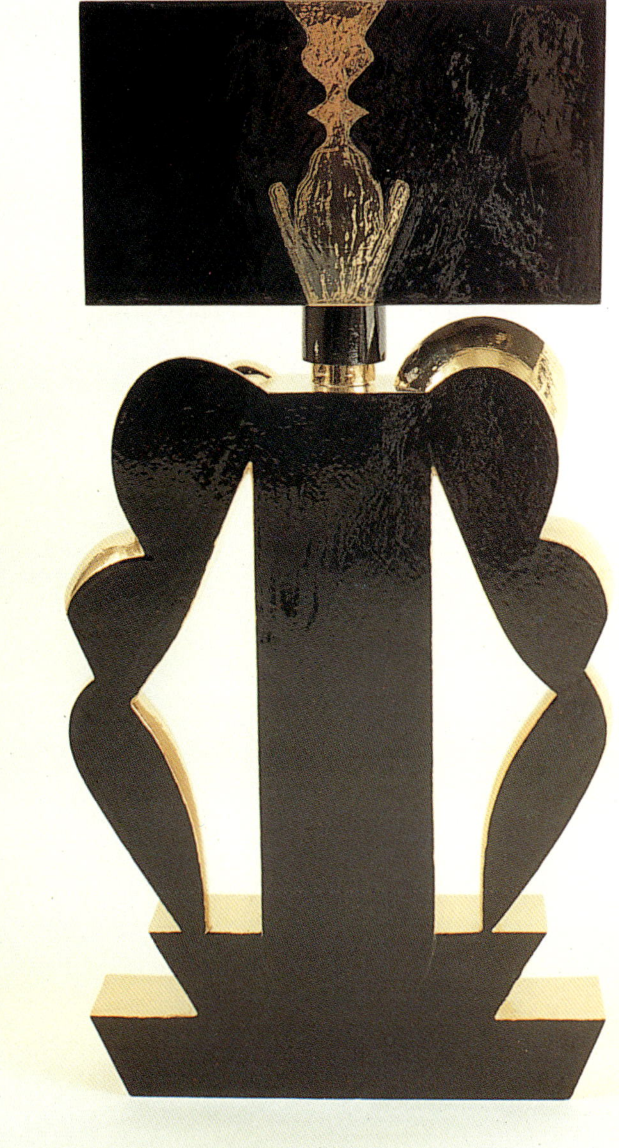

(Left) 4.41 *Kottler Posing as a Cubist*, 1987. Whiteware, 33½ x 16½. Collection Seattle Art Museum. Gift of Anne Gould Hauberg; (Right) 4.42 *Kottler Posing as a Cubist*, 1987. Rear view

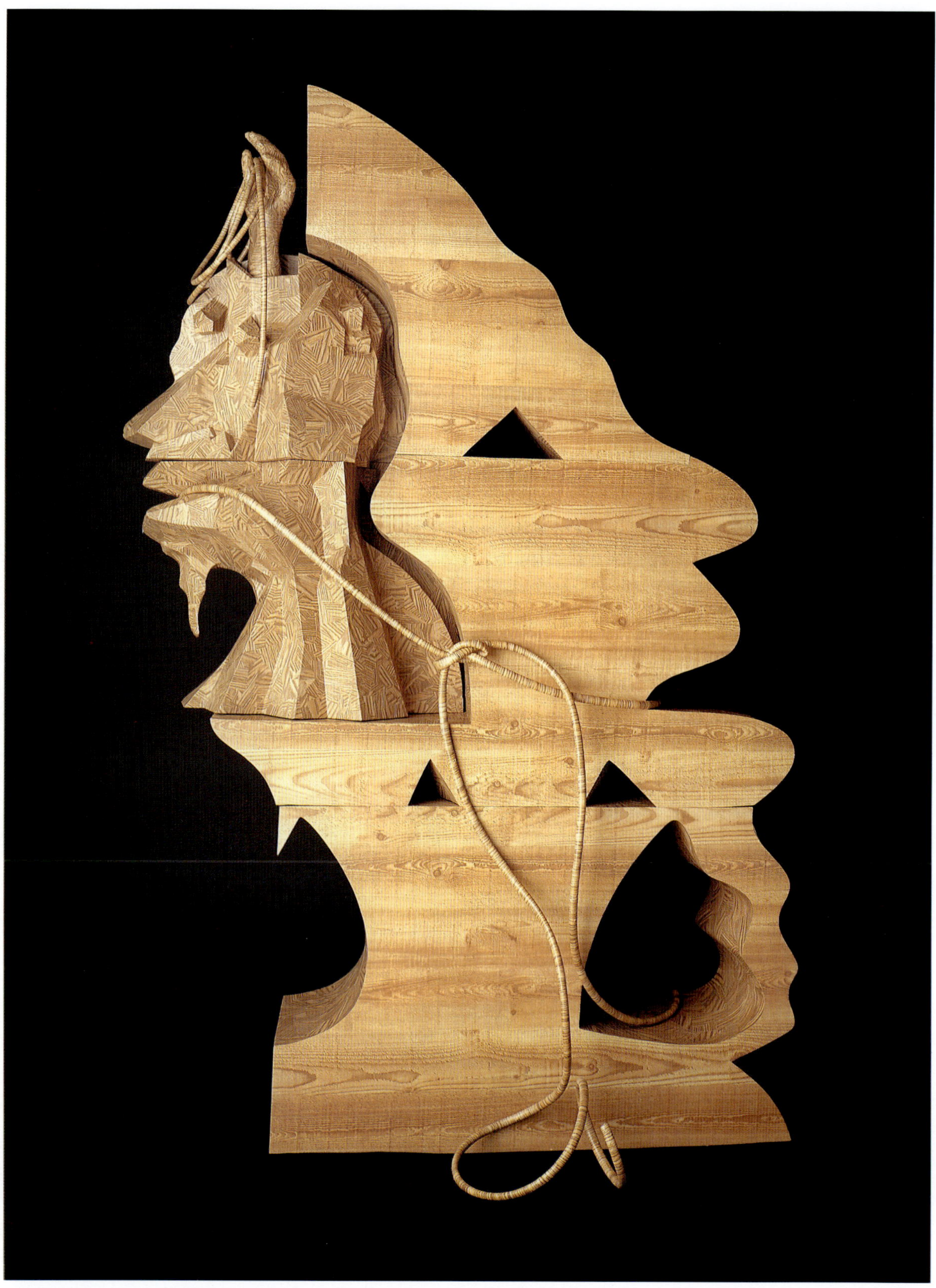

4.43 *Bent,* 1986. Mixed media, 69 x 39

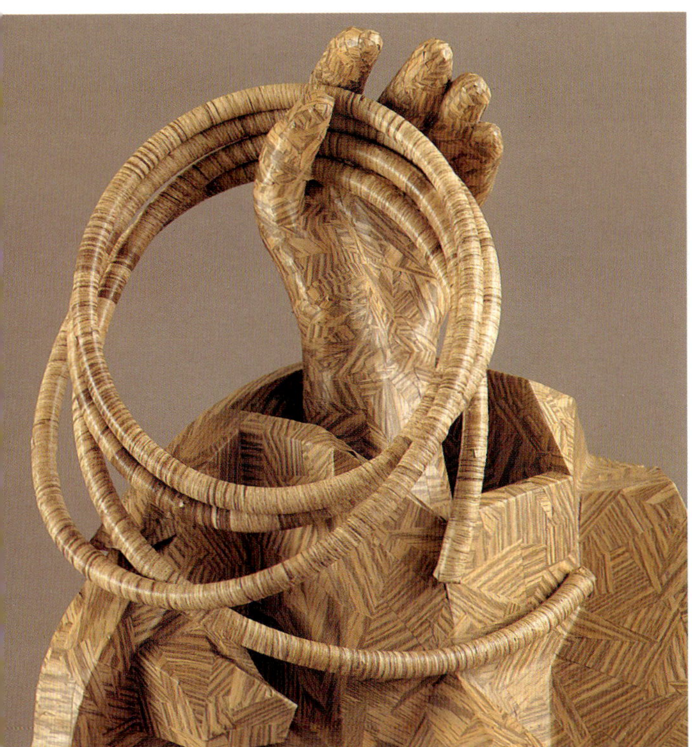

4.44 *Bent,* 1986. Detail

ecuted in 1986 and 1987 which re-present animal figurines from Kottler's collection of 1920s knickknacks. *Waiting for Master,* for example, is based on a geometrized dog figurine with ears transformed into big green leaves (figs. 4.47, 4.48). "I wanted to see what would happen if I took a kitsch object and glorified it by blowing up the scale and changing the surface," Kottler said. "I put the dog in its proper art-historical context by resting it on a little cubist landscape. Then I covered the surface with simulated gold leaf so there is no reference to clay—the base material is irrelevant. On one level the sculpture is about fine art and kitsch and how that relationship can be shifted."[42]

Physical clues on the exterior of *Waiting for Master,* however, suggest other strata of meaning. The body is clearly divided into three sections, the top one accented by the fingers of a black hand that slices through the animal's neck. Lifting up the head of the figure, the full form of the master's hand is revealed. Removing the middle section exposes the dog's dream in the form of an

interior landscape. The reclining Hellenistic goddess in Giorgio de Chirico's *The Soothsayer's Recompense* reappears here as a dog on a pedestal contemplating a strongly foreshortened building. An attached written message reads, "Waiting for master is waiting for life." The references to alchemy in the simulated gold surface and in the circulation of visual signs moving from high art to low have analogues, according to Kottler, in the paradoxical dynamics of human relationships (figs. 4.49, 4.50). "We're all in attendance on someone," he observed, "whether it's a master waiting for a dog to come home, or a husband waiting for a wife, even if the husband is the dominant figure. Our pets control us, just as we control them."[43]

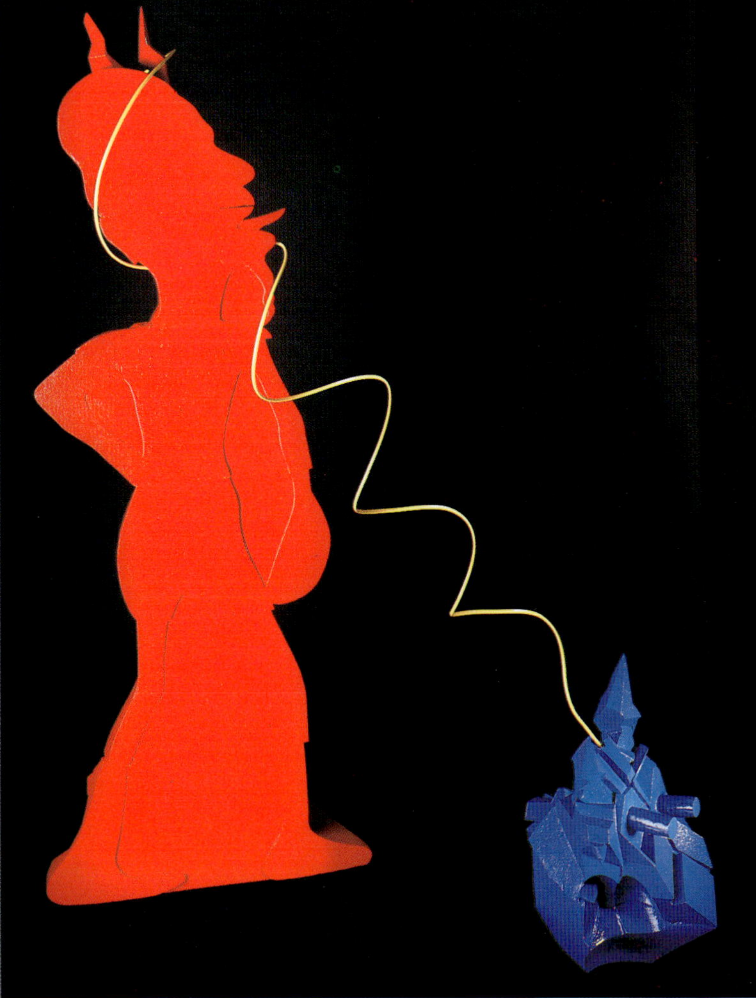

4.45 *Devil Walk,* 1986. Mixed media, 90 x 62

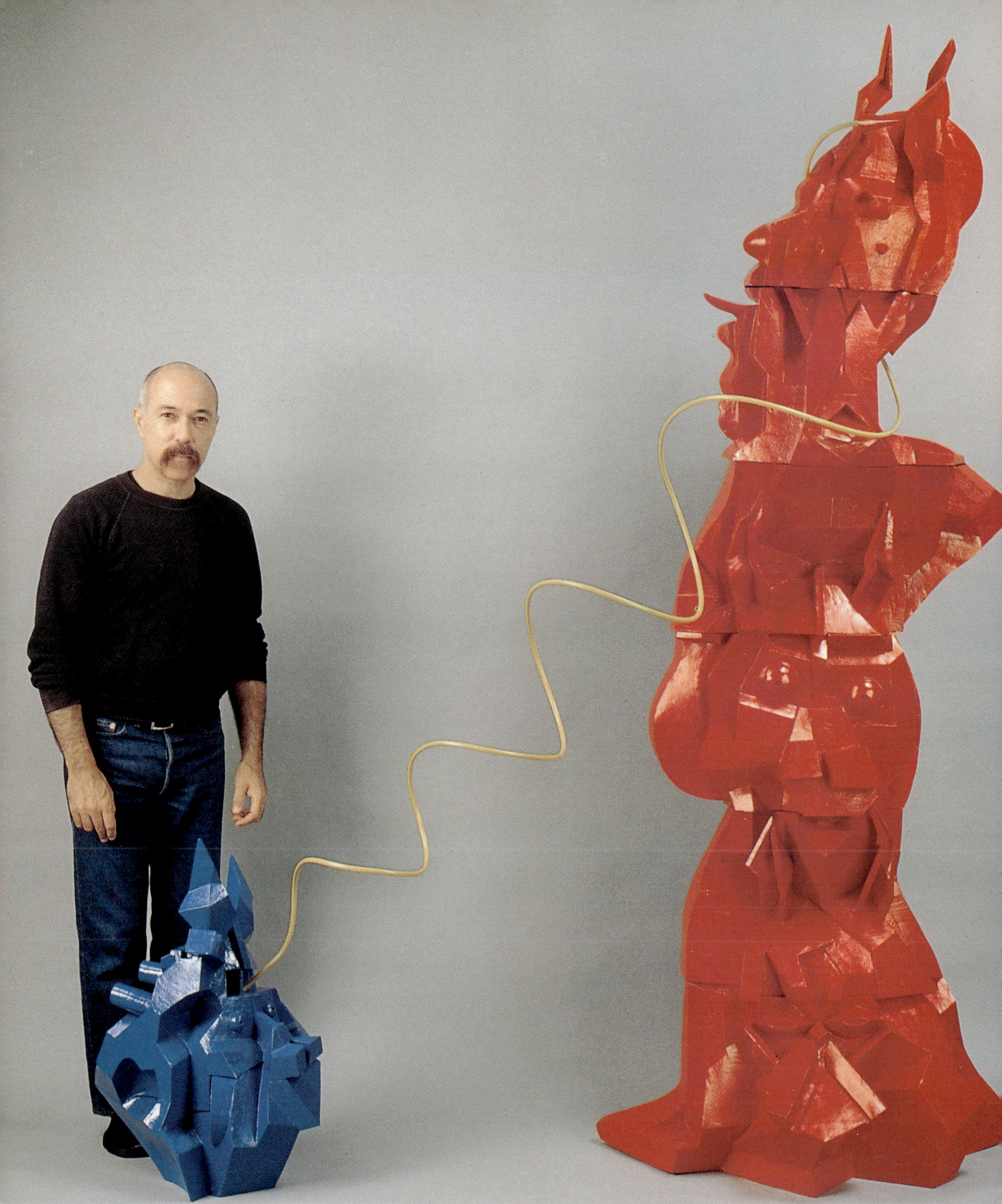

4.46 Kottler with *Devil Walk*, 1987

A similar conflation of art-historical commentary and sexual politics inspired *Screwball* (1986), a dog portrait also derived from a cubist-styled 1920s knickknack (fig. 4.51). Apparently howling at the moon, the cubistic canine is tethered to the same large screwball form introduced a year earlier in *Face Vase*. Covered with a façade of marble contact paper, the dog amplifies its howl with a long rippling tongue. "You can read this image in a variety of ways," Kottler said. "Is the screwball tugging away at the dog and opening its mouth? Is it howling because its sexual needs are being repressed?"[44] These questions remain even when one penetrates the dog's interior by dismantling the separate sections of its anatomy: inside are three-dimensional representations of a blue human penis and testicles and a stylized phallic core (figs. 4.52-4.54). These phallic forms are the keys, literally and metaphorically, that hold the body together.

In several respects Kottler's re-presentations of manufactured ceramic art in his dog sculptures presage the work of sculptor Jeff Koons, who hired Italian craftsmen to enlarge mass-produced ceramic novelty figurines. When Koons's garish relics were first exhibited in New York in 1988, several critics interpreted the work as a trenchant but cynical exposé of art-world commercialism and the declining myth of artistic originality.[45] Kottler's enlarged figurines, in contrast, offer more complex levels of commentary. In his work, the appropriation of cubism by industrial designers of the 1920s and its reclamation by a high-art ceramist of the 1980s is only the outermost edge of several concentric rings of meaning. At the center are Kottler's conclusions about the situational definition of master and slave, high art and kitsch, owner and pet, animal and human, reality and falsehood. His extensive research on the history of Noritake provided a theoretical preface for many of these observations, and must be credited as an oblique but pervasive influence in his late work.

One category of Kottler's canine sculpture, however, more closely parallels Koons's ceramics: the dog-in-ashtray series. In these sculptures Kottler enlarges 1920s ashtray figurines to heights of two or three feet.[46] With this shift in scale, the cute little creatures and the innocu-

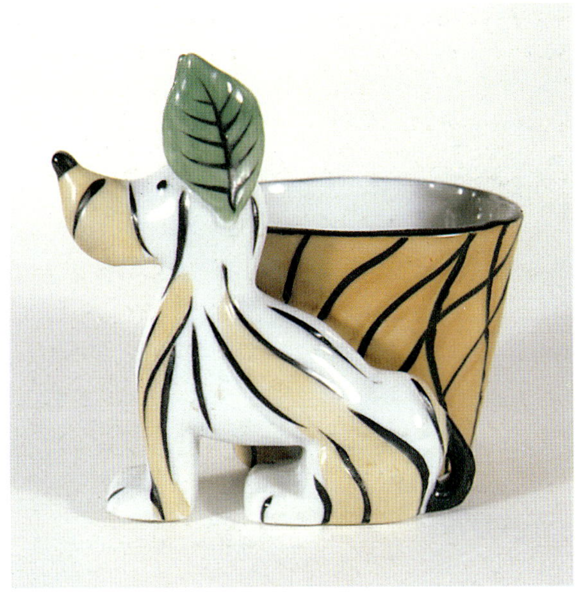

4.47 Japanese figurine, 1920s, prototype for *Waiting for Master*

ous ashtrays become strikingly ominous and absurd (figs. 4.55-4.57). Yet even these enlarged figures lack the confrontational cynicism that characterizes Koons's appropriations. They reflect another sensibility, perhaps best described in Susan Sontag's well-known 1964 essay, "Notes on Camp."[47] Camp taste, writes Sontag, is "above all a mode of enjoyment, of appreciation—not judgment. Camp is generous. It wants to enjoy. It only seems like malice, cynicism. (Or if it is cynicism, it is not a ruthless, but a sweet cynicism)." The experiences of Camp, she continues, "are based on the great discovery that the sensibility of high culture has no monopoly on refinement. Camp asserts that good taste is not simply bad taste; that there exists, indeed, a good taste of bad taste. . . . This discovery is very liberating." The ultimate point of Camp, she adds, is to "dethrone the serious. Camp is playful, anti-serious. More precisely, Camp involves a new, more complex reaction to 'the serious.'"

Comparing Pop Art with Camp, Sontag articulates some of the differences between Kottler and Koons. Pop Art embodies an attitude that is related to Camp, she observes, but it is still very different. Pop Art [like Koons's work] "is more flat and more dry, more serious, more detached, ultimately nihilistic." Sontag also emphasizes

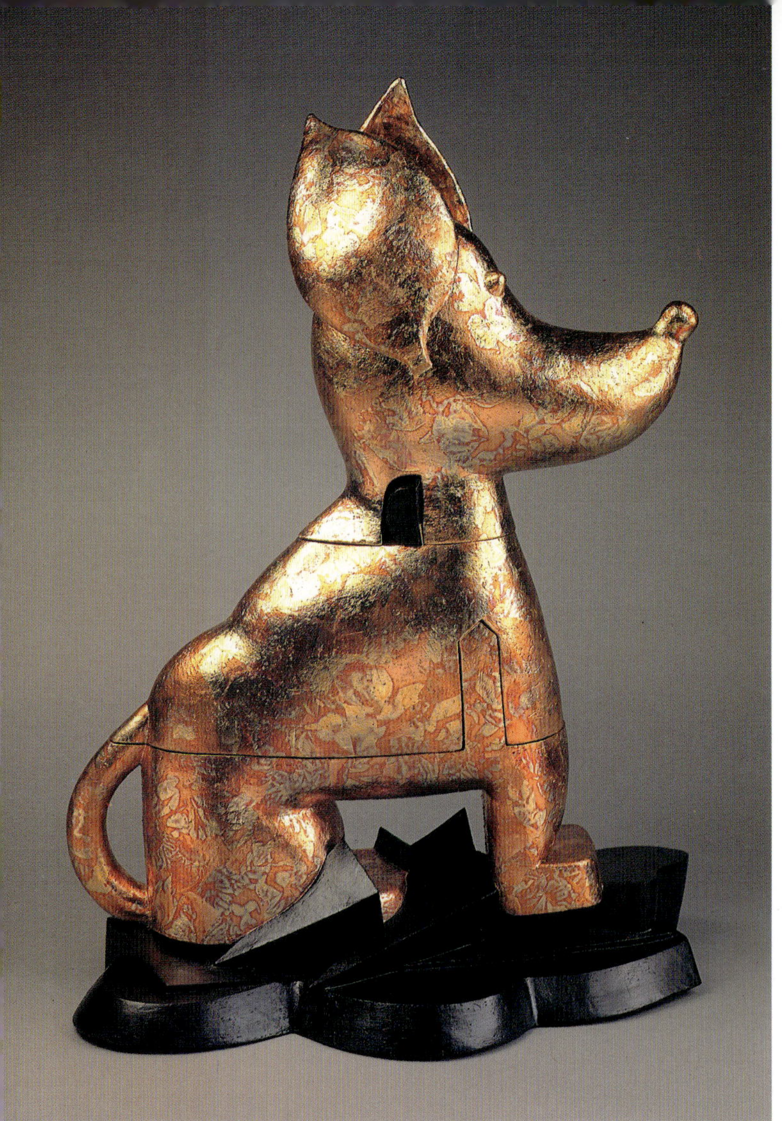

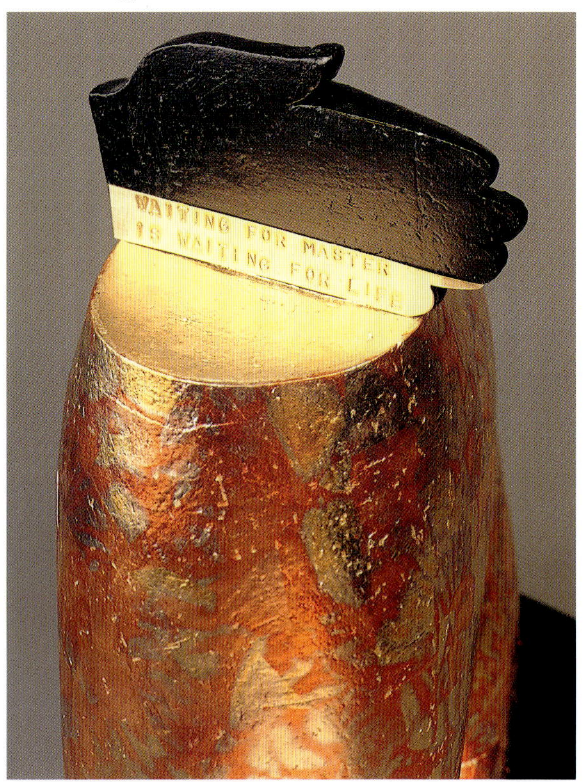

4.48 *Waiting for Master*, 1986. Earthenware, 38 x 26½. Collection National Museum of American Art, Smithsonian Institution. Bequest of the artist

4.49 *Waiting for Master*, l986. Detail, interior section

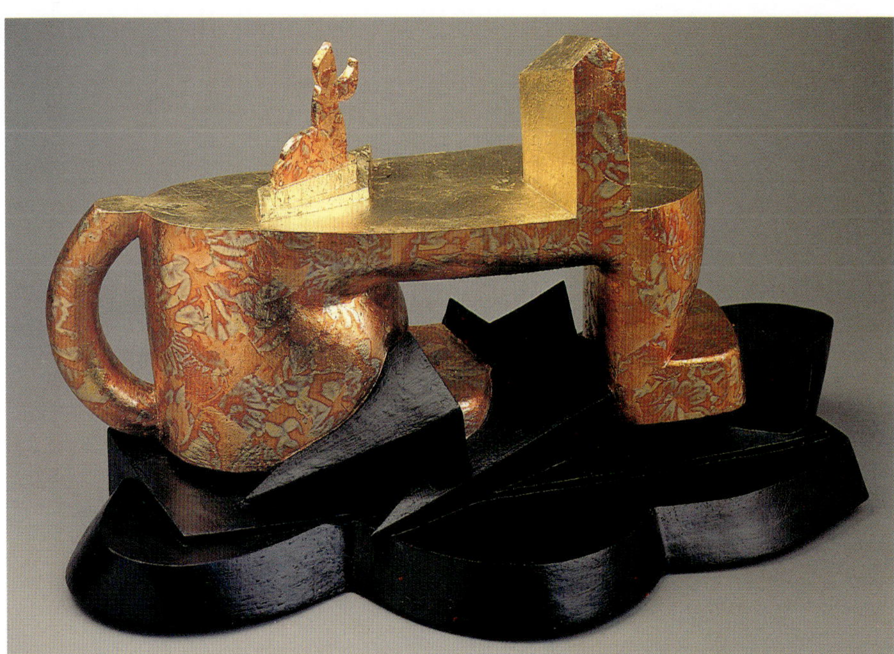

4.50 *Waiting for Master*, 1986. Detail, interior section

the special relationship between Camp taste and gay culture.

> While it's not true that Camp taste is homosexual taste, there is no doubt a peculiar affinity and overlap. Not all liberals are Jews, but Jews have shown a peculiar affinity for liberal and reformist causes. So, not all homosexuals have Camp taste. But homosexuals, by and large, constitute the vanguard—and most articulate audience of Camp. (The analogy is not frivolously chosen. Jews and homosexuals are the two outstanding creative minorities in contemporary western culture. Creative, that is, in the truest sense: they are the creators of sensibilities.) The two pioneering forces of modern sensibility are Jewish moral seriousness and homosexual aestheticism and irony.[48]

Kottler's pattern of artistic development reflects aestheticism and irony more than moral seriousness, yet compared with Koons, his work is informed by a certain courageousness derived from, as Kottler put it, laying more and more of himself on the line. According to several of his friends, he was never entirely comfortable with his identity as an acknowledged homosexual, yet he refused to be equivocal about his allegiances to gay culture. From the time he began to find his own voice in the mid-1960s, he frequently approached ceramics as a medium for doublespeak, utilizing physical materials with increasing sophistication to reveal his feelings about the operations of human desire within the daily disguises of a multifaceted personality. Kottler was correctly characterized as a "supermannerist" and "slick comedian," but he was also a political commentator in the decal plates, a neo-Surrealist in *Bushel and a Peck* and *Knotty Pine*, a Duchampian conceptualist in the word sculptures, a subtle expressionist in portraits such as *Bent*, and a postmodern explorer in his late sculptures. The multifaceted self he laid on the line in his work, furthermore, was often presented under the guise of Camp, a form of dandyism in the age of mass culture which finds pleasure, as Sontag indicates, in the arts of the masses, in

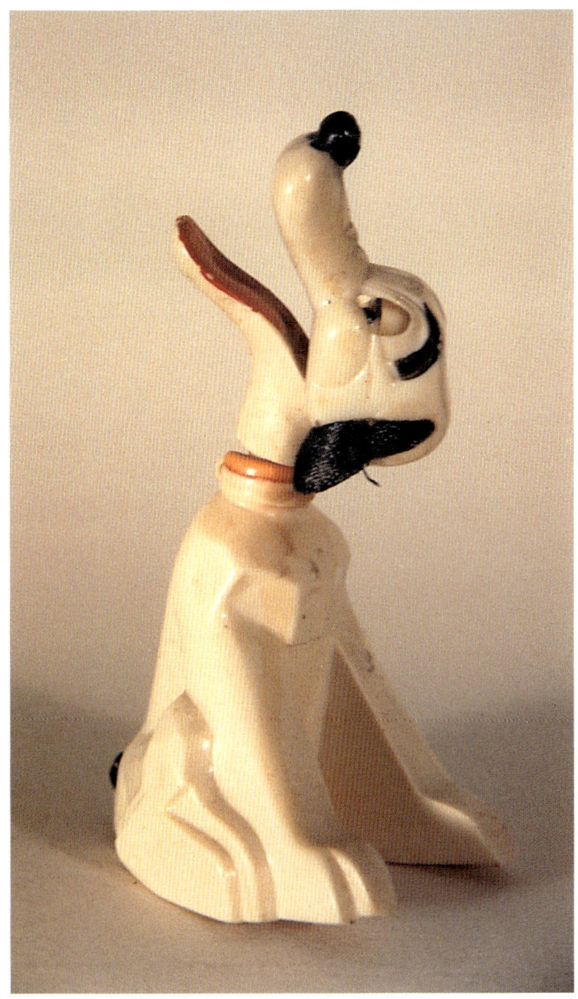

4.51 Japanese figurine, 1920s, prototype for *Screwball*

things-being-what-they-are-not, in seriousness that fails, in the theatricalization of ordinary experience, and in the tongue-in-cheek affection that produces art forms such as the Busby Berkeley musical.

The distinctions that can be drawn between Kottler's achievements and those of other artists involved with related forms of ironic connoisseurship were not sorted out during his lifetime, however. Early in 1987 LaMar Harrington mounted a major exhibition of Kottler's new work at the Bellevue Art Museum, along with selections from his Noritake collection.[49] Included were the ball-and-shaft vases, large-scale portrait sculptures such as *Bent* and *Devil Walk*, and multicomponent dog figures such as *Waiting for Master* and *Screwball*. Local reviewers were generally appreciative but addressed the

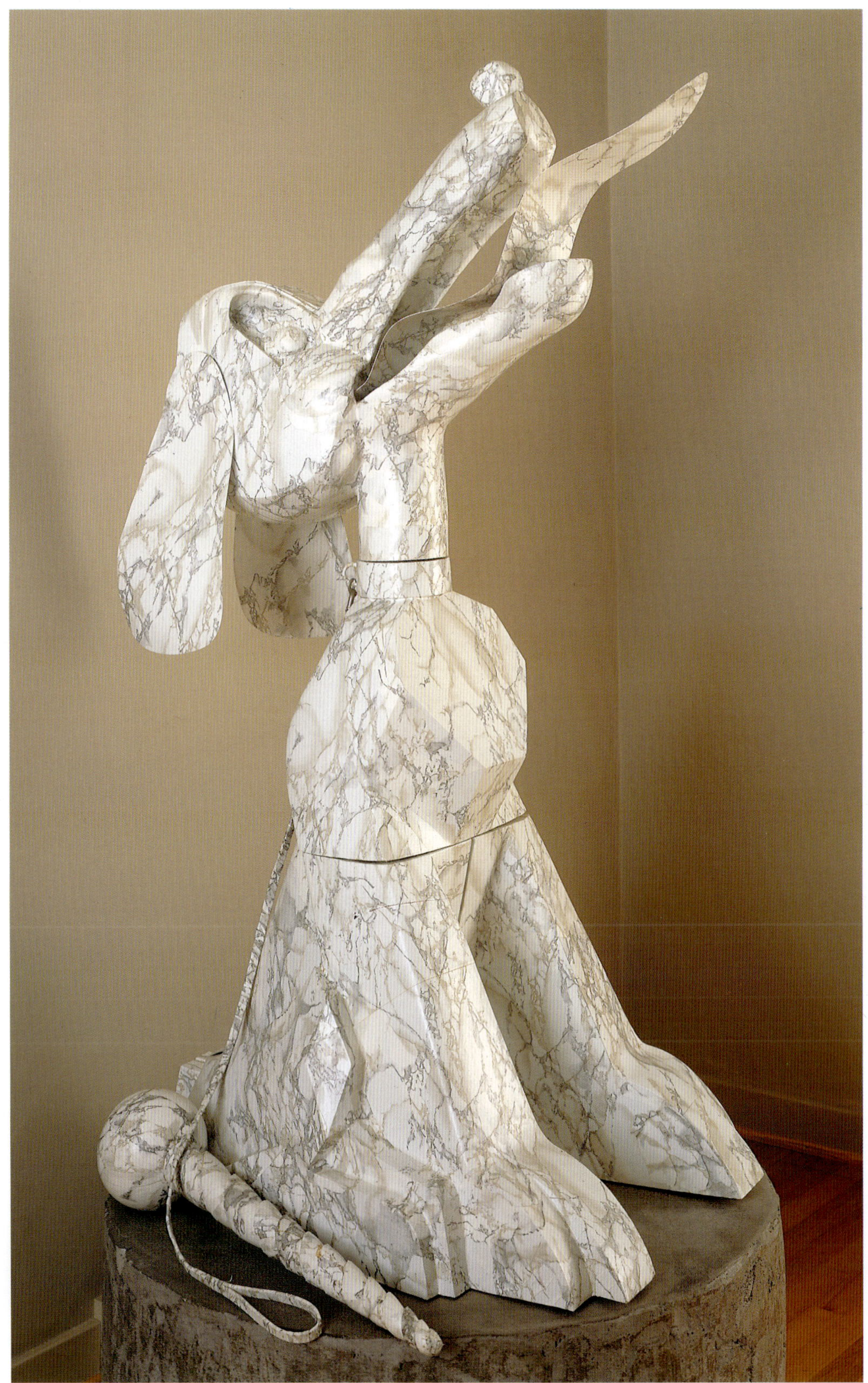

4.52 *Screwball*, 1986. Mixed media, 58 x 40

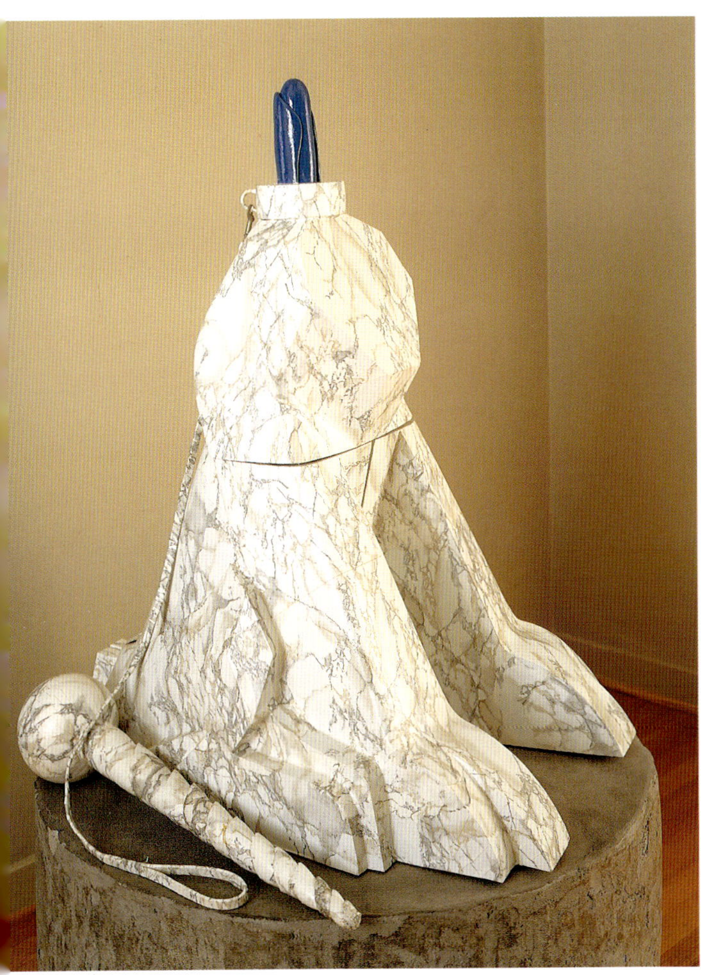

4.53 *Screwball*, 1986. Detail, interior section

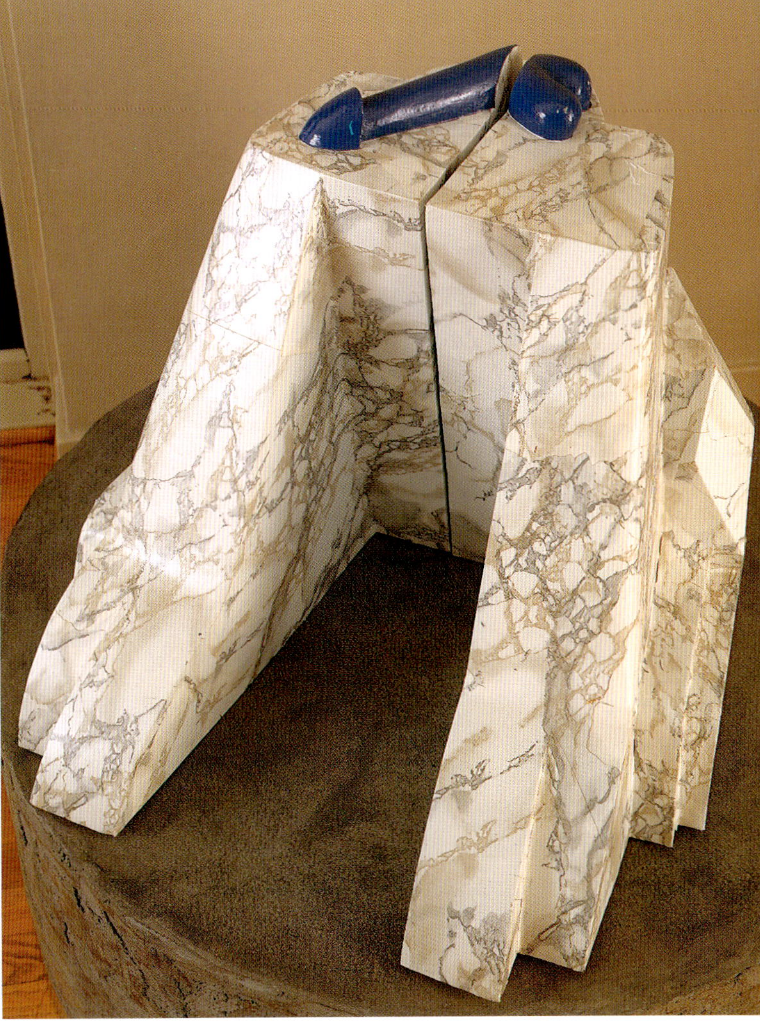

4.54 *Screwball*, 1986. Detail, interior section

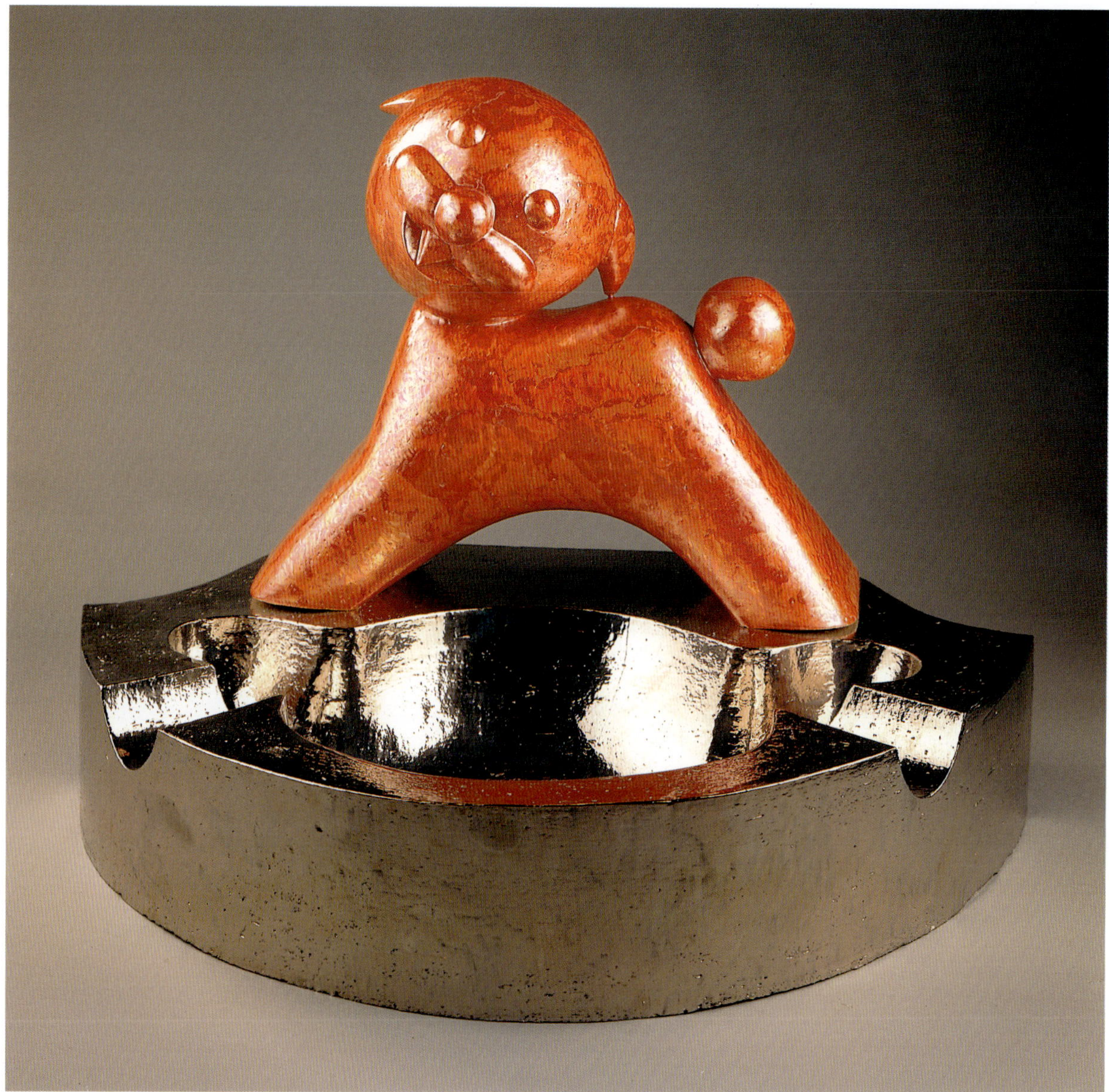

4.55 *Cute Kal,* 1984-89. Earthenware, 24½ x 33.Collection Seattle Art Museum. Gift of Howard Kottler Testamentary Trust

work primarily as the "pun-filled phallic humor" of a notorious prankster. Even Matthew Kangas, often a perceptive critic of Kottler's work, was less than enthusiastic about the canine figures and did not mention their secret interiors. The dogs seem to "push the conceit of the giant knickknack too far," he wrote. "If it is a lightweight, trivial image to begin with, why compound the error by making it literally heavyweight and big?"[50] The most insightful review of the show was not published. In a handwritten note on the bottom of a museum form letter,

Harrington wrote, "Howard—your show has meant many things on many levels we will not fully understand for a long time."

After early 1988, when he learned that he was afflicted with inoperable lung cancer, which may have been caused by long exposure to toxic art materials, Howard Kottler spent little time in the studio. But he conferred frequently with his assistant Dan Neish, who continued to execute a number of works in progress, including several vases and sculptures that were finished posthu-

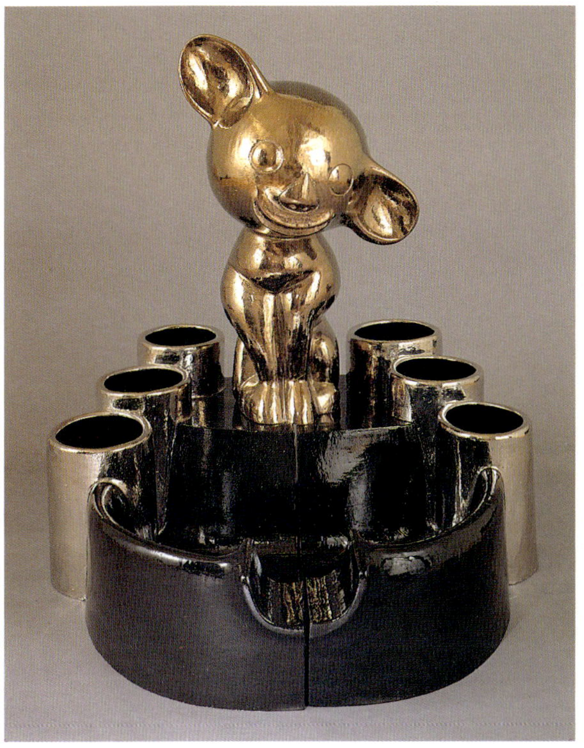

4.56 *Spot*, 1984-89. Earthenware, 35½ x 31½

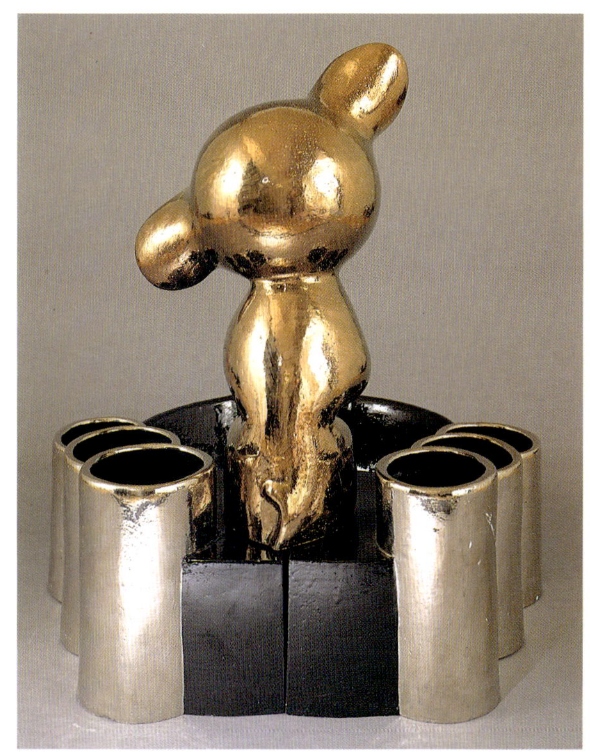

4.57 *Spot*, 1984-89. Rear view

mously. Among these were self-portraits in the form of horizontal cubist landscapes, such as *Baroque Braque* and *Northwest Braque*, and dog-in-ashtray sculptures and portrait heads containing inner landscapes, such as *Kottler's Picasso* and *Legacy*.

In these compositions, as well as in other sculptures of the 1980s, Kottler was working toward a witty and sometimes poignant synthesis of postmodern irony, robust theatricality, and nuanced expressionism. He was in full command of his artistic resources, like a clipper ship, all sails set, heading majestically out to sea. All the new beachheads he might have established for ceramics, however, would undoubtedly have been shaded by the witty hedonism and affectionate good humor of Camp, for as Sontag has observed, "Camp taste is a kind of love, love for human nature. . . . Camp taste identifies with what it is enjoying." In her estimation, those who share this sensibility, as Howard Kottler surely did to a significant degree, "are not laughing at the thing they label as 'Camp'—they are enjoying it. Camp is a *tender* feeling."

Notes

1: Early Years in Ohio

1. Howard Kottler, interview with author, January 4, 1988.

2. Howard Kottler, "The Search for Noritake," in *Noritake Art Deco Porcelain: Collection of Howard Kottler* (Pullman: Washington State University Museum of Art, 1982), p. 31.

3. Howard Kottler, interview with author, January 4, 1988.

4. Ibid., May 17, 1987.

5. Ibid.

6. Mel Bernstein, "University Impact on Ceramics: Charles Fergus Binns at Alfred University," *NCECA Journal* (vol. 5, 1984), p. 38.

7. Judith Schwartz, *Contemporary American Ceramic Sculpture: Satire in Selected Works of Robert Arneson, David Gilhooly, and Howard Kottler* (Ph.D. diss., New York University, 1983), p. 169.

8. Howard Kottler, interview with author, January 4, 1988.

9. Ibid.

10. Ibid., May 23, 1987.

11. Ibid.

12. Ibid.

13. William Milliken, "Review of the Exhibition," *Bulletin of the Cleveland Museum of Art* (May 1956), p. 81.

14. Howard Kottler, interview with author, May 23, 1987. The Seattle Art Museum acquired one of these cats from Kottler's estate.

15. Howard Kottler, *The Waisted Cylinder Form in the History of Ceramic Art* (M.A. thesis, Ohio State University, 1956), p. 36.

16. Howard Kottler, interview with author, May 23, 1988.

17. Kottler, *The Waisted Cylinder Form*, pp. 5-9.

18. Garth Clark, *American Ceramics: Eighteen Seventy-Six to the Present* (New York: Abbeville Press, 1988), pp. 31-32.

19. Ibid., p. 49.

20. Howard Kottler, interview with author, May 17 and May 23, 1988.

21. Ibid., May 17, 1988. In 1956 Kottler was awarded the Ellen Scripps Booth Memorial Scholarship at the Cranbrook Academy of Art.

22. Ibid., May 23, 1988.

23. Ibid., May 17, 1988. A group of Kottler's Takaezu-esqe bottles was included in the 1957 "Midwest Designer Craftsmen" exhibition organized by the Art Institute of Chicago and circulated by the Smithsonian Institution Traveling Exhibition Service.

24. Ibid., May 10, 1988.

25. Ibid.

26. Howard Kottler, "General History of My Use of Ceramic Decals," 1980. Typescript, artist's files.

27. One of these branch pots later won first prize for pottery at the Cleveland Museum's 1960 May Show. See *Bulletin of the Cleveland Museum of Art* (May 1960), p. 102.

28. Howard Kottler, interview with author, May 25, 1988.

29. Ibid., May 17, May 25, 1988.

30. Ibid., May 3, 1988.

31. Paul Bogatay, in Art Institute of Zanesville exhibition flyer, October 1960. Artist's files.

32. Carlton Atherton, in Ohio State University Faculty Club exhibition flyer, January 25-February 18, 1960. Artist's files.

33. Louise Bruner, "Kottler Ceramics on View at BGSU [Bowling Green State University]," *The Blade* (Toledo, Ohio), December 4, l963. Clipping in artist's files.

34. Howard Kottler, interview with author, April 19, 1988.

35. Howard Kottler. *An Exhibition of Pottery in Support of Three Processes in Ceramics* (Ph.D. diss., Ohio State University, 1964), p. 17.

36. Ibid., pp. 12-13.

37. Ibid., pp. 17-18. The Mason quote first appeared in *Craft Horizons* (October 1957), p. 41.

38. Howard Kottler, *An Exhibition of Pottery*, p. 21.

39. Howard Kottler, interview with author, May 25, 1988.

2: Seattle and the 1960s

1. Howard Kottler, interview with author, May 25, 1988.

2. LaMar Harrington, *Ceramics in the Pacific Northwest* (Seattle and London: University of Washington Press, 1979), p. 66.

3. Ibid.

4. Ibid., p. 69.

5. Howard Kottler, interview with author, May 23, 1988.

6. Howard Kottler, *An Exhibition of Pottery in Support of Three Processes in Ceramics* (Ph.D. diss., Ohio State University, 1964), p. 5.

7. Howard Kottler, in Lee Nordness, *Objects: U.S.A.* (New York: Viking Press, 1970), p. 118.

8. Harrington, *Ceramics in the Pacific Northwest*, p. 95. In 1965 Myers's work was featured in an exhibition at the University of Washington's Henry Art Gallery.

9. Howard Kottler, interview with author, May 31, 1988.

10. Nancy McCauley, "Artist Explores Six Conceptions," *The Oregonian* (Portland), April 30, 1967, p. 14.

11. Harrington, *Ceramics in the Pacific Northwest*, p. 93.

12. Jeff Perrone, "Madness, Sex, Exhaustion," *Artforum* (January 1990), pp. 98-101.

13. Ibid.

14. Howard Kottler, interview with author, May 31, 1988.

15. Ibid. For a technical description and illustrations of Egyptian paste compositions by Kottler and Warren Maruhashi, see Peter Raven, "Egyptian Paste," *Art Education* (February 1968), pp. 22-25.

16. Howard Kottler, interview with author, May 31, 1988.

17. Ibid.

18. Ibid.

19. Ibid.

20. Ibid.

21. Ibid., June 1, 1988.

22. Ibid.

23. Ibid.

24. Ibid., May 31, 1988. Kottler's fur pots were featured in the Museum of Contemporary Crafts "Fur and Feathers" exhibition in New York, January 23–March 28, 1971.

25. The Funk exhibition was held at the University Art Museum, University of California, Berkeley, California, April 18–May 29, 1967. Several artists in the show incorporated fur into their work, among them Joan Brown, David Gilhooly, and Don Potts.

26. Fred Mitchell, "Ceramics by Howard Kottler," exhibition flyer (New York: Museum of Contemporary Crafts, 1967). Artist's files.

27. LaMar Harrington, "Howard Kottler," *Craft Horizons* (March/April, 1967).

28. Howard Kottler, interview with author, June 10, 1988. The two glass workshops conducted at the Toledo Museum of Art in 1962 are often cited as pivotal events in the history of the modern studio-glass movement in America.

29. Ibid. One of the "tongue" compositions exhibited at the Cone 10 Contemporary Crafts Gallery in Seattle (November 16–December 4, 1968) was illustrated in an article by Sally Hayman, "Crafts Enter the 20th-Century," *Seattle Post-Intelligencer*, November 24, 1968. Kottler's work in glass was also reviewed by Theo and Peter Raven in "Letter from Seattle," *Craft Horizons* (January/February 1969), p. 41.

30. Howard Kottler, interview with author, June 10, 1988.

31. Katherine White, "Howard Kottler," *Craft Horizons* (May/June 1968).

32. "Extended Sensibilities," *Discourses: Conversations in Postmodern Art and Culture* (New York: New Museum of Contemporary Art, 1990), p. 146.

3: Vessels and Sculpture of the 1970s

1. Howard Kottler, interview with author, August 26, 1988, and January 4, 1989.

2. Ibid., January 5, 1989. The frank acknowledgment of gay sexuality in Art Deco, as in George Barbier's drawings of lesbians, for example, also contributed to his affinity for the movement.

3. Howard Kottler, "General History of My Use of Ceramic Decals." Typescript (2 pp.), artist's files, 1980. The hobby-shop decals Kottler used were silk-screened and impregnated with a low-fire glaze. Transferred to a ceramic surface and fired in a kiln at 1,250 degrees, the decals were permanently affixed.

4. Howard Kottler, interview with author, June 10, 1988.

5. *Ode to a Cherry* was included in the 1971 "Fur and Feathers" exhibition at Museum of Contemporary Crafts (see chap. 2, n. 23). In one reviewer's assessment, "Howard Kottler's *Ode to a Cherry* is just obscene." "Ecolerotica," *New York Magazine* (January 25, 1971), p. 51.

6. Several cast sculptures were shown in Kottler's 1970 one-person exhibition at the Galeria del Sol, Santa Barbara, California. He subsequently lost track of most of these compositions.

7. "Coffee, Tea and Other Cups," Museum of Contemporary Crafts, New York, September 30-January 3, 1971. Kottler's

cup, *Colonial Rockettes*, was decorated with collaged decals similar to those on a plate series with the same title begun in 1967.

8. Howard Kottler, interview with author, August 26, 1988.

9. Constance W. Glenn, *Roy Lichtenstein, Ceramic Sculpture*, exhibition catalogue (California State University at Long Beach Art Galleries, 1977), p. 17.

10. Howard Kottler, interview with author, August 26, 1988.

11. Vicki Halper, *Clay Revisions: Plate, Cup and Vase*, exhibition catalogue (Seattle: Seattle Art Museum, 1987), p. 39.

12. Howard Kottler, "Notes on my Work: 1965-1982." Typescript (2 pp.) in artist's files. One version of *Mug Shot* (1973) included a toy metal gun. In another variation the gun was made from clay and painted to match the decals.

13. Howard Kottler, interview with author, August 26, 1988.

14. Howard Kottler, "Notes on my Work: 1965-1982."

15. In another variation, the base of *Bushel and a Peck* is covered with wood-grain contact paper.

16. Howard Kottler, "Statement, April 1986." Typescript, in artist's files.

17. Several of Kottler's observations parallel those expressed in a recent study of faux surfaces and American culture by Susan G. Lewin, *Formica and Design: From the Countertop to High Art* (New York: Rizzoli, 1991.)

18. Elaine Levin, *Illusionistic Realism Defined in Ceramic Sculpture*, exhibition catalogue (Laguna Beach, Calif.: Laguna Beach Museum of Art, 1977), unpaginated.

19. Howard Kottler, interview with author, October 4, 1988.

20. Ibid.

21. Howard Kottler, "Notes on My Work: 1965-1982."

22. Howard Kottler, interview with author, October 4, 1988.

23. *Eleven Updates: A profile of the Slocumb Gallery's interest in and enthusiasm for the craft renaissance*, exhibition catalogue (East Tennessee State University: Slocumb Gallery, 1978), unpaginated.

24. Howard Kottler, quoted in exhibition catalogue, *Illusionistic Realism Defined in Ceramic Sculpture*, unpaginated.

25. The sculpture illustrated in the *Illusionistic Realism* exhibition catalogue is actually *Dream Street* (1976), a variation on *The Old Bag Next Door Is Nuts*, in which the paper-bag cast is covered with wood-grain decals. A second version of the *Old Bag Next Door Is Nuts* was executed in 1977.

26. Garth Clark, *American Ceramics: Eighteen Seventy-Six to the Present* (New York: Abbeville Press, 1988), p. 275. *The Old Bag Next Door Is Nuts* was illustrated in the September 1977 issue of *Ceramics Monthly*.

27. Ruth Poris's letters were published in *Ceramics Monthly* (November 1977), p. 7, and (March 1978), p. 7.

28. The letter is dated March 3, 1978. Copy, artist's files.

29. Clark, *American Ceramics*, p. 275.

30. Harold Rosenberg, "Inquest into Modernism," *New Yorker* (February 20, 1978), p. 103.

31. The self-portrait series is discussed in chapter four.

32. Howard Kottler, interview with author, October 4, 1988. An alternative title for *Knotty Pine* was *Source of Deep Trouble.*

33. Ibid.

34. Clark, *American Ceramics*, pp. 117, 153.

35. Ibid., p. 158.

36. Howard Kottler, interview with author, October 4, 1988.

37. Howard Kottler, "General History of My Use of Ceramic Decals." Typescript (2 pp.), artist's files.

38. Kottler also created a container for the four leather envelopes with the series title stitched across the front.

39. C. E. Licka, "Prima Facie Clay Sampler: A Case for Popular Ceramics," *Current* (August/September), 1975.

40. Howard Kottler, interview with author, August 24, 1988.

41. Clark, *American Ceramics*, p. 129. Jan Axel and Karen McCready make a similar point about the plate containers' "old-fashioned craftsmanship," in *Porcelain: Traditions and New Visions* (New York: Watson-Guptill Publications, 1981), p. 123.

42. Howard Kottler, interview with author, August 24, 1988.

43. Ibid.

44. Ibid.

45. Jean Lipman and Richard Marshall, *Art About Art* (New York: E. P. Dutton, 1978), p. 144.

46. In 1987 and 1988 Kottler was formulating plans to update the decal plate series. In the new work, the decals were to represent icons of modernist ceramics, such as Voulkos's stoneware plates of the early 1960s. He also reproduced some of the decal plates as "picnic ware" by gluing color-Xerox copies of the altered decals on paper plates.

47. Howard Kottler, *An Exhibition of Pottery in Support of Three Processes in Ceramics* (Ph.D. diss., Ohio State University, 1963), p. 4.

48. Howard Kottler, interview with author, April 27, 1988. Kottler purchased most of his blank plates at Pier One, a retail import store. According to ceramist Irvin Tepper, "Howard was so cheap he would never pay retail for the plates—he would buy seconds. He often went to the store and picked up twenty plates or more. The owners began to recognize him, not as Howard Kottler the ceramist, but as this guy who threw great parties—parties where everyone would smash the plates after dinner. That's what he had told them."

49. Ceramics historian LaMar Harrington and Seattle critic Matthew Kangas have written perceptively about Kottler's work, but neither has published an in-depth review of Kottler's decal plates. The most perceptive and serious study of the plates to date is by Judith Schwarz in *Contemporary American Ceramic Sculpture: Satire in Selected works of Robert Arneson, David Gilhooly, and Howard*

Kottler (Ph.D. diss., New York University, 1983).

50. Howard Kottler, interview with author, May 5, 1988.

4: The Last Decade

1. Howard Kottler, interview with author, May 23, 1988. According to several of Kottler's friends, some of his University of Washington colleagues had argued that he should not be granted tenure because he was gay. These sentiments undoubtedly contributed to his uncertainty about settling in Seattle.

2. Howard Kottler, interview with author, May 3 and May 5, 1988.

3. Ibid., January 5, 1989.

4. LaMar Harrington, *Ceramics in the Pacific Northwest* (Seattle and London: University of Washington Press, 1979), p. 99.

5. Irvin Tepper, interview with author, August 16, 1992.

6. Howard Kottler, interview with author, January 5, 1989.

7. Kottler had mixed feelings about the workshop format because, in his estimation, the instruction usually emphasized technique over ideas. In the 1980s Kottler presented slide lectures about his work at these gatherings but declined to give technical demonstrations. Howard Kottler, interview with author, May 10, 1988.

8. L. P. Levine, "Together, Wherever We Go-O: Colorado Mountain Clay Symposium." Typescript, artist's files, dated July 11, 1978.

9. Richard Notkin, interview with author, July 1990.

10. Howard Kottler, interview with author, September 3 and 4, 1987. Many pots from this series are dated 1981-1985 or 1982-1986, indicating the temporal distance between conception and execution. Several of these vessels, such as *Romaine*, were made in various sizes.

11. Suzanne Slesin, "Memphis Mania," *New York Times Magazine* (October 5, 1989), p. 44.

12. Howard Kottler, interview with author, December 19, 1989.

13. According to Dan Neish, several vases in this series, among them *Ramrod* and *Encore*, were named after gay bars. Dan Neish, interview with author, August 25, 1992.

14. Howard Kottler, interview with author, December 19, 1989.

15. Ibid., September 3 and 4, 1987.

16. Ibid., December 19, 1988.

17. Sanford Shaman and Patricia Watkinson, "Introduction," in exhibition catalogue, *Noritake Art Deco Porcelains* (Pullman: Washington State University Museum of Art, 1982), pp. 11-14. The exhibition originated at the Washington State University Museum of Art.

18. Howard Kottler, "The Search for Noritake," in *Noritake Art Deco Porcelains*, pp. 31-36.

19. Howard Kottler, interview with author, May 3, 1988. The 1987 "Eloquent Object" exhibition, organized by the Philbrook Museum of Art, was accompanied by a lavishly illustrated, hard-cover catalogue with essays by major critics. Kottler's 1967 *Hustler's Delight Pot*, on loan from the Daniel Jacobs Collection, New York, was included in the show.

20. Howard Kottler, interview with author, May 17, 1988.

21. Ibid., May 5, 1988.

22. Ibid., January 5, 1988

23. Ibid., May 10, 1988.

24. William Hunt, "Graham Crackers: Revisiting the exhibition 'Clay Revisions,'" *NCECA Journal* (Fall 1988), pp. 18-19.

25. Rob Barnard, "Kitsch as avant garde," *New Art Examiner* (September 1988), p. 29. Similar arguments about modernism versus crafts were elaborated by Bruce Metcalf in "Replacing the Myth of Modernism," *American Craft* (February/March 1993), pp. 40-47.

26. Derek Guthrie, "The Eloquent Object gagged by kitsch," *New Art Examiner* (September 1988), p. 29.

27. Howard Kottler, interview with author, November 16, 1988

28. Ibid., December 19, 1988.

29. Ibid., November 16, 1988. When Kottler conceived *Dinner for Me*, he was not aware of the parallels between his treatment of the table and the work of Richard Artschwager.

30. Ibid. In a 1984 exhibition at the Palm Desert Museum, which included work by artists such as George Herms, Terry Allen, Roland Reiss, Red Grooms, and George Segal, Kottler's *Dinner for Me* was presented as an example of the "return of the narrative" in contemporary sculpture. The *Dinner for Me* Dymotape text was also reprinted in the show's catalogue, *Return of the Narrative* (Palm Springs, Calif.: Palm Desert Museum, 1984), p. 65.

31. Howard Kottler, interview with author, November 16, 1988.

32. According to Kottler, who corresponded with the author in selecting the texts, Jack Fritscher's "Dog Dik" first appeared in *The California Action Guide* (October 1981).

33. Howard Kottler, interview with author, April 27, 1988.

34. Matthew Kangas, *Shattered Self: Northwest Figurative Ceramics* (Pittsburgh: The Society for Art in Crafts, 1988), pp. 3-4.

35. Howard Kottler, interview with author, May 5, 1988.

36. Kottler often showed slides of Robert Arneson's *A Hollow Jesture* to his students. The portrait was acquired by Joseph Monsen, one of Seattle's prominent art collectors. Monsen and his wife Elaine began developing an important collection of contemporary ceramics in 1965. Kottler was one of Monsen's early advisors and, says Monsen, "helped me move away from my somewhat conservative

taste." Joseph Monsen, interview with author, March 1992. Also see *A Decade of Ceramic Art 1962-1972: From the Collection of Professor and Mrs. Joseph Monsen* (San Francisco: San Francisco Museum of Art, 1972).

37. Howard Kottler, interview with author, May 5, 1988. Kottler also parodied his "devil tongue" in the cubist self-portrait, *Tongue Twister* (1986).

38. Donald Kuspit, "Robert Arneson's Sense of Self: Squirming in a Procrustean Place," *American Craft* (October/November 1986), pp. 37-44, 64-68.

39. "Extended Sensibilities: The Impact of Homosexual Sensibilities on Contemporary Culture," *Discourses: Conversations in Postmodern Art and Culture* (New York: The New Museum of Contemporary Art, 1990), p. 134.

40. Howard Kottler, interview with author, September 3 and 4, 1987.

41. Howard Kottler, "Artist's Statement, December 1986." Typescript, artist's files.

42. Howard Kottler, interview with author, September 3 and 4, 1987.

43. Ibid.

44. Ibid.

45. For example, see the discussion of Koons's ceramics by K. Varnedoe and A. Gopnik in *High and Low: Modern Art and Popular Culture* (New York: Museum of Modern Art, 1991), pp. 395-98.

46. According to Dan Neish, this series was begun in 1984. "The first assignment Howard gave me when I was hired in 1984," he reported, "was to enlarge one of the dog-in-ashtray figurines. Most of these pieces sat around in the studio, though, because he couldn't make up his mind about the surfaces. Should he play up their original colors, or play them down, or do something altogether different? It was typical of him to agonize over surfaces for a long time—he was never as secure about color as he was about form." Dan Neish, interview with author, August 25, 1992.

47. Susan Sontag, "Notes on Camp," *Partisan Review* (Fall 1964), pp. 515-30.

48. Ibid., p. 529.

49. The 1987 Bellevue show was divided into three sections: "Howard Kottler: Recent Ceramic Sculpture;" "Noritake Art Deco Porcelains;" and "New Vistas: American Art Pottery." The latter was a small traveling exhibition of American ceramics from 1880-1930.

50. Matthew Kangas, "A fresh look at decorative arts," *Seattle Weekly* (February 4-10, 1987), p. 37.

Works in Public Collections

A SELECTED LIST

American Craft Museum
New York, New York

Bellevue Art Museum
Bellevue, Washington

Butler Institute of American Art
Youngstown, Ohio

Cleveland Museum of Art
Cleveland, Ohio

Cooper-Hewitt Museum
New York, New York

Cranbrook Academy of Art
Bloomfield Hills, Illinois

Dayton Art Institute
Dayton, Ohio

De Pauw University Art Center
Greencastle, Indiana

Detroit Institute of Art
Detroit, Michigan

Everson Museum of Art
Syracuse, New York

Henry Art Gallery
University of Washington
Seattle, Washington

Kansas City Art Institute
Kansas City, Missouri

Los Angeles County Museum of Art
Los Angeles, California

Mills College
Oakland, California

The Museum of Ceramic Art at Alfred
Alfred, New York

Museum of Fine Arts
Boston, Massachusetts

National Museum of Modern Art
Kyoto, Japan

Portland Art Museum
Portland, Oregon

Renwick Gallery
Washington, D.C.

Seattle Art Museum
Seattle, Washington

Syracuse University
Syracuse, New York

Tacoma Art Museum
Tacoma, Washington

University of Manitoba
Winnipeg, Canada

Utah Museum of Fine Arts
Salt Lake City, Utah

Victoria and Albert Museum
London, England

Whitney Museum of American Art
New York, New York

Bibliography

Unpublished Archival Material and Dissertations

Kottler, Howard. Notes and statements in the artist's files.

———. *The Waisted Cylinder Form in the History of Ceramic Art*. M.A. thesis, Ohio State University, 1956.

———. *An Exhibition of Pottery in Support of Three Processes in Ceramics*. Ph.D. diss., Ohio State University, 1964.

Schwartz, Judith. *Contemporary American Ceramic Sculpture: Satire in Selected Works of Robert Arneson, David Gilhooly, and Howard Kottler*. Ph.D. diss., New York University, 1983.

Interviews by the Author

Interviews with Howard Kottler, September 3 and 4, 1987, and April 19, 1988-January 5, 1989. Individual dates are cited in the notes. Other interviews by the author quoted in the text include: Dan Neish (February 1990 and August 1992); Richard Notkin (July 1990); Joseph Monsen (March 1992); and Irvin Tepper (August 1992). An interview with Patti Warashina (February 1990) and conversations with LaMar Harrington, Judith Schwartz, and Arna Goffe provided additional background material used in this text. Dan Neish also supplied answers to many questions about the genesis of individual compositions.

Books, Catalogues, and Articles

Axel, Jan, and Karen McCready. *Porcelain: Traditions and New Visions*. New York: Watson-Guptill Publications, 1981.

Barnard, Rob. "Kitsch as avant garde," *New Art Examiner* (September 1988).

Bernstein, Mel. "University Impact on Ceramics: Charles Fergus Binns at Alfred University," *NCECA Journal* 5 (1984).

Bruner, Louise. "Kottler Ceramics on View at BGSU [Bowling Green State University]," *The Blade* (Toledo, Ohio) (December 4, 1963).

Bulletin of the Cleveland Museum of Art (May 1956).

Clark, Garth. *American Ceramics 1876 to the Present*. New York: Abbeville Press, 1987.

Clay Revisions: Plate, Cup and Vase. Seattle: Seattle Art Museum, 1987.

Crow, Thomas. "Modernism and Mass Culture in the Visual Arts." In *Pollock and After: The Critical Debate*. Editor, Francis Frascina. London: Harper and Row, 1985.

A Decade of Ceramic Art 1962-1972: From the Collection of Professor and Mrs. R. Joseph Monsen. Exhibition catalogue. San Francisco: San Francisco Museum of Modern Art, 1972.

"Ecolerotica." *New York Magazine* (25 January 1971).

Eleven Updates: A profile of the Slocumb Gallery's interest in and enthusiasm for the craft renaissance. Exhibition catalogue. Johnson City: Slocumb Gallery, East Tennessee State University, 1978.

"Egyptian Paste." *Art Education* (February 1968).

"Extended Sensibilities." In *Discourses: Conversations in Postmodern Art and Culture.* New York: The New Museum of Contemporary Art, 1990.

Glenn, Constance W. *Roy Lichtenstein, Ceramic Sculpture.* Exhibition catalogue. Long Beach: Art Galleries, California State University at Long Beach.

Harrington, LaMar. "Howard Kottler." *Craft Horizons* (March/April 1967).

———. *Ceramics in the Pacific Northwest.* Seattle and London: University of Washington Press, 1979.

Hayman, Sally. "Crafts Enter the 20th-Century." *Seattle Post-Intelligencer* (24, November 1968).

Hunt, William. "Graham Crackers: Revisiting the Exhibition 'Clay Revisions.'" *NCECA Journal* (Fall 1988).

Illusionistic Realism Defined in Ceramic Sculpture. Exhibition catalogue. Laguna Beach, Calif.: Laguna Beach Museum of Art, 1977.

Kangas, Matthew. "A fresh look at the decorative arts." *Seattle Weekly,* 4-10 February 1987.

———. "Howard Kottler." *American Ceramics* (January 1988).

———. "Shattered Self: Northwest Figurative Ceramics." *American Craft* (August/September 1986).

Kuspit, Donald. "Robert Arneson's Sense of Self: Squirming in a Procrustean Bed." *American Craft* (October/November 1986).

Leach, Bernard. *A Potter's Book.* London: Faber and Faber, 1945.

"Letters." *Ceramics Monthly* (November 1977, January 1978, and March 1978).

Levin, Elaine. *The History of American Ceramics.* New York: Harry N. Abrams, 1988.

Licka, C. E. "Prima Facie Clay Sampler: A Case for Popular Ceramics." *Current* (August/September 1975).

Lipman, Jean, and Richard Marshall. *Art about Art.* New York: E. P. Dutton, 1978.

McCauley, Nancy. "Artist Explores Six Conceptions." *The Oregonian* (Portland), 30 April 1967.

Metcalf, Bruce. "Replacing the Myth of Modernism." *American Craft* (February/March 1993).

Milliken, William. "Review of the Exhibition." *The Bulletin of the Cleveland Museum of Art* (May 1956).

Nordness, Lee. *Objects: U.S.A.* New York: Viking Press, 1970.

Noritake Art Deco Porcelains: Collection of Howard Kottler. Pullman: Washington State University Museum of Art, 1982.

Perrone, Jeff. "Madness, Sex, Exhaustion." *Artforum* (January 1990).

Raven, Peter. "Egyptian Paste." *Art Education* (February 1968).

Raven, Theo, and Peter Raven, "Letter from Seattle." *Craft Horizons* (January/February 1969).

Return of the Narrative. Exhibition catalogue. Palm Springs: Palm Springs Desert Museum, 1984.

Rosenberg, Harold. "Inquest into Modernism." *New Yorker* (20 February 1978).

Shattered Self: Northwest Figurative Ceramics. Exhibition catalogue. Pittsburgh, Penna.: The Society for Arts in Crafts, 1988.

Sontag, Susan. "Notes on Camp." *Partisan Review* (Fall 1964).

Varnedoe, Kirk, and Adam Gopnik. *High and Low: Modern Art and Popular Culture.* Exhibition catalogue. New York: Museum of Modern Art, 1991.

Wechsler, Susan. *Low-Fire Ceramics: A New Direction in American Clay.* New York: Watson-Guptill Publications, 1981.

White, Katherine. "Howard Kottler." *Craft Horizons* (May/June 1968).

Index